WHO'S YOUR CADDY?

ALSO BY RICK REILLY

Missing Links

Slo-Mo

The Life of Reilly

WHO'S YOUR CADDY?

LOOPING for the GREAT, NEAR GREAT, and REPROBATES of GOLF

RICK REILLY

DOUBLEDAY NEW YORK LONDON TORONTO SYDNEY AUCKLAND

PUBLISHED BY DOUBLEDAY

a division of Random House, Inc.

DOUBLEDAY and the portrayal of an anchor with a dolphin are registered trademarks of Random House, Inc.

Book design by Chris Welch

Library of Congress Cataloging-in-Publication Data

Reilly, Rick.

Who's your caddy? : looping for the great, near great, and reprobates of golf / Rick Reilly.— 1st ed.

p. cm.

Includes index.

1. Caddying—Humor. 2. Golfers. 3. Reilly, Rick. I. Title.

GV977.R45 2003

796.352—dc21

2003040940

ISBN 0-385-48885-8

PRINTED IN THE UNITED STATES OF AMERICA

June 2003

18 20 19

For John,

who showed me

how much fun the

stupid game can be.

CONTENTS

Acknowledgments ix

Introduction: Jam Boy 3

1. The Masters: Get Your Mouth off My Ball! 7
2. John Daly: Unzipped 30
3. Donald Trump: The Search for True Trumpaliciousness 56
4. Tom Lehman: By the Way, You're Fired 77
5. David Duval: The Maniac Behind the Shades 105
6. Dewey Tomko: Just a Lil' Ol' $50,000 Nassau 126
7. Jack Nicklaus: We'll Always Have Vail 150
8. Deepak Chopra: The Seven Spiritual Laws of Double Bogey 169
9. Casey Martin: Hell on Wheels 185
10. Bob Newhart: The Anti-Trump 206
11. Jill McGill: Where's Your Caddy? 222
12. Bob Andrews: The Blind Approach 246

ACKNOWLEDGMENTS

The author would very much like to thank his editor Bill (Scratch) Thomas; his agent Janet Pawson, from whom all good checks come; his great friend and sounding board Gene Wojciechowski, who has caller ID and still takes his calls; his wonderful family, many of whom will be giving him strokes soon, both golfing and neurological; his mook pal Sky, who came up with the blind idea; his magazine bosses, Bill Colson and Terry McDonell, who pretended not to notice columns coming from Buy.com tournaments and two-day pro-ams; Frantic Ralph, who somehow got him all these places; Norma Foerderer, who is even more fun than Trump; Justice Sandra Day O'Connor, who gave him the nicest "no" of many dozens; Two Down O'Connor, who actually exists, which is a great help in itself; Sean (One Down) O'Connor, who subcaddied; Tammy Blake, who is to publicity what Godiva is to chocolate; and Amy Arnold, great friend and assistant. To all of you, remember, this is only thanks. There is no tip involved.

WHO'S YOUR CADDY?

INTRODUCTION: JAM BOY

You ever notice anybody standing next to Boston Red Sox pitcher Pedro Martinez as he's firing cheese at the Yankees?

Ever notice any reporters kneeling down in the huddle as Brett Favre calls, "Red right, x-cross, y-drag wheel" in the huddle?

Ever notice any slow white guys helping Allen Iverson decide which direction the air conditioning is coming from as he sets up for a three-pointer?

Me, neither.

Only golf lets you do it.

Only in golf can a schmoe like me lurk right there next to David Duval, in the middle of the fairway, as he decides what he's going to hit to a green surrounded by 10,000 people. Only in golf can a hack like me read a putt at the Masters as a huge gallery watches in absolute silence. Only in golf can a pest like me help Jack Nicklaus decide whether it's a hard 7 or an easy 8. "Personally," I told Jack, "I'd skull a 9."

Which is the main reason I wanted to write this book. I'll never play golf like those guys. I'll never play it like those guys' gardeners. But as a caddy, I can be closer to great athletes without actually *being* one than in any other sport.

But I didn't want to just be inside the head of great golfers. I wanted to be inside the head of golf itself—awful golfers, blind golfers, gambling golfers, celebrity golfers, crazed golfers, and guru golfers. Carrying a bag for 18 holes is known in caddyese as a "loop." And I wanted to find The Perfect Loop, The Funniest Loop, and The Worst Loop.

Besides, when you caddy, you get to hang out with caddies. That's the other reason I wanted to write it. I happen to love caddies. It's about time somebody stood up for them. Do you realize, in the early 1920s in this country, rich guys would hire two caddies—one to carry the bag and one to cover himself in jelly in order to attract flies *away* from the golfers? They were known as "jam boys." Can you imagine doing that to anyone now? Except, of course, members of Congress?

I happen to think caddies deserve better, mostly because caddies are more fun than strippers and firehouse poles. When I cover a golf tournament for *Sports Illustrated*, I'd be toast without caddy quotes. I'll send a limo for the caddies. All the stuff you hear from the players, agents, swing coaches, mind gurus, flex trainers, and masseurs don't equal one cigarette-smoking caddy going, "Sumbitch is golfin' his ball" or "My man is hookin' like Divine Jones."

By the way, I never took any money out of any caddy's pocket. The deal was the same whenever I approached a pro: I couldn't be paid. The player could do anything with my percentage he wanted, including keeping it, giving it to his caddy, or lighting cigars with it. But I couldn't get a dime.

I was stunned at the kind of people who took me up on it. I mean, would *you* want me near your sticks? I can't imagine what they got out of it, but I know I learned as much about golf from these two years as I had in 22 years of covering the game before then.

From Tommy Aaron at the Masters, I learned silence. From

Casey Martin, guts. From Tom Lehman, family. From John Daly, humor. From Nicklaus, mortality. From David Duval, I learned how easy the game can be, and from Bob Newhart, how hard. From Jill McGill I learned how tough it is to play with skill but not enough passion, and from Deepak Chopra, passion but not enough skill. I still don't know what I learned from Donald Trump. And from Bob Andrews, who is blind, I learned how much I love the game itself, for itself.

Oh, one last thing. You're sitting there, going, "How come you didn't ask Tiger?"

I did.

I asked Tiger 100 ways. I asked him if I could substitute for his usual man, Stevie Williams, in a tournament, or an exhibition, or a practice round, or a casual round, or even nine crummy practice rounds at his home course of Isleworth in Orlando. And he'd always say the same thing: "No."

"Why not?" I asked.

"Because," he explained. "I suck. I need good help."

This is a guy who can make a wad of balata do the rumba on the tip of a flagstick from 208 yards away. How much help does he need?

After I'd accepted the fact I was never going to get Tiger, I saw in the paper that Warren Buffet, the legendary investor and one of the richest men on the planet, paid $100,000 to caddy for Tiger as part of a one-day charity. Six months later, I happened to be at an AIDS benefit in Lincoln, Nebraska, saw Buffet there, marched right up to him and said, "What gives?"

He said Tiger didn't *really* let him caddy. "I pretty much just sat in the cart," he said. But on the 18th, Tiger said, "Mr. Buffet, I want to play you this last hole for some serious money."

"Uh-oh," said Buffet, who happens to be worth billions. "How much is 'serious'?"

"Five bucks," said Tiger.

Buffet thought about it and said, "That wouldn't be too fair, do you think? You against me? I'm a 20 handicap!"

And Tiger said, "Yeah, but I'll be playing on my knees."

So they bet. Tiger got down on his knees and hit a rope-hook 260-yard drive down the fairway, made bogey on the hole, and took the five dollars off Buffet.

But then Buffet cleared his throat and said, "Aren't you forgetting something?"

Tiger couldn't think what it might be.

"My 10 percent," he said. "That's fifty cents."

And *that's* how you get to be a billionaire.

1

THE MASTERS

Get Your Mouth off My Ball!

Having never caddied in my life, I needed a smallish place to start out, away from the spotlight, a podunk kind of tournament.

Naturally, I chose The Masters.

In front of thousands of people, in the greatest tournament in golf, I made my professional caddying debut, looping for 64-year-old Tommy Aaron, the 1973 champion. I think he'd tell you it went quite well, unless you count tiny, little nitpickings, such as my dropping the towel eleven times, the headcover four, the puttercover six, standing in the wrong place at the wrong time, standing in the right place at the wrong time, forgetting to give him his putter, his ball, his driver, being too close to him, being too far from him, letting the clubs clink too much as I walked, letting myself clink too much as I walked, the infamous "mouth" incident, and the awful, shameful thing that happened on No. 5 that none involved shall ever forget.

This was Friday. We were paired with "Sponge," who caddies for New Zealander Michael Campbell, and "Fanny" Sunneson, who won six majors with Nick Faldo and now is the bagwoman for Notah Begay, who hates me very much, despite the fact that I've never caddied for him.

Sponge and Fanny. Sounds like a British sex club.

I say, Nigel, didn't I see you last night at The Sponge and Fanny?

What happened was, Aaron hit a 3-iron at No. 5 into the left greenside bunker, then splashed out. I handed him his putter and then nervously set about my raking duties. The crowd was huge around that green, as they are around most Augusta greens, and nobody was ready to putt yet, so I could feel all the eyes on me. I had dropped my towel once already that day and had 500 people yell, "Caddy! Caddy! Towel!" as though I were President Bush's Secret Service agent and had dropped my gun. *Caddy! Caddy! Uzi!* So I knew they were watching. I raked as I have raked my own bunkers far too many times, climbed out, then placed the rake on the grass behind.

That's when I noticed Aaron staring at my rake job, then glancing at Fanny. Aaron nodded at her. She nodded back. Begay nodded. Sponge nodded back. For all I know, the huge crowd nodded. Only one of us had no idea what all the nodding was about. Suddenly, Fanny dashed over to the rake, picked it up, got back in the bunker, and did it again. Completely.

I was to suffer the ultimate caddy humiliation: Re-raked.

I was left with nothing to do but stand there and watch, humiliated. It was like a coach calling time-out in the middle of the Super Bowl and showing a quarterback how to put his hands under the center's butt.

And that's when I realized the horrible flaw in this book idea: Just because somebody "lets" you do something, doesn't mean you necessarily should go out and "do" it.

THE FACT THAT I, an absolute novice know-nothing, could get a bag and traipse my size 12s across the hallowed ground of Augusta National tells you how dangerously easy this whole idea was.

At the 2000 Masters, every past champion got a lifetime invitation, even if they were 111 years old. The rule has changed now, but then, it meant if Byron Nelson, then 89, felt like playing in next year's Masters, he could play. Naturally, since 1966, he has had the good sense not to.

Luckily, guys like 1957 champion Doug Ford (then 78) did not have good sense. He played every year until they made him stop in 2002. In the 2000 Masters, he went out there, threw a little 94 at them, and then withdrew. Meanwhile, a very good player sat home and bit his putter.

Naturally, figuring Ford was not exactly "counting" on winning and therefore might suffer an insufferable caddy and get in a book, I called him first.

"Mr. Ford," I began, "I'm doing a book on caddying and—"

"Already got a caddy," Ford snapped. "Had him for 25 years."

"Sure," I said, "but I was thinking, just this once, you might allow—"

Click.

May his bunions burst.

Finally, the agent for Aaron called back and said Aaron would let me caddy Wednesday only, as a tryout for the next year. Said we'd play nine holes and then the par-3 contest and that would give him an idea of exactly how horrible I was.

Yes!

I started researching Aaron, who, it turns out, is famous for three things: 1) Saving the Masters from having to put up with J. C. Snead every year by beating him by one shot in 1973; 2) Writing down an incorrect par "4" instead of a birdie "3" on the 17th hole for Sunday playing partner Roberto De Vicenzo in 1968. De Vicenzo signed the card anyway, causing him to keep that one-stroke higher score, causing him to miss his rightful spot in what would've been a two-man playoff with Bob Goalby, who was then declared the winner. When told of it, De Vicenzo did not blame Aaron. Instead he said, "What a 'stupid' I am." 3) Not being Hank Aaron's brother, though people ask him all the time anyway, despite the fact that the baseball Aarons are black and this golfing Aaron is white. ("No," Tommy tells them, "I'm taller.")

He'd played in 37 Masters, won the par-3 tournament one year with a five-under 22, and had missed more cuts than a drunk surgeon. However, in 2000, Aaron became the oldest player ever to make the cut—63 years, one month—when he shot 72-74–146, three under the cut, the first two days. Of course, he wound up dead last by five shots at 25-over, but still, on that Friday night, he was three shots better than Ollie, seven than Daly, and nine than Ben Crenshaw.

My man!

I reached him on his cellphone. "Meet me at the bag room at 7:30 sharp tomorrow morning," he said. "We'll play a practice round and then we'll play the par 3."

Having slept not at all, I was at the holy place by 7A.M., and by this I mean the Augusta caddyshack. It was a white brick building, with lockers, tables, a TV playing ESPN, and a little caddyshack grill where a huge black man cooks delicacies for the caddies, such as hamburger ($2), cheeseburger (also $2), soup (50 cents), and fries (50 cents). Of course, business was a little slow this week on account of—for Masters week only—a giant cake-display case being brought in and filled with pimento-cheese sandwiches, fruit, Gatorade, pop, and candy. Now who is going to pay a whole 50 cents for soup when you can get free pimento-cheese sandwiches?

I saw Pete Bender, who carried Ian Baker-Finch at the 1993 British Open—which tells you how good Bender is—and he said that Augusta is good, but the best caddy room in the free world is the

Players Championship. "Oh, man, hot breakfasts, hot lunch, big-screen TV, couches," Bender said wistfully. Here's a guy carrying Rocco Mediate and probably making $100,000 a year, and he's thrilled at the idea of being able to actually eat a meal during his 10-hour workday. The worst, he said, was Arnold Palmer's tournament, Bay Hill. "They got nothin'. Zero. Not even a room to change in."

Shame, Arnie, shame.

I put on the classic all-white painter overalls with the green Masters hat they give you (free!). It's the classiest uniform in golf, with the player's number Velcroed on the left breast (I got No. 411—the defending champ's caddy always gets "1"), the Augusta logo on the right breast pocket, and the player's name on the back. Beautiful. Like a fool, I forgot to steal it when I was done.

I tried to ignore the sign that read, "Caddies are required to wear white flat-soled sneakers." All I had were black Softspiked golf shoes. This made me stand out like a bridesmaid in construction boots. Also, I found out later, on hot days, guys wear nothing but boxers underneath. There have been rumors of guys going "commando" under them, and I can only pray that: a) it isn't true and b) if it is true, I didn't get Fluff's old overalls.

They handed me a yardage book, which looked like Sanskrit. It made no sense, just numbers and swirls and acronyms. It must be how *The New Yorker* looks to an illiterate. I was standing there, looking like Rubik's twit brother, when Cubby, Davis Love's caddy, said, "Don't even bother, Rook, you'll never understand it."

Cubby is one of the great lads. When not caddying, he's always got the sports section in one hand and an unlit cigar in the mouth. His breakup with Brad Faxon was one of the most tragic in tour history—13 years together. But that's how it is. No alimony, no keeping the china. Just like that, everybody notices you're not lugging the old bag with you everywhere you go.

Cubby and Faxon used to be quite a pair. They had a language all their own. For yardages, for instance, Cubby would say, "OK, you got 123 plus Elway, and a little Reagan." Which meant, "You have 123 yards to the front of the green, plus another seven yards (Elway's jersey number) to the flagstick, with the wind throwing your ball a little to the right (Reagan's politics)." Or Cubby would say, "You got 214 (yards to the front) plus Michael (Jordan, which is 23 yards), and a little Clinton (wind going left)." What, you don't speak fluent Cubby?

Cubby has a jersey number for every conceivable yardage, but I always thought there were more they didn't use. For instance, what about: "You got 134 plus Hal (four, for the number of Hal Sutton's wives)," or "You got 189 plus O. J. (Simpson's two murders)," or "It's 201 plus Anna (Kournikova, a perfect 10)."

The yardages in the book were from every conceivable place you could think of—sprinkler heads, bushes, benches. You half expected to see distances marked to Martha Burk's offices written in. But there were also strange numbers way to the sides of the hole drawings accompanied by strange letters—like ICYFU: 219. And ICYRFU: 174. Cubby explained it to me. "ICYFU means 'In Case You Fuck Up.' And ICYRFU means 'In Case You Really Fuck Up.' "

Then somebody came up to him and said, "Cubby, did you get those bad numbers on 11?"

"What bad numbers?" Cubby said.

And the guy said, "Where it says 64 and 56, it's really 60 and 51." I made a secretive note of it in my book, which Cubby slyly noticed. Then Cubby said to the guy, "And did you get the one on 16? It's 144 from the front tee there, not 164." And his buddy goes, "Yeah, I got it. But did you get the one on 18? That first bush isn't there anymore, so that 128 is really 182." And I'm flipping frantically through the pages, trying to find the stupid 16th hole when I hear them both suddenly break up into hysterics. Great fun to con The Rook.

As God is my witness, I will get them someday.

I jammed the yardage book in the overall pockets, plus some sandwiches and apples, plus I had my wallet in there, my notepad, four pens, and a cellphone, which I forgot to leave in the car and is strictly forbidden at Augusta. I walked out of there looking like a man shoplifting porcupines.

I checked my watch. It was 7:29. I started sprinting for the bag room. Then I was reminded of one of Augusta's big rules: No running. I sprint-walked. People suddenly started parting seas for me. People jabbed each other. I was wondering what was going on when I heard: "There's Aaron's caddy." The overalls were, it turns out, a big deal. I was Augusta royalty. I was wearing the white, the green, the logo. I was the real deal. You know, if a guy were single . . .

I made it by 7:30. Luckily, Aaron wasn't there yet.

And he wasn't there by 7:45 either. Or 8. Or 8:30, 9, or 9:30.

"Welcome to the Pro Gap," Joe LaCava, caddy for Fred Couples, told me.

"What's the Pro Gap?" I asked.

"The difference between when the pro *says* he'll meet you and when he actually shows up."

Of course, caddies accept the Pro Gap as part of caddy life. But, as they pointed out, let "you" be late and you're as fired as Anna Nicole Smith's dietician.

Still, it was sort of caddy *Star Wars* outside that bag room. Fluff was there (for Jim Furyk). LaCava was there. Jim Mackay, the world-renowned "Bones," my personal caddy hero who had hauled Phil Mickelson for 10 years by then. And, of course, the Joe Namath of caddies, Bruce Edwards, Tom Watson's longtime Sancho Panza.

Edwards happened to be the person Tom Watson told, "I'm going to chip this in," on the 17th hole at Pebble Beach at the 1982 U.S. Open, which he did, to beat J. W. Nicklaus himself.

Finally, at 11:30, four hours late, Aaron showed up. He was much taller than I thought he'd be. Maybe 6–1, still slender, elegantly dressed, curly gray hair, glasses, and a visor.

"I'm just going to go into the Champion's Room (the locker room at Augusta reserved for past champions) and then we'll go. Meet me on the range in, what, 45 minutes?"

"Sure," I said, cheerfully. *Sure! What's another 45 minutes!?! No problem! Perhaps I'll knit another sweater!*

The bag was simple and blue, with no sponsor on it, and heavier than Meatloaf. What's this guy got in there, anvils? I remembered the time British golf writer Bill Elliott spent a day caddying for Faldo for a story. Elliott struggled under its weight all day, until he discovered, afterward, that Faldo had snuck a brick and three dozen extra balls into the bottom of the bag for a laugh. There is nobody that will crack you up like that madcap Nick Faldo.

I made my way past the ropes, into forbidden territory—the range—the place where no writer is allowed to go at the Masters, nor fan, nor photographer. Self-conscious and thrilled, I tried to think of what to do so as not to appear self-conscious and thrilled. So, naturally, I decided to eat.

I sat on the bench and pulled a pimento-cheese sandwich out, and an apple and a Gatorade. I was about to take my first bite when I noticed, for the first time, approximately 1,000 people watching me. The bleachers behind the range were full of fans and, at that moment, nobody was actually hitting balls, so they were watching me. I tried not to spill.

Just then, Bruce Edwards sat down next to me. Sitting on that bench, him waiting for the great Watson and me waiting for Aaron,

I, naturally, ruined the moment by hounding him desperately for advice.

"Just remember the three ups," he said.

"Three ups?" I asked.

"Show up, keep up, and shut up."

I asked Edwards if he ever wished he'd have done something else for a living.

"Never," he said. "In fact, in 1976, Tom wanted me to quit caddying for him and go to school. He even offered to pay for it. He wasn't winning much then and he said, 'Look, go get your degree and have a real life.' So I thought about it and I came back to him and said, 'No. I like *this* life.' And I'm sure as hell glad I did. Because that next year he won four times and the next year five." And went on to a career that has so far paid like a winning Lotto ticket and kept Edwards in cold beer and nice boats ever since. Finally, Watson himself showed up, about an hour late.

"I'm sorry," Edwards chided. "Did you mean 12 o'clock, Kansas City time?"

Caddies 1, Pro Gap 0.

They walked off and Edwards grinned at me. I thought maybe I should say that to my man. "I'm sorry, did you mean 7:30 A.M., sharp THURSDAY?" but then I thought, perhaps this is a wisecrack one might try after caddying 30 years, not 30 seconds.

Aaron came striding onto the range and I came striding after him, holding a bag of balls which I—ever the sharp caddy—had secured and made ready. Except when we got to our stall on the range and I plopped them down, they turned out to be the wrong balls. "I play Callaway," he said, staring at me. I jog-walked (no running!) back to the ball boys and said, "I need Callaway, fast!" and they said, "Red or blue?" And I said, "Bloody hell? You have red or blue?" I took a bag of each.

Aaron was accompanied by his coach, 79-year-old Manuel de la Torre, the head pro at Milwaukee Country Club, one of the foremost teachers of the "swing the club" school of golf. And already, he was tutoring Aaron on how to swing the club.

"What happened there?" Manuel said.

"I felt like I swung it a little right of the target."

"And where did it go?" said Manuel.

"Right of the target."

"Correct," said Manuel.

Whoa, this is the magic that they're discussing? This is the inside conversation that we're all dying to get up close and hear?

We went through two bags of BLUE Callaways, went through another bag in the bunker—where I learned upon receiving a dirty look that you want to flip the practice ball to him so that he doesn't have to move his feet—putted for a while, and then, suddenly, miraculously, we were on the first tee at Augusta National during the 65th playing of the Masters Tournament. It was wonderful . . . until Aaron uttered five awful words: "Do you know Scott Hoch?"

"Uh . . ."

"He's got nobody going with him, either, so we're going with him."

Suddenly, I was turning around to shake the hand of a man I'd mocked to 21 million readers more than once in print for: a) skipping the British Open every year because it's too "expensive"; b) missing a 2-foot putt that would've won him the 1989 Masters; and, c) being voted Least Liked Player on Tour in a poll of his peers.

Hoch looked at me. I looked at him. He knew.

"Scott, Rick Reilly," I said, holding my hand out.

He looked at me, looked at the hand, said, "I know who you are," and began to tee up his ball.

Oops.

Aaron gave me a look. I stared at my shoes. Not a shot hit yet and I was already causing him problems.

Still, I was thinking that Scott Hoch has had to play with people he dislikes and who dislike him quite often in his career. Like, say, on the order of every Thursday through Sunday. So, off we went.

Of all the signs in the world, the most ignored has to be the little white-and-green sign on the first tee at the Masters that reads, "Play Only One Ball Please." In fact, about the only place only one ball is played during practice rounds is at that first tee. Otherwise, players play about eight balls. Players hit all kinds of second shots, third shots, dozens of chips, putts, bunker shots, pitches, and lags from every possible angle on every green.

This makes practice days very difficult for your average everyday caddy and absolute, pure Dante's *Inferno* for your basic Rook. It was "throw those back to me" and "rake those spots" and "let me hit those again, Rick." If I'd had a methamphetamine habit, I couldn't have done it all: clubs to be cleaned, clubs to be exchanged for different clubs, balls to be cleaned, balls to be retrieved, bunkers to be raked. And that was just the stuff I *knew* I should be doing. God knows what I *wasn't* doing. I almost quit. If it hadn't been the first hole, I might have.

At one point on No. 1, I got so confused I put our 8-iron in Hoch's bag—they were both white—until Hoch's caddy cleared his throat. Caddy etiquette. If it were one day later and Hoch played the hole with the club in there, it would've been a two-shot penalty—on Hoch. And then he really wouldn't like me.

Exhausted and dehydrated by the time we reached the No. 2 tee box, I stood the bag up and went for a cup of water. When I came back, Tommy was pissed. "You *never* take your hand off the bag when it's standing up," he growled. "It can—and will—tip over at the worst possible time and place, like on my golf ball." Good point.

That would be another two-stroke penalty, wouldn't it? Played one hole, nearly caused four shots in penalties. Nice start.

Tommy Aaron is just slightly more finicky than the Sultan of Brunei. For instance, he informed me on the second hole not to hand him his putter until he reached the green. I always thought there's nothing better than a long walk with your putter, meaning you've hit the green, life is good, but, no.

One time, on No. 5, he hit a chip that looked like it was going to be short.

"Get up!" I said to it.

He turned to me. "Keep your mouth off my ball."

I was confused.

"I don't use my mouth," I said, earnestly. "I'm using this wet towel here." I held it up for him as proof that I wasn't popping his ball in my mouth to wash it.

"No, no. Keep your mouth off my ball. Don't talk to it. I want it to get up as much as you do. It doesn't help me to know that you're over there, telling it to get up or get down or whatever. It just adds to the pressure."

I said OK, and I thought about it. It "adds to the pressure"? You'd think he'd want to know that somebody is cheering him on, rooting for him "and" his stupid ball! How is that "more" pressure? It seems to me it's dividing the pressure in half, you and me, pal, a team! But the more I thought about it, the more I understood what he was trying to say. What he was saying is, "If I hear you urging my shots to do a certain thing—Sit! Bite! Run! Cut!—and they *don't*, I'm going to feel like I've let *you* down, too. I've got a family to support, and friends here, and fans, and press. The last thing I need is a caddy piling on, OK?"

It's like me. I write a weekly sports column. The "last" thing I want is my wife to call at the office and say, "Hey, how are you doing this week? Is the lead going to be good? The kids and I are really hoping it's going to be funny!"

Still, there were other things. He'd hit a drive and people would applaud and we'd walk down the fairway and he'd say to me, "I can't understand that."

"I'm sorry?" I said, fingering my wet towel, in case I needed it as evidence again.

"The gallery applauding. Can't they see I hit that one in the heel? I mean, don't they know anything about golf?"

I wanted to say, "Well, you're 64 years old. You've already told me you're playing with a painful hammertoe, an arthritic hip, a bone spur in your neck, a little vertigo, and insomnia. I suppose they're just glad you got it airborne."

One time, somebody in the crowd hollered, "Hey, Tommy!" and Tommy gave them the tiniest of waves.

"That's funny, isn't it?" he said.

"I'm sorry?" I said, for the 116th time.

"If I were at a tournament, I don't think I'd speak unless I was spoken to. I'm trying to work here, you know? How would they like it if I hung around the insurance office all day while they were working and said, 'Hey, Fred, way to go!' "

I agreed, of course. They should all be hung from the old tree on the clubhouse veranda.

On the third hole, Aaron said, "Seemed like there was some tension between you and Scott on the first tee." Uh-oh. Here it comes. I've got no chance now. I'll get the rest of this day and see ya later.

"Yeah, well, I noticed that, too," I said. "Not sure what that was about."

He stared at me for a second and then walked on.

Uh-oh.

At the end of nine, Aaron had played well. I had us at one-over-par 37. But he suddenly decided to quit for the day. He also said he wasn't going to play the par-3 tournament. "And I'm afraid I'm going to stay with the caddy I was given," he said. "You can take the clubs to the bag room. Thanks for your help."

Crushed. Heartbroken. Untipped.

Sacked after nine practice holes at the Masters. If not Aaron, who would ever let me out? My book advance flashed before my eyes. I was doomed.

Desperate, I said, "You sure? Because I'll be here all week. Maybe if your caddy comes up hurt or something?"

He just smiled and said, "I doubt it."

I hung around in my beloved caddy overalls as long as I could. A few Japanese people took my picture. I finally had to take them off. I didn't see how a caddy could ask Tiger Woods a question in the press conference.

"Uh, Tiger, how do you feel about people's mouths on your balls?"

The next day, Thursday, I followed Aaron and his caddy, a local, a few holes. I felt like a jilted lover.

But then I noticed something wonderful. I couldn't hear, but Aaron was jawing at him animatedly. I thought maybe it was the dreaded Mouth-on-Ball Syndrome, but it seemed worse. Aaron was walking away, shaking his head. And the caddy was shrugging his shoulders.

Could he have accidentally said, "Good shot?"

Aaron shot 81. I found him in the clubhouse after lunch and said it looked like he'd played fairly well, but something seemed to be bothering him.

"That caddy," he said, shaking his head, "has the *worst* damn attitude of any caddy I've ever had. Just a *piss-poor* attitude. He was pouting the *whole* time. He gave me a read that was just flat wrong on 16 and I told him so and he pouted. He had his head down all the time. The most miserable, worst goddamn *horrible* attitude I've ever seen."

Hope springs anew.

I cleared my throat. "Well, if he's that bad, how about this? I'll 'pay' him to stay off your bag the rest of the week and I'll work for you for free!"

Aaron thought about it and thought about it some more and finally said, "OK."

Pinocchio, you're a real boy.

On the way to the pressroom, higher than Tokyo rent, I saw Carl Jackson, Ben Crenshaw's Masters-only caddy, the one who gave Crenshaw the little ball-positioning tip before the 1995 Masters that Crenshaw credited for helping him win. I imagined me doing that for Aaron.

Aaron to Press: I know it's incredible, a 64-year-old man winning, but it never would've happened without my caddy, Rick. He noticed my left pinky knuckle was pronating slightly and it made all the difference in the world. Rick, I want you to have the jacket.

Me: No, I couldn't.

Aaron: Oh, nonsense. Try it on!

Me: Well . . .

I paid the old caddy $150 for the day he missed on Wednesday and another $150 for the day he was going to miss Friday, and I said I'd pay him $150 for any day after that, although, after the 81, Masters chairman Hootie Johnson was going to vogue across the 18th green naked before that happened. Still, the guy made $300 for sitting on his couch watching on television while I humped the bag up Augusta's hills for bupkus. OK, I undermined him, but I ain't holding any telethons for him.

Friday morning came and as Aaron met me, he warned, "Now, don't get too excited out there."

"I'm sorry?" I said.

"If the caddy gets all nervous and excited, it seeps into me. So just be quiet and calm."

Got it.

When we got to the first tee, Aaron said, "Rick, do you know Notah Begay?"

Uh-oh.

I did know Begay and he knew me and I could tell that from the glare I was getting. Begay had spent a week in an Albuquerque prison after his second DUI, only it wasn't exactly the gulag. He was part of a "work-release" program, so he was allowed to get up in the morning, go hit balls at his club, have lunch at the club, then play 18 holes in the afternoon, then dinner at the club, then back to the prison to sleep. I said they ought to call the jail Swing-Swing. I said that for most guys, that wasn't prison, that was a week at the Myrtle Beach Red Roof Inn. I'd heard Begay was ticked off about it. Still, unlike Hoch, he begrudgingly shook my hand. I made a note to stay very clear of his tee shots.

Aaron might have said something to me like, "I noticed some tension between you and Notah there," except for the fact that he found something that annoyed him about Begay and Campbell right off. He canned a 40-footer on No. 1 to save par, walked over to me, and whispered, "Did you see that?"

"I'm sorry?" I said, nervously fingering my wet towel and trying to figure out what I'd done now.

"Neither of those guys said, 'Nice putt.' That's the way it is with these younger players. They don't see any shot but their own."

"Selfish," I said, shaking my head. For once, he was mad at somebody other than me. It didn't last long.

On No. 2, Aaron had a little chip back from above the green. I gave him the wedge and stood there a second and then realized I better get the bag to the side of the hole that would lead to the next tee box, as all good caddies do. He was still eyeing the chip from behind the shot and he gave me a dirty little look. I froze. Then he chipped.

Going down the third fairway, he said, "The clubs are making too much noise."

"I'm sorry?"

"They're making too much noise. Listen to the noise they're making. Quiet them down."

He walked ahead of me in a kind of huff. I wandered over to Fanny. "I can't *believe* this guy!" I complained to her, struggling up the hill at No. 3. "He says my clubs make too much noise when I walk. I mean, Christ, what am I supposed to do, buy fourteen mufflers and—"

"Yes," she said. "Yours do make too much noise."

I stared at her. She stared at me. "Take your towel and wrap it through the middle of the irons, like this. Then walk with your hand over them."

I tried it. They quieted right down. Fanny Sunneson is a goddess.

On No. 4, the par 3, he was standing in the middle of the tee box, about eight feet from where I was standing with the bag, just to the left of the tee markers. "Rick, come over here," he said.

I had a flutter of excitement. He was finally trusting me enough to ask me advice. Maybe he wanted to talk wind. Maybe yardage. Maybe club selection. So I stood the bag up where it was and walked over to him. He looked at me like he'd just swallowed a cockroach. "*With* the bag," he said, irritated.

I didn't understand why he wanted me to drag the bag the eight feet out to the middle of the tee markers when it was much easier for him to simply take the club himself. Fanny and Sponge weren't doing that. Their guys would stand by their bag, pick the stick, and walk the eight feet. But so be it. I got the bag and brought it to him. He took his club. I went back to where I was and he hit it.

But on the sixth hole, another par 3, I forgot and the same thing happened. "Rick, bring the bag," he said sharply, and I schlepped it out there again. He took a 6-iron and made the most gorgeous swing, nearly making a hole-in-one, missing by inches left. As the huge crowd roared, he came over to me and looked me right in the eye. I figured he was going to say something clever or snappy, something like, "Pulled it." Or, "Take a suck of that!" But instead he yelled—YELLED—"Now, goddammit, I'm not gonna tell you again! I don't wanna have to walk clear over there to get a goddamn club!" There was a hush around the crowd at the tee box. Caddy whipping. All I could do was clean my little 6-iron and stare at the bottom of the bag.

I would ask Couples' caddy, Joe LaCava, about this later. I said, "Why would a guy want me to pick up the bag and take it to the middle of the tee box when he could just take it with him when he steps out there?" And Joe LaCava said, simply, "Because he is a professional golfer."

I didn't know what that answer meant then. But I'd learn. I'd learn.

On No. 8, I watched Sponge and Fanny give their guys 3-woods so they didn't have to walk clear back to the tee, so I did the same. I was kneeling there, trying to catch my wind, when I felt a tap on my shoulder. It was Begay. "Here is where he lets me have it," I thought. Here is where he spikes my kidneys. Or gets me with a homemade prison shiv. Instead, he said, "You should go wait with the others." I looked around and Sponge and Fanny were 150 yards up the 8th fairway, resting happily in the shade.

Left the Rook behind.

After that, it all fell apart for us. Aaron bogeyed the par-5 8th despite being right in front in two and then doubled 10, where he chunked a chip into a bunker, then three-putted.

Then we headed into Amen Corner and it was a thrill to be inside the ropes at the most famous section of holes in golf. "Nobody" gets inside the ropes at Augusta except players and caddies and the scorer. Not coaches. Not photographers. Not press. Not rules officials. Nobody. It's virginal land, pristine. If Ansel Adams were around, he'd shoot it. Walking down 11 fairway, I was struck by the hugeness of the place, the vast "space." I'd covered thirteen Masters and yet I'd never noticed how deep the woods went to the left of 11 and 12. It looked like *Blair Witch 3* in there.

Another odd thing. Since the crowds are so huge at Amen Corner, I was aware that every time I moved a step, I was blocking the views of maybe 100 people or more. It was an odd feeling. Move one yard this way and those 100 can't see. One yard that way and those 100 can't see. Great, great fun. I was the God of Views, free to give and take away as I saw fit. "Oh, you drove the Dodge Dart clear from Manitoba for your first Masters? Sorry. I choose to stand . . . *here.*"

All my life I'd wanted to stand on the 12 green during The Masters. I'd always wondered what it's like out there, viewed by thousands of fans, but all from 160 yards away—every movement watched through binoculars but not a sound heard. For fans, it's like watching a silent movie. But on the green, so far away from the thousands watching, you find out. "Fuck me," Begay said when his par putt missed. Aaron missed a four-footer for par, but, to his credit, did not say, "Fuck me." The thousands back in the gallery probably assume they're saying, "Well played there, Tommy," and "Oh, a spot of bad luck there, chum," and instead they're going, "Fuck me."

There is nothing in golf like the 13th tee box, either. Set back into the azaleas and dogwoods, it must be the most beautiful inland tee in the world. And yet, to the players, it is more famously known as the home of the "pee bush." Players and caddies go back behind a huge bush and pee. There are not many Porta Potties at Augusta and the ones they have are packed, so 13 has become the traditional whizzing ground. Not wanting to piss on history, I also loosed the lizard back there, and as I was doing so it hit me that some of the great names in golf history—Jones, Snead, Hogan, Nicklaus—had all squirted on this very bush. It made me proud. It also made me want to throw out my shoes first chance I got.

We made an awful double bogey at 13, but it wasn't our fault. We wound up in a divot after our second shot, had to blade it out of there and over, putted way, way by in 4, half-lagged it up in 5, and missed a three-footer for 6. I still feel if I could've spoken to his ball, it would've helped. Now we were 10 over par with five holes to go. We were headed for 90. Doug Ford, here we come.

But at 14, 15, and 16, we made great pars—nearly made three birdies—and it was a privilege to carry the bag of a man who can play that well at 64 years old with more ailments than the Mayo Clinic. The pars made him so chipper, in fact, that I offered a small bit of chitchat. "This place has great memories for you, huh?"

He said it did. He said he hated to come and play so badly as he did this week. "Shooting in the 80s is not my idea of fun," he said. He said he loved Augusta and loved the memories of his win here, when he made birdie at 18 and had no idea he'd won until later, since he wasn't in the last group.

I offered up a potential grenade, seeing as how we were coming to the 18th tee box. "How did the whole De Vicenzo snafu happen?" I said, walking just out of swinging-putter range.

He was quite happy to talk about it. "It was really so ridiculous," he said. "In those days, you'd check your scorecard at a little card table they set up, right out in the open, under the sun. Roberto was a little mad that he'd made bogey on the last hole and so he just signed the card without even looking at it. He threw it on the table and left. Whoosh. Now, I'm *very* meticulous about my scores. I double and triple-check them. My card checked out and I was about to leave when I looked up at the scoreboard and saw that it said 'De Vicenzo, 11-under.' And it hit me that something was wrong. I had him at one 'higher' than that, 10-under. I checked it against the scoreboard and realized what had happened. I said to one of the officials, 'Better get Roberto back here. This isn't right.' I felt bad, but people make mistakes on your scorecard. Happens all the time. You *have* to check it."

At 18, Aaron made an unbelievable chip shot, a purposely bladed chip from against the collar that he aimed 180 degrees away from the hole, ran over the green, down the hump, over the fringe on the other side, and back to within six inches of the hole. It was the kind of shot only a man who'd played 37 Masters could've made, and even Begay and Campbell put their putters down to applaud.

Tommy checked his card, meticulously, then gave me a tour of the Champion's Locker Room, which is the tiniest locker room you've ever been in, yet with the greatest collection of nameplates ever in one room. His was under Jimmy Demaret's. Then he had a lunch and a couple vodkas and I had a beer, and suddenly he was the nicest man you'd ever want to meet, chatty, funny, cordial.

He gave me his critique of my maiden loop. "For a first-time caddy, you weren't *that* bad," he said. "It seemed like you wanted to get rid of the bag at all costs. Most caddies walk right up on the green with the bag on their shoulder, wash the ball, make sure everything's right, and *then* get rid of the bag. You just wanted to get rid of the bag right away, no matter what, get rid of the bag, then come and check on me."

That was true, of course, for two reasons. One, I was taught you don't walk on the green with your bag on your shoulder as it makes deep footprints in the green. Guess not. And two, that stupid bag was heavier than a lead piano.

I asked him if there were any scorecard problems this time, 33 years later. "As a matter of fact," he said, "Michael Campbell had two incorrect scores for me—on 2 and on 8. I had sixes on both and he had me for fives. I'm telling you, it happens all the time!"

What a stupid Campbell is.

We could've used those fives, by the way. We finished fourth worst in the tournament at 163, just 27 shots behind Tiger's two-day 136, which would lead to his four-day 16-under 272, which would merely win him the Consecutive Grand Slam is all. Only Billy Casper had a higher two-day score at 167. Gay Brewer had an 84 the first day and withdrew. We were 90th out of 96 in driving distance at 241 yards (66 yards behind Tiger), and 90th in greens in regulation (13 total), but we were 30th in putts. Then again, we did a whole helluva lot better than the charming Doug Ford, who made a six on the first hole, withdrew immediately, took his $5,000 participant's honorarium, and went home. Class guy. I'll bet he voted against Lincoln, too.

Actually, $5,000 to play one hole is about what third-place finisher Phil Mickelson ($380,000) made per hole after playing 72.

Maybe he's not so dumb after all.

A CADDY DICTIONARY

If the caddy says . . .

"So we go Yogi Bear on the last six holes and he goes Helicopter City with every one of his bats right there, straight into the Jacques Cousteau. Then he gives me the bullet, bang, just like that. Looks like I'm trollin' at Westchester."

He means . . .

"So, we played each of the last six holes in one-over-par bogey. This made my player very angry and he began throwing each of his clubs in a whirling manner into the nearby body of water. This is the point at which he fired me. It appears I'll be in the parking lot asking players if they need a caddy at the next tournament on the schedule, which is Westchester."

2

JOHN DALY

Unzipped

Some people parachute off skyscrapers. Some scuba under the polar ice cap. Me, I spend 24 hours as John Daly's caddy.

7 P.M. Sunday

Daly is supposed to be here at the 4,000,012th celebrity pro-am kickoff dinner of his life. This one is at Willowbend Country Club in Mashpee, on Cape Cod, in June 2001.

I want to caddy for Daly because absolutely nothing about him says golf. Look at that swing. Like his life, it's *way* past parallel. Look at that hair. The classic mullet: business in front, party in the back. Look at that body. Like some balls after he smashes them, it's *way* out of round. Can you imagine what he'd look like if he gave up smoking?

But it's also more than that. Daly is so human it hurts. There is nothing that hasn't happened to him, no weakness he doesn't have, no demon he doesn't duel every day. No athlete today comes with higher highs and lower lows than John Daly. If *Psychology Today* ever runs a centerfold, he'd be it. And yet, against all odds, he's still out there, making it.

7:21 P.M.

There is a buzz across the great country club hall. Everybody's favorite train wreck, the 35-year-old Daly, has been spotted. In a room where Boston sports heroes Bobby Orr, John Havlicek, and Dwight Evans are hanging, Daly is the one people want to see in the flesh. Every rich guy in the room wants for his partner tomorrow a confused Arkansas redneck who hasn't won a tournament in six years.

As he tries to make his way across the room, you notice he doesn't look like anybody else here, a little like Mayberry's Otis in a coat and tie, a bit awkward around country-club folk, itching to get away from the stares.

And boy do they stare. Nobody else in the history of golf has had their life flayed open on the rocks and devoured the way Daly has. The ongoing wrestling match with alcohol. The three demolition-derby marriages. The undefeated and untied record against hotel furniture. The gambling losses approaching the GNP of Chile. The 18 he took at Bay Hill. The troika of U.S. Open disasters: walking off after 9 at Congressional, swatting a moving ball at Pinehurst, the 14 he took on the 18th hole at Pebble Beach. The unforgettable image of him shivering and crying on an 85-degree August day at a tournament.

He should be doubled-over in a little ball in some Idaho cabin by now, refusing to shave or speak. And yet he stays in front of the cameras. He stays because he has this amazing talent that even he can't kill. He's the longest player in golf. He's got the softest hands. He did not check into the Hotel Orville Moody after he won the 1991 PGA out of Absolutely Nowhere, USA. Instead, four years later, Daly won *another* major. And he won a B.C. Open in between. And a BellSouth. And two European Tour events. And those wins kept him out in front of a public and a press that keeps waiting under his window, wondering when he'll jump.

And it's not just golf. I've thrown footballs with him. He can throw a 50-yard spiral that will hurt your hand for two days. When he was eight and nine, he made it to the semifinals of the national Punt, Pass & Kick contest two years in a row. Represented the New Orleans Saints. Wonder if Archie Manning remembers he met the kid? Twice. He kicked a winning 46-yard field goal in high school. He once made 36 straight free throws. He was a Babe Ruth all-star baseball player. He's a helluva water skier. Hell, he's even a good dancer.

8:33 P.M.

Having dinner next to John Daly is to watch a lot of food go cold. Everybody wants to talk to him, pat him on the back, say good luck. Daly is America's Project Hope.

The world approaches. There's nobody that doesn't like Daly. They know he's not particularly dangerous. Mostly, the only person he ever hurts is himself. And so everybody's got the cure.

Look, a few of us get together every morning and talk about our alcoholism. Why don't you stop by tomorrow?

Hey, I know you struggle with your weight. I've got this diet I've developed . . .

John, I know you've lost a few sponsors. I work with this management firm in . . .

They mean well. They do. They see a man with a gift trying desperately to pitch it all in the Dumpster and they reach out. They all want to be his mother, his father, his big brother, his AA sponsor.

But help is what Daly runs from the fastest. He's so sick of help that he blew off millions in sponsor money just so he wouldn't have to go to any more rehabs and AA meetings, just so he could be left alone with his demons.

Daly listens intently, takes their cards, says he'll think about it. Later, he'll ash-can the cards on the way to the bar.

9:31 P.M.

Gary McCord is emceeing the live auction. He's trying to pump up a one-day spa treatment in New York City.

"J.D.!" he yells from the stage. "What about it? You could drive the Winnebago right through the front window and never have to leave the front seat!"

Daly flips him off.

"And we have a $1,000 bid from John Daly!"

9:57 P.M.

Daly gets in some face time with Paul Fireman, owner of Willowbend and CEO of Reebok, the Boston-based shoe Godzilla. The whole event is Fireman's baby. That's the reason Daly is here, to pay his respects to Fireman, try to show him he's not a lawn-and-bottle club waiting to happen. Reebok used to pay Daly millions, then stopped when Daly kept losing TKOs to hotel rooms, engaging in fistfights with tour players' parents, and checking out of alcohol rehab farms before he'd warmed a pillow.

"I'm hoping maybe if he sees I'm fine," Daly says, "he'll take me back."

10:29 P.M.

Uh-oh.

Tour player Rocco Mediate has persuaded everybody to go to a bar, this little dive 15 minutes from the club—a lot of coeds, a lot of golf groupies, a bad little band, $2 longnecks, more potential trouble than Ray Lewis's limo. In other words, John Daly's kind of place.

Here, in one room, is nearly all of his favorite addictions: alcohol, cigarettes, cheeseburgers, and women. If the joint had an M&M's machine and a pharmacy, we'd have The Big Six covered. Bringing Daly here is like bringing a dieting fat woman to the Sara Lee factory.

"No problem," Daly says as we enter. "I do it all the time."

Tonight's trapeze act will be performed without a net.

11:09 P.M.

I suggest to Daly that today is the first day of the rest of his booty life, considering he has just broken up this very day with his fiancée, Shanae Chandler. "No way," he says. "I ain't lookin'." Of course, he's a man, so it will take time to recover and open up emotionally again. Maybe in an hour or so.

It's odd that he and Shanae are history, since the *Golf Digest* currently on the newsstands has an 18-page spread detailing how blissfully happy they are together.

"Fuckin' bitch," Daly grumbles. "I had a buddy of mine from the FBI tailin' her for three weeks. Bitch was cheatin' on me! She was lyin' to me! And I got proof!"

I muttered sympathetically.

"I've just been trampled by women my whole life," says the man who once wrote a song entitled "All My Exes Wear Rolexes." "Everybody tells me, 'You treat 'em too damn good, John.' I mean,

I bought this one a brand-new car, a $50,000 ring! Man, I paid her way thru college!"

And what did you get out of it? I ask, just trying to be the good caddy.

"Well, yeah, she did take care of me through the lowest point of my career." He thinks for a while. "Damn! I just don't get 'em! Maybe I try to buy love, I don't know. I just thank God I didn't marry the bitch."

Daly and any one woman generally have a freshness date of about 18 months. He's always hopelessly in love one time you see him and lovelessly in hate the next time. When he was 21, he married a girl named Dale Crafton of Blytheville, Arkansas. They divorced two years later. He then married Bettye Fulford, only to find out that she was eight years older than she told him and was still married when he proposed. Although that's not exactly what broke up the marriage. What broke up the marriage may have been Daly coming home to their Castle Pines, Colorado, house on a December night in 1992 and busting it apart like a TinkerToy town—and nearly Bettye with it. They had a daughter, Shynah.

Then he married the "LER" in a walking, curvy, three-girl CHRYSLER billboard at the Bob Hope Chrysler Classic in Palm Springs. Her name was Paulette Dean. They had a daughter, too, Sierra. I told him it seemed like he was always happy with Paulette.

"Yeah, until after Sierra was born, and she stopped havin' sex with me," he complained. "Man, that hurt. What did I do that was so wrong she doesn't want to be with me? I mean, I think I'm a damn good lover. I'm a very slow lover. I love oral sex. Not just on me, both ways! I'm very giving! I'll make a woman come five or six times before I have intercourse with her! Why did I deserve that?"

I did what all guys do when another guy bares his soul. I took a long glug from my beer bottle in order not to say anything.

"Someday, my kids are going to read about what these women did to their dad," Daly says, "and they're not gonna be too happy. They're gonna finally see how bad their moms treated me. How money-hungry they all were."

Just a guess, but here, he may be referring to the estimated $35,000-a-month alimony and child support he pays.

"I'll find the right one someday. Maybe I just need an 80-year-old woman who'll just take care of me. But, I mean, damn, where's a woman who will fight for you?"

If Daly would look up, he'd have about six ready to do just that right now.

Midnight

Still no alcohol has gone into Daly. Mediate is blotto. I'm a good sheet and a quarter to the wind. But Daly is sober as an Amish librarian.

It's weird because Daly used to be *such* a drunk. He was a Jack Daniel's guy—thus, the "J.D." nickname that still sticks with him. And the more J.D. and J.D. became one fluid, the more he'd hate himself. He used to drive full-speed through red lights, as a kind of self-punishment. Problem was, Bettye and their little girl would be in the car. He'd bust shot glasses in his hand just out of anger. If you look at his hands, you can see the scars from all the times he punched mirrors—hotel mirrors, bedroom mirrors, car mirrors. Mirrors showed him all the things he didn't want to see. In fact, later, during the 2002 British Open, Daly's hand was killing him. He went to a doctor, who found a piece of glass that had been embedded in a bone for years. They stitched him up, but the stitches came out and Daly used his own method of keeping them together: Super Glue.

"You and I both know I can't drink whiskey," he says. "I was a mean drunk on whiskey. The last time I drank whiskey was when I was 25 years old. I drank it from the time I was 14 until I was 25. Even today, the smell of whiskey makes me sick. I'll never drink whiskey again. Never."

Of course, as the song lyric goes, " 'Never again' is what you swore the time before."

12:18 A.M.

The guitarist comes over during a break and asks Daly if he'd mind playing a song with them. They ask Daly this in nearly every bar he goes into anywhere in the world, and he almost always obliges them one song. And that song is usually Dylan's "Knockin' on Heaven's Door." Daly can play other songs. He's actually pretty good on the guitar. Unfortunately, Daly plays the Dylan song no matter the situation. Once, at a Make-a-Wish dinner for terminally ill children at the Bethpage U.S. Open, they begged him to get up in front of the kids and play something. So he whispered to the band what he wanted. Pretty soon, they were wheeling into "Knockin' on Heaven's Door."

Oops.

2:15 A.M.

Time for mullet-wearing legends to find a pillow, and still no recipe has made its way down Daly's famous gullet. Alcohol everywhere and Daly has not had a sip.

When was your last drink? I ask just before he piles in the car as the designated driver.

"August of last year [2000]," he says. "I had three beers that night at Ruth's Chris steak house. I was having dinner with Shanae. I'm not sayin' I'm never having another drink. I might. You never know. But it's not something I want in my life.

"It's just all these people had all these expectations for me. But deep down, I just didn't think they had the answers. I mean I went to AA meetings. They helped me, the 12 steps, with other stuff—the cigarettes, the pills, the gambling, the food. And, you know, alcohol, too, I guess. I mean, I still talk to my mentor all the time.

"Finally, it just hit me. This is my life. Fuck the money. I was miserable. I couldn't live with the world's expectations anymore. I'm just a guy who's tryin' to get his life back together. I'm not gonna worry about what people think about me."

And the millions you kicked away?

"Fuck the money," he says. "I couldn't have spent all of it anyway."

I look at him.

"OK," Daly says, "*I* could."

7 A.M. Monday

Daly shows up at Willowbend, right on time. My first job, he says, is to find him a Diet Coke.

John Daly is not an orange juice guy. He is not a coffee guy. He is not a breakfast guy. He is a Diet Coke guy. He will drink them all day and all night. When he is lying on his deathbed someday, his i.v. will drip Diet Coke.

It's not unusual for him to have 20 in a day. "I just love the taste of 'em," he says.

He's also got a Marlboro going. He's a two-packs-a-day guy except when he's a three-packs-a-day guy. John Daly is one of the great consumers in American history.

"Somebody tried to get me to quit smoking," he says, shrugging. "They gotta be fuckin' kidding."

But aren't you afraid of lung cancer?

Daly nearly does a spit take. "Do you know how much stuff I could worry about? Hell, alcohol kills your liver. We're all dyin' every day. I'm know I'm gonna be in a box someday, six feet under."

8:36 A.M.

Waiting for him on the range, there's time to rifle through his bag, as all good caddies must do.

There's two dozen Titleist Pro VI balls, five Zippo lighters, a large can of Zippo lighter fluid, a bottle of Bayer, a bottle of Allegra, a bottle of sunblock, a box of Band-Aids, 15 fricking gloves, and five cigars packaged with lighters.

Apparently, if we are all somehow trapped overnight on the 11th hole, Daly wants everybody to be able to smoke.

As for clubs, everything is Titleist, including three Vokey wedges—60, 52, and 48 degrees—forged Titleist 981 irons 2–9, a 12.5-degree Titleist 975J 3-wood, and a Scotty Cameron putter. He's got no 5-wood. The Big Boy everybody wants to see him hit, the Johnny Wadd Holmes of drivers, is a Titleist 975J 7.5 degree that he's bent down to 6.5. Six point five is damn near the loft of most putters. It's got a very stiff Pinley shaft, with gobs of lead tape on the bottom. It's covered by a big lion headcover, which is Daly's idea. He says the lion rules the jungle "and I want to control my jungle."

What's mind-blowing is that Daly is playing Titleists for free. Nada. Scratch. Can you imagine that? The longest hitter on tour (eight yards longer than Tiger in 2002) getting *nothing* to play his brand of clubs? It'd be like Miles Davis playing on a street corner, his horn case open for change.

He used to have one of the richest club deals on tour—with Callaway. Daly just kept screwing up, time after time, and each time the late owner Ely Callaway stuck with him. Ely agreed to pay off all of Daly's gambling debts—rumored to be $9 million—and let him continue with his deal, which still had $3 million left, on one condition: He stop gambling, stop drinking, and attend regular AA meetings.

That was in the summer of 1999. Every week was another rumor. Daly was seen guzzling here. Seen playing craps there. Seen playing craps and guzzling here and there. "I got so sick of callin' and having to tell 'em, 'Hey, I wasn't there. That's just a rumor.' "

But in September of that year, Callaway had enough proof to insist that Daly check into a San Diego rehab. He'd already done two rehab stretches—one in Tucson and one at Betty Ford—and he was looking forward to it the way a Wisconsin nudist looks forward to mosquito season.

Daly tried to like it. He really did. He checked in. Of course, he brought his fiancée, but he checked in. They even stayed a night. But it was just too much. Something in his brain just snapped. So he did something only John Daly could do. He jumped back in his car, picked up his cellphone, and called Ely himself.

"Just cain't do it, Mr. C," Daly said, as he put the joint in his rearview mirror. "That place ain't for me."

Ely begged him to turn around, but no. Daly went straight to Las Vegas, where he gambled, drank, and partied for all he was worth, which, right about then, was suddenly very little. He not only walked away from the $3 million but also was handed back the $1.7 million in gambling debts he owed. Didn't matter. It was worth it to him.

"I just got sick of listening to anyone and everyone," Daly says now. "I just got tired of playin' that whole game. For the first time in my life, I'm takin' care of myself."

9:05 A.M.

For the clinic, with 2,000 people watching, emcee McCord knows enough to save Daly for last. There's been no time to hit balls. All the players just sit in director's chairs until McCord calls them forward to hit their specialty shot and make fun of them. And now McCord wants Daly to step up and rip one. Stiff as a corpse, Daly gets up anyway and crunches one 310. McCord is disappointed.

"Aw, hit another one," says McCord. "That one just broke the adhesions."

9:25 A.M.

As we make our way to the first tee, I notice that we're being followed by Daly's regular caddy, Mick Collins, 40, a 2-iron-thin six-foot-two Iowan with a hangdog face. "The Mickster" as Daly calls him, can usually be found with a cigarette in one hand, a beer in the other, and a second on the way. But right now, on a day when he could be away from golf, away from Daly, he's following us, making sure I don't caddy his man off a cliff, I guess.

This is how it works in pro golf now. Nearly every pro bag I'll take, the regular caddy comes along anyway. It would happen with David Duval, too, and Jill McGill on the LPGA Tour. It's because in big-time golf today, one of the simplest things a caddy does is work on the golf course. They also serve as travel agent, shrink, bodyguard, chauffeur, navigator, valet, butler, and father confessor. Isn't that right, Mick?

"Nah," he says, "I just do all John's drinking for him."

They're the Tour's odd couple—the beer hound and the alcoholic; the splinter and the barrel—and it's working. Before Mickster came along, Daly had missed nine straight cuts and fallen to No. 507 on the Official World Golf Ranking, just below the deceased Jack Lemmon. Since then—going into this week's tournament at Hartford—they've made a Lazarus-like comeback, surviving 18 of 24 cuts and, two weeks ago, finishing fifth at Memphis. Now Daly was into the top 100 in the world.

"I got every caddy on this tour pullin' for J.D.," says Mick. " 'Cuz if we win, they know the Mickster is gonna throw the greatest party this tour has ever seen!"

Uh-oh.

9:31 A.M.

We tee off. I've been appointed official scorer. As usual, Daly has drawn the big enchiladas of amateur partners—the CEO of Kmart, the CEO of JCPenney, the CEO of Choice Point, and former Boston Bruin great Cam Neely. They all want to see what I want to see: little balata-covered spheres go hideous distances.

Last night, I went over the yardages with Mick, sort of the way a dressmaker wants to go over Pam Anderson's measurements, just for the sheer fun of it.

"Man, I've seen him hit a 2-iron 260 yards, no problem," Mick said. "When he gets really fired up, he goes nuclear. At Memphis, he carried a 6-iron 235 yards. That was *carry*."

This is a man whose genes are *literally* nuclear, since his daddy worked at nuclear power plants his whole life. This is a man who, through the 2002 season, has led the Tour in driving distance 11 straight years, the most any player has ever led a single category. This is a man who once hit a drive 440 yards at Royal St. George's in England. "You've got to really pay attention to fairway bunkers and lakes," Mick says. "Stuff that other caddies don't have to think about. I mean, he'll *cut* drivers 315 yards."

I realize I'm drooling.

9:47 A.M.

A local TV crew comes up to us on the second fairway. The reporter asks, "What's the secret to hitting it so far?"

"Well," says Daly, "you gotta have a lot of ex-wives. I just think of them and hit it."

10:24 A.M.

It's a pretty decent team we've got. Neely is very good and very long. The executives aren't half good, but not all the way bad. But there is nothing anywhere like the game I'm carrying.

It's an absolute joy to work for Daly. He plays fast, like a man getting in a quick nine holes after robbing a bank. He flops everything from 25 yards in, and each one is a thrill, because he flops off tight lies, chunk lies, everything. Daly would flop off airport tarmac. The man seemingly has never hit a bump-and-run shot in his life, and yet he won the British Open. Figure that!

The backswing is a kick to behold up close, too. It's longer than Tolstoy and yet somehow precise.

His talent weakens your lower-jaw muscles and yet, "Nearly every teacher I had when I was younger wanted to change it," he says. "They'd say, you're too feely. Your backswing is way too long. Your grip is too strong. I had this pro once work with me and basically tell me, 'Son, you're never gonna make it.' "

Yeah, and people told Eminem he was too white to rap.

That's Daly's whole point. Maybe the people always wanting to help, help, help, have no idea what they're talking about.

11:07 A.M.

On the fifth hole, Daly hits a drive that I pace off as 331 yards. That was probably the last of the adhesions. Unfortunately, Long John Daly is playing too long today, having flown two of the first five greens. It's possible this may be the fault of his rookie caddy, who thought the yardage was to front when it was to middle.

What? You never had a hangover?

11:20 A.M.

On the sixth, Daly hits a sweet shot that cozies up to about eight feet from the pin.

"Good swing, Boss," I say.

"Yeah," he says, picking up his cigarette. "Imagine how good I could be if somebody would clean the dirt out of my grooves."

Oops.

Still, it's a chance to ask him about one of his old caddies, Jeff (Squeeky) Medlen, with whom Daly won the 1991 PGA title. Medlen was free because his regular boss, Nick Price, was with his nine-months-pregnant wife. Squeeky would win it three years later, in 1994, with Price. Three more years later, Squeeky would die of leukemia.

"Every tee box that whole week, he'd say the same thing," Daly says, then goes into Squeeky's helium voice: "Rip it, John."

On the last day, on the last hole, a par 4, with a three-shot lead, some caddies thought Squeeky was crazy to let Daly hit driver. "Hell, Squeek wasn't gonna let me take nothin' else *but* driver!"

Daly remembers. "We both figured: why not? I hit it all week. And even if I hit in the water, I'd be so far up there, I could drop and still be on in 3. Two-putt for a five, at worst a six, and I still win by two." As it happened, he flushed it right down the middle, made par, and won the tournament.

Being his caddy for one day, I can see it. You get addicted to the distance. It's a rush, a jolt, a fix, and you *need* it. You're constantly pulling the lion off the driver, hoping he'll get the hint. You find yourself saying, "Hell, yeah, I think you can hit it over that house. Just blow it over the whole damn *cul de sac*!

11:28 A.M.

At every tee box, there lurks something sinister and dangerous to my man—Twix bars.

Actually, anything made of chocolate is dangerous to my man as he is unable to resist such things and they go straight to his gut without passing Go.

There has rarely been a love affair like Daly and chocolate. It might stem from his favorite meal—his mother's biscuits and chocolate gravy. When he won the British Open, he came to the winner's press conference and delivered one of my single favorite moments in interview history. All these half-dead Royal and Ancient dandruffs were there in their Windsor knots. The prospect of having Daly represent them for all time looked like it might completely do them in. Who'd win next year, Jed Clampett? And Daly said he owed the victory to the homemade chocolate donuts that some local was selling out on the 10th hole. "I got one every day," Daly told the world. "You know those Otis Spunkmeyer chocolate-chocolate chip ones you can get at the Shell stations back home? Well, these were even better 'n those."

I thought the dandruffs were going to have a group stroke right then and there.

I say, Nigel. Who is this Spunkmeyer chap Master Daly refers to?

One time I was with him on a Thursday evening after the first round of the Masters. He was laid out in a Barcalounger, stuffing himself with peanut M&M's and Diet Coke and double-chocolate cake. Fifty-three-year-old Jack Nicklaus was on TV discussing his opening-round 67, which tied him for the lead. Nicklaus was saying that he was motivated by "all these young players hitting the gym after every round, working out, eating the right foods." That nearly caused Daly to choke on the cake he was cramming in his mouth at the time. "Yeah, Jack! That's right! Here I am sitting with my 104th Diet Coke and my fifth goddamn bag of peanut M&M's, looking like a big bag of shit. Yeah, Jack, let me light up another cigarette on that!"

It was funny, but just barely.

12:55 P.M.

I think Daly is starting to respect my caddying abilities.

Just a moment ago, I asked him, *Do you feel the world expected you to be famous for your 15 minutes and then disappear?*

And he looked at me and said, "Do you feel you could just go get me the yardage, Dumbshit?"

You know you've arrived when Daly gives you a nickname.

1:30 P.M.

As I hand Daly his ninth Diet Coke of the day, I ask him how it is the caffeine doesn't affect him.

"Shit, yeah, it affects me!" he laughs. "Why the hell you think I drink 'em?"

1:44 P.M.

It's no wonder Reebok put its big swinging dicks with Daly. He's one of the best I've ever seen at schmoozing with amateurs. He laughs with them, tells stories, gives them tips. He goes to every tee box and discusses the shot with them. Most don't. He reads every putt for them. Most don't. Hell, most pros would rather shave their tongue than play in a pro-am. But these guys each paid $6,000 to get into this event and Daly has given them their money's worth.

This is his fourth outing in four days and he hasn't missed so much as a photo op. Of course, with the way Daly gambles, he *better* work. One year, Daly announced to the press that he'd won $42 million gambling around the world. "Problem is," he added, "I think I lost 'bout $51 million."

In South Africa, Europe, Vegas, and Mississippi, Daly was dealing himself directly into bankruptcy, hand by hand. He was famous for playing seven blackjack hands at once, at $15,000 per. That's $105,000 at once. He took $500,000 markers like some people take swizzle sticks. A certain gambling friend of mine told me that the day Daly won the British Open in 1995, Jack Binion, owner of the Horseshoe Casino in Tunica, Mississippi, threw a party to celebrate. It seems Daly owed him $4.2 million in markers. "He knew then he'd get the $4.2 million back and another $10 million besides," says my buddy.

"They call it a cross-addiction," Daly says. "I used gambling instead of alcohol. I admit it. It got out of hand."

You think?

But he's working on it. "I still love to gamble. I just don't exceed what I can't afford now. And I don't ask for markers now, either. But I still go into casinos. I ain't afraid."

Like his notion that he should be all right drinking beer, just not whiskey, Daly figures he is safe if he gambles on just the slots, not the tables. Of course, Daly's idea of slots is like Meatloaf's idea of lunch. He plays the $500 ones. If you figure a spin takes 10 seconds, start to finish, that means Daly can bet $3,000 a minute, or $180,000 an hour.

Life without a net.

The day I caddied for him, he'd just been through Tunica and turned $30,000 in cash into $180,000 on the slots. At Meadowbrook Country Club in West Memphis—Daly's home course—he and his buddies play $10,000 a hole some days. "My buddy, Kent, brings guys down and we play 'em. I made $88,000 off a guy the other day. All cash."

I'm sure what he meant to say, Mr. IRS Investigator, is that it *felt* like $88,000 in cash. Sir.

What Daly doesn't blow gambling, he likes to just blow. Today, he's wearing a $21,000 Rolex. He drives a $121,000 Mercedes-Benz 600 and parks it in the driveway of his 9,000-square-foot home in Dardanelle, Arkansas (pop. 3,909). He's got his $1.4 million motor home, which he often parks next to Davis Love's monster at tournaments, if you can imagine those two as neighbors. And he's got a $57,000 Hummer, and a $15,000 golf cart.

Sadly, he's already told me what my tip is going to be.

"Zero, Dumbshit."

2:05 P.M.

Waiting on the 18th hole to hit, Daly has a thought. He has the 50-plus signed guitars, including ones from Eddie Van Halen, Glenn Fry, and Joe Walsh. Plus, he has over 120 framed and signed jerseys. "I could open a bar!" he says. "You know, like Cheers. I'd be Sam Malone! I'd own the bar, but I wouldn't drink!"

And Mick could be Norm!

2:26 P.M.

The team is not going to finish in the money—hard to believe with an 18-under 54—but the day is more fun than nitrous oxide. Individually, I have Daly down for a 74, but when he sees that, he goes, "Hold on a second, pardner."

He asks me to change a 4 he made on a front-nine par 3 to a 3, and a bogey 5 he made on the back to a par. "I don't want to embarrass Paul [Fireman, the Reebok boss]. He was nice enough to invite me, y'know? And I don't want him to think I wasn't trying."

Daly really did play much better than 74. He had stretches of absolute genius. He made some bogeys only because Neely hits it so damn far and straight, he could afford to take crazy chances. His caddy kept talking him into hitting it over bogs and around barns and thru holes in trees a robin wouldn't attempt to thread.

So, I figured, it doesn't affect the team score, and the players aren't competing against each other for anything, why not?

So I did it.

What a stupid I am.

3:33 P.M.

As we're standing at the entrance of the club, waiting for Mick to pick us up, a brunette walks up who is by no means difficult on the eyes, maybe in her early 30s. She shakes his hand, leaving a small note in it. Later, it will turn out to say, "John, I really think you and I could hit it off. Call me anytime, day or night."

For an odd-looking guy with more problems than the *National Enquirer*, this guy gets more women than a Clinique counter.

3:57 P.M.

We're in the Hertz van I rented to get us all to Hartford. Mick's at the wheel, I'm in the second row with the computer out, and Daly is ready to talk.

That was the bargain: I rent the van, Mick drives, and Daly puts up with questions lobbed from the middle row. But Daly seems like he *wants* to talk. He really seems himself now, finally away from all the people out to save him. He's got his jeans and T-shirt on and a thicker Southern accent than before. He's got three hours to be exactly who he is—a wild-ass Arkansas country boy who happens to love people and just wants to have some fun.

It's about three hours to Hartford and we've already driven-thru one McDonald's. Mick warns we'll probably do it again before the trip is over.

Daly is a guy who loves his red meat. If he doesn't get at least two helpings of red meat a day, he starts feeling like Richard Simmons. Some dinners will be The Angioplasty Special: six cheeseburgers and a box of Oreos. He gets two Big Macs, fries, and a Diet Coke, supersized.

I count the Diet Coke as two, which makes 14 so far.

4:11 P.M.

Naturally, the talk turns to sex, as it always does, and Daly's stories would make Hugh Hefner blush. Tragically, he refuses to let me write them down.

You ever get any wild mail? I ask.

"Hell, yeah," he says. "Lotta nude pictures. Some pretty good ones and some really bad ones."

Any of them from women? I ask.

"Funny, Dumbshit."

What kinda mail do you get, Mick?

"Mick doesn't get any mail," Daly interjects.

Why not?

"None of his friends can write."

5:05 P.M.

Daly has to piss like an elephant now, but he won't let Mick stop. He wants to get to Hartford. So, to save time, he simply pulls out his crank and pisses into his now-empty giant Diet Coke cup.

Hey, nobody said this was 24 hours with Martha Stewart.

He does a masterful job, no spills, even sealing it with the plastic lid. I think he secretly hopes Mick will mistake it for his Coke later in the trip.

Suddenly, he turns in his chair and he's laughing and I realize Daly's got something huge and white and massive in his hand. It's his dick.

"This is why they call me Long John Daly!" he screams. Mick is howling and Daly's howling and I'm stunned silent, mostly because the thing is colossal. It looks like a Hebrew National or perhaps the leg of a very large beechwood credenza. It's flabbergastingly large, an instrument Chicago police could break down doors with. Slather it with pine tar and Sammy Sosa could use it.

I had no idea McDonald's could supersize *everything.*

5:28 P.M.

When a man has shown you his penis, many emotional barriers come down. I asked him if it were true he became addicted to his antidepression medications, including Lithium, Prozac, Xanax, and Paxil.

"Damn right," he said. "You name it, I was on it. I was like a damn rat." He said the pills sapped his energy and bloated his gut. He said he got up to 260 pounds and stared down depression every day, and, once, suicide.

"For awhile there, I was like, 'Man, I can't drink. I can't gamble. I got no money. I look like shit. I mean, what's the point?'

"But ever since I left there (the San Diego rehab), I've been happy. This is the happiest I've ever been in my life, really. I'm a great father. I love my girls. I'm not trying to prove anybody right or wrong about me. I'm just trying to live my life and take care of myself. I guess it's selfish in a way, but I don't care. My girls come first and then me, my parents, and my brother. That's it."

Something other than Super Glue is keeping Daly together?

"I mean, I know there's hard stuff ahead. I've got to be ready for the lonely nights. I used to hate being alone. Maybe that's because I didn't like the company I was with. But now I do. I don't mind being alone now at all. I get on the computer. I play my guitar. I feel young. Hell, I don't feel 35 at all."

How old do you feel?

"Thirty-four and a half, tops," he says.

Ever smash mirrors anymore?

"Nah, I kinda like what I see now," he says. "I realize maybe I'm not that bad a guy after all."

6:38 P.M.

After getting lost a few times, we finally find his Hartford hotel.

I thank him and Mick both. I tell them how much fun these 24 hours were, which they were, times two. I also mention to Daly that if The Mickster ever wants a week off, I'm available.

"Dumbshit," Daly says warmly, "you'll be the 100th guy I call."

Epilogue

I saw Daly six weeks later, at the Tour's Castle Pines stop outside Denver.

"Hey, Dumbshit!" he hollered from the middle of the 17th fairway, waving me over with his cigarette. The Mickster was on the bag and Daly was beaming.

"Guess what?" he said. "I got married!"

To the girl you tailed with the FBI?

"No!"

To the girl who gave you her cellphone number?

"No, you dumbshit!"

Well, who?

Turns out it was a completely new woman, one he'd met and married in the six weeks. She's the daughter of a Colliersville, Tennessee, car dealer, a woman named Sherrie Miller, 25 years old with a two-year-old son named Travis. They were married in Vegas, naturally, at Bally's. I met her, too. Lovely woman. Shortish in height.

Drop-dead body. Dripping Arkansas accent. Still, if I were her, I wouldn't make any long-term plans. Like, nothing past next Thursday.

"And I got other news!" he said.

She's pregnant?

"No!"

YOU'RE pregnant?

"No, Dumbshit! I won $330,000 in slots one day and $300,000 the next!"

And I felt ashamed for wondering, *Any of it left?*

Here now, your Daly recap: Married a woman he'd known less than six weeks. Still gambling like a maniac. Still smoking like a coal fire. Still eating like twins.

But still sober, he said.

Hey, with Daly, you take any fairway you can find.

A month after that, he busted through, winning the BMW International Open in Munich, his first win in six years. He'd go on to win $1.5 million worldwide in 2001, $828,000 on tour, his richest season ever, and climb into the top 50 in the world rankings.

That calls for a toast.

Anybody got a Diet Coke?

If the caddy says . . .

"Guess how we end up trunk slammin' last week? We're on 18, right? So we bring this sweet 7 straight down the chimney with some hellacious sauce on it. 'Cept it jizzes into the Johnny Cat and the sumbitch knits us a sweater in there. We take two scoops and it's DTR, baby."

He means . . .

"Would you care to know how we missed the two-day cut at last week's tournament? Well, on the last hole, my player hit an extremely high 7-iron to the green, only perhaps he applied too much backspin to the ball because when it hit the green, it spun backward into the sand bunker. There, he did not perform well under pressure. In fact, he wound up scoring a two-over-par double bogey on the hole. Soon, we were driving in our cars, down the road, to the next tournament, friend."

3

DONALD TRUMP

The Search for True Trumpaliciousness

You do not interview Trump. You just try to be in the Doppler radar when his tornado blows by and sucks you in.

You needn't even ask a question. Trump will take over from here. Your job is to simply try to keep your hat on and your Bic working. At the end of a 12-hour day, you will be spit out of a black stretch limo on a Manhattan street corner, unsure of what you've seen, your notes scattered, your mind severely Trumped.

So you try to piece it together. Was it real? Any of it? All of it? So many lies. So many truths. So much bullshit. So much beauty. It all rolls into one colossal Trumpalooza.

TO TRUMP, WHOM you've known almost 20 minutes, you are now simply "Baby." Of course, Trump calls everyone "Baby," as in, "Oh, you don't think I hit that one, Baby? Damn right I did! That's a little thing we like to call *talent!*"

There are two others along with us here at Trump's preposterously wonderful Trump National Golf Club in Briarcliff Manor, New York: his blond, pig-tailed, purse-wearing eight-year-old daughter, Tiffany, whom he calls "Baby"; and Trump's code-blue, neck-snapping, brown-haired, walnut-eyed, high-cheekboned, cantaloupe-breasted, gazelle-legged Austrian goddess girlfriend Melania Knauss, who is just so damn centerfold beautiful she ought to come with staples. Trump refers to her as "Baby" as well. Also, the head pro is known to Trump as "Baby," the waitress is "Baby," the stoneworker is "Baby," and the limo driver is "Baby."

So when Trump says, "Throw me another ball, will ya, Baby? My foot slipped on that one," three people konk heads trying to reach for a ball out of his bag.

Of course, when he's introducing you to, say, the greens superintendent, you are no longer "Baby." Now you are suddenly "the King," as in the phrase, "This man is the King! He's the guy who runs *Sports Illustrated*, Baby!"

"Well, no, not rea—"

"Sure you do, Baby! This is the top man at *S.I.*!"

"Well, actually, no, I'm—"

"Can you believe the stonework at this place? Brought in the best guy in the world, Baby. When I do things, it's only the best!"

That's the other thing. When you enter the tornado, all things are suddenly "the best" "the absolute best" "the most incredible" "no. 1" "unsurpassed" and "top of the line, Baby." It doesn't matter. It can be his watch or the guy who waxes the lobby or the Hefty bags in the trash cans. Trump is mayor of Superlative City. It's a constant string of "Nobody's ever done this before" and "Finest in the world" and "You just can't buy it any better than that, Baby." If it's not "the greatest" then it's the "biggest" the "richest" the "nicest" the "farthest" and "most expensive" "most beautiful" and "absolute top of the A list, Baby."

This includes lunch.

"How 'bout this cheeseburger, Baby?" he is raving. "Can you tell we brought in the best cheeseburger chef on the entire Eastern seaboard?"

Who knew cheeseburger chefs were ranked?

IT'S A TUESDAY in the office with the single greatest view in New York—up the Hudson, down the Hudson, all the way up the park past Yankee Stadium, across New Jersey. Trump is sitting at a huge glass desk yelling things out to his genius executive secretary, Norma Foerderer, who looks perhaps like Miss Hathaway only better dressed and funnier. "Norma! This is crazy, right? Me playing golf on a Tuesday? I never play golf on a Tuesday! I'm usually in here, ranting and raving on a Tuesday, right, Norma? Can you believe I'm going to play golf on a Tuesday?"

Says Norma, "Mr. Trump, I'm thunderstruck."

On his desk are not piles of business deals but stacks of color Xerox copies of articles about himself and his two golf courses, soon to be four, and his company. He is not just the CEO, he is the greatest public relations agent in the world. He gathers one off each pile and hands them to you, like college syllabi.

"OK, time to go, Baby! No idea why I'm doing this! I never do this, right, Baby? I never, ever, not once, have I ever played during the week, right, Baby?"

"Never," coos Melania, who has suddenly materialized. "Except for Fridays."

"Right! Except for Fridays!"

Why not during the week? I ask.

"Bad for business," says Trump. "You start missing weekdays, you start to like it too much, your whole empire goes kaput."

As he goes, people hand him this and that—his suit coat, his brief-case. They straighten his coat as he walks, brush off lint, trying to keep pace. Suddenly we are escorted by two large men in impeccable suits. It's unclear what these men do, but it seems a good bet that it involves some kind of pinching of men's heads off like Sunday chickens. And now we're going down the elevator with them and then across the lobby of the glass-and-brass-and-fabulousness of the Trump Tower and up a new elevator bank to the residences of Trump Tower. Elton John lives here and Steve Spielberg, and, of course, on the top two floors, facing north, west, and south, Trump himself.

We enter his apartment and it's more glass and ivory and marble than you could find at the Vatican. It screams at the top of its lungs: Arbitrage! Below us, Spielberg's apartment is not like this at all because once, I happened to get a tour of it. It's homey and cozy and full of plush couches and toys and rugs. Of course, Spielberg has a wife and many kids and no achingly beautiful supermodel girlfriend. For that, you need an apartment that looks like Liberace's ring box.

He's got young Tiffany with him. Mother Marla Maples lives in L.A., but once in a while, Trump sends his 727 for her and they have a day or two together. "If I can see my daughter for dinner once every two months, I'm happy," Trump says. "I don't have to be around all the time to be a good father."

Hey, do you know how much *time* empire-running takes?

"Make yourself at home," he says as he takes the steps two at a time, to change. But this is not the kind of place where you make yourself at home. What are you going to do, cozy up to the marble busts? No, this is the kind of place where you might sign a disarmament treaty or eat vichyssoise, but that's it.

There are two Renoirs, an Andy Warhol of Trump himself, long white couches that look virginal, and a gorgeous white piano completely out of tune. There is a 14-seat dining table in a dining room with 25-foot-high ceilings. There's frescoes on the ceiling of angels and harps. Welcome to the Sistine Trump.

And this is only one crib of three. Trump has a home in Seven Springs, New York, in the former home of Katharine Graham. And in Florida, he lives in one wing of his private club Mar-a-Lago, which is the former oceanfront estate of Mrs. E. F. Hutton and so over-the-top fabulous that Michael Jackson and Madonna go there to hide out as ostentatiously as possible. Each bungalow comes with a pool table and a hot tub.

It's got to be fun to be Trump. He says he can't remember the last time he paid for a ticket to any sporting event. He flies everywhere in that 727, in which he's ripped out the 180 seats and reconfigured it for a more comfy 22. He gets $175,000 for his speech, which is titled: How to Get Rich. *Lesson No. 1: Charge $175,000 for a speech.*

LIMO LOADED, WE leave from in front of Trump Tower and drive by what soon will be Trump Park Avenue, though we do not drive by Wall Street's Trump Building or Trump World Tower or Trump Parc, or, in Atlantic City, the Trump Plaza Hotel and Casino or the Trump Marina Casino Resort or the Trump Taj Mahal Casino Resort, or, in Indiana, the Trump Casino, or, in Palm Springs, Trump 29 Casino. You get the feeling that it wouldn't take much digging to find out that Trump has even named his personal toilet Trump Dump. Then we drive by six huge apartment buildings with room for six more right on the Hudson River, which are called Trump Place. Admiring them, Trump says to Tiffany Trump, "Enjoy it, Baby! Someday you'll own 'em!"

She doesn't seem all that excited.

McDONALD'S IS HERE to film a commercial. All Trump has to do is eat a Big and Tasty and attest to its deliciousness. For this he gets $1 million. If it runs more than 3 months, he gets another million.

But this is not what Trump is excited about. He's excited about the little yellow card McDonald's has given him.

"With this little baby, I can eat McDonald's free the rest of my life!" he announces. "They say there are only nine in the world, Baby. Michael Jordan's got one, too. So I can be totally tapped out, fucking broke, living on the street, and still be able to eat!"

Thank God. We won't have to throw a telethon.

IN THE LIMO, there are three phones. Trump admits he needs three, "so I can be going fucking crazy on them."

And after a while you see exactly how crazy is achieved. You mention another writer you both know. Suddenly he's got Norma trying to get hold of him. Then he remembers that you have just written a controversial piece about Sammy Sosa, the balloon-biceped Chicago Cub. He's reaching for the other phone and yelling, "Norma, get Sammy Sosa on the phone, quick!"

Thankfully, neither can be found. You make a mental note not to bring up, say, Jeffrey Dahmer.

OUR LIMO DRIVER is named Tony. He's a dark-sunglasses, bent-nose mook with a big moustache that covers a mouth of very few words. He's built like a small Wal-Mart and his arms look like they could bend a Yugo in half.

As we approach the baroque gate of Trump National, a man in a guardhouse comes out. Tony rolls the window down, jerks his head ever so slightly toward us, and grunts, "Da Boss."

PROBLEM IS, TRUMP wants you to play instead of caddy. He seems to want this more than anything else in the world. He's already got his caddy, Billy, ready to go—"Best caddy in the world!" he declares—and since the EuroBabe and Tiffany don't even play, Trump would have to play by himself and he just won't have that under any circumstances. You don't get the feeling Trump is a guy who requires a lot of personal quiet time.

"But, see, the book isn't about playing, it's about caddying for—"

"Did I tell you Bruce Willis is a member here? And Sylvester Stallone. And Rudy Giuliani. And . . ."

So that settles that.

"Any chance maybe you'd have a game tomorrow I could caddy for?" I ask.

Trump stops and looks me square in the eye.

"Believe me," Trump says. "One day of me is enough."

LORD, THE MONEY Trump put into this golf course. He bought an old Jewish country club, Briar Hall, and tore every hole out. Every single hole. He moved three million yards of earth, "the largest earthmoving project in the history of Westchester County," Trump brags.

Now, really, how are you going to check that?

Or this: "Look at those suspension bridges. No column supports! Those are $400,000 each!"

Or this: "Look at these bunkers! We take all the sand out and pad them! That padding will last 100 years!"

Not unlike his hair.

This story is absolutely true, though: When architect Jim Fazio, slightly less famous brother of architect Tom Fazio, was finished looking at the property and drawing up plans, he called Trump and said, "We can have 16 great holes."

"Whaddya mean, 16?" Trump says.

Fazio explained that there wasn't enough land for the first two holes he wanted to build.

"Why not?!" Trump bellowed.

"Because people's houses are there," Fazio said.

Trump told Fazio to hold, picked up the phone, called somebody, and bought the houses.

Fazio got his holes.

You think Fazio doesn't know how to play his Trump?

Building your own course must be more fun than being locked in a room with the Rockettes and a box of Lady Gillettes. For instance, Trump insisted the range be built between the 9th green and the 10th tee. See, when he's playing badly, he likes to go to the range and figure out what's wrong. It's quite illegal, but what are you gonna do? He's Da Boss.

Trump says he spent "$40 million on this baby" and guarantees it will host majors. "It's only a matter of time."

If you want to join, win Lotto. It's $300,000 up front (Trump International is now $350,000), plus $9,000 dues a year. "But this'll be $500,000 before long," says Trump. "I only want 300 and we've got 250 already."

Has he mentioned the celebs who've joined?

TRUMP REALLY DOES love golf. When asked to list the top 10 things that helped him climb his way back from $9.2 billion in debt in the 1990s—the largest financial comeback in history, according to the *Guinness Book of World Records*—Trump's No. 1 was: "Play golf."

"It helped me relax and concentrate," he once wrote. "It took my mind off my troubles."

See, at that point in his life, he didn't get the free cheeseburgers.

TRUMP VERY MUCH likes attention. For himself, yes, but also for his hotels, his apartments, his casinos, his office buildings (he owns the GM building now), and his golf courses. He understands the value of free publicity. He *craves* it, lives for it, screams for it.

To show the world Trump International—which *Golf Digest* architecture writer Ron Whitten called, "The finest new course I've seen since Muirfield Village"—Trump let the LPGA host the ADT Championship there in November 2001. This is the tour wrapup for the top 30 women, with a $1 million purse.

And, boy, did Trump put on the dog for them. And, boy, did the players put out the snarls for Trump.

"It was awful," says LPGA player Nancy Scranton. "It was tricked up. It was contrived, ridiculous, and stupid. He kept going around, pestering everybody: 'Is this the toughest course you've ever played? Is it? Is it?' But, I have to admit, Mar-a-Lago was beautiful and Donald was a wonderful host."

Trump decreed that some of the mounds in front of lakes be mowed down to the height of cue balls so that short shots would all roll right back into the water. Trump was like a little boy melting ants with a magnifying glass. "I kept going around asking them, 'When was the last time you scored this high?' And they kept saying, 'When I was nine.' "

During the first round, Trump walked right down the middle of the fairway with the players, who would sooner be followed by wolf-whistling construction workers than Trump. "You'd think he'd have better things to do," grumbled Annika Sorenstam, the tour's best player.

When Sorenstam tripled the first hole, Trump said, "Oops, looks like she just threw up on herself. You know, we *could* make this course more difficult if we wanted."

Then there was the whole prison incident. According to written reports, inmates at the Palm Beach County Criminal Justice Complex, which is close to Trump International's third hole, got word that women pros were just across the way. So they started screaming things that might make hockey players blush, much less LPGA players.

"That never happened!" Trump yells. "Never happened! That was put out by my enemies. The wall of the prison that faces the course doesn't even have windows!" Still, he put up a huge row of 200 palm trees to serve as a barrier. Cost him $1 million, which is a lot for something that never happened.

YOU'VE GOT ENEMIES?

"Many, many, many," he says. "Too many to name."

WELL, WHAT ABOUT the dead swan, Trump?

"True" he says, shaking his head morosely. "All true."

Pause.

"See, the famous real estate guy, Ed Gordon, gave me four black swans (for the ponds at Trump International). Best swans in the world! And I've got a bunch of white ones to go with them. Well, the one swan loses its mate to an alligator. So, after that, the swan gets more aggressive. He even scared one of our caddies, a 6–5 guy, scared him backward into a bunker. So some guy, a guest of the No. 1 plastic surgeon in Palm Beach, is out on the course and he's having a terrible day. And this black swan comes at him like it's going to attack him and this guy starts swinging at him with his iron and whacks it dead. The poor guy, it was the only thing he hit well all day.

"OK, so one of these very rich, fancy women comes along next and sees a black swan there dead and bleeding and she freaks out. I mean, it was a real mess. And because it had something to do with me, it became this international incident. This poor guy gets arrested and gets six months' probation and has to pay this big fine. And, of course, I had to sanction the doctor. I'm telling you, it was terrible. But, actually, I probably sold 20 memberships from it. I guess people found out I had a course."

See? Things tend to work out!

JUST A WORD on Trump's hair.

There are those who do not like Trump's hair. My softball buddy, B-Square, asks, "The guy is worth billions, so all I can figure is that he must *want* to look like that!"

And I admit, when I asked Trump to let me caddy for him, I was thinking maybe we would need a separate caddy for the hair.

Up close, though, it is much less threatening and possibly real. It resembles red cotton candy. It seems to have been spun off a wheel and then fired. Maybe it's fiberglass. Remember making model cars when you were a kid, how the glue froze in cool, solid wisps? That is Trump's hair. I cannot imagine the teams of artists it must take to do his hair each day, but I know they must arrive by the busload. Somehow they've managed to make his hair look like the moment when you open a bottle of aspirin and you can't quite get the cotton ball out and it only comes partially out, all teased. That's Trump's hair.

TRUMP PLAYS GOLF fast. And well. We're on 11 and he still hasn't missed a fairway. OK, there's been a stray mulligan or two, but mostly he hits it low and far and straight. On 3, he drove it 310 yards, I kid you not. Three hundred and 10. Man is 56 years old. Doesn't matter how much hellajack you've got, you can't buy a golf game.

He owns the joint so he parks the cart all the places he wants the rest of the world *not* to—edges of greens and backs of tee boxes. This makes for a very fast round. We will end up going 18 in three hours and 15 minutes and that includes stopping often to harangue the stonemason, the path paver, and the greenskeeper to redo the bricks, or retrim a tree, or repave a path that is not absolutely, immaculately Trumpalicious.

Right now it's some finished brickwork along a cart path that Trump declares is not a graceful enough arc. He's got the course superintendent over, and the stonemason and the general manager. And he's hot.

"Am I fuckin' nuts here with these bricks or what?" he yells.

If you can't rant and rave at the office, why not do it on the golf course?

Yet when we come back two hours later, the bricks have been all ripped out and the stonemason is starting over. Even Trump is amazed at his power. "I nod and it's done!" he says.

Trump drives people crazy that way. His magnificent par-3 waterfall 13th hole was perfect, until Trump decided he wanted the green 10 feet lower. They dug it up and started over.

As Fazio said once: "Nobody tells Donald Trump what to do. You make suggestions and he improves on it."

Of course, when he sees work that *is* Trumpalicious, he is practically moist. Just now he saw five workers doing a job he liked on a cart path.

"Beautiful!" he said.

So now we gotta go over and tell them.

They're all from Chile and don't speak a syllable of English. He whips out three $100 bills and gives it to them. They smile melon slices, shocked at their good fortune. Trump climbs back in the cart, pleased mightily.

"Now those guys are the Donald Trumps of Chile!" he announces.

DID YOU EVER have a friend in high school who would just tell you the most outrageous lies? Stuff like, "You know, my aunt is Farrah Fawcett." And you and your buddies give him a wedgie because you know it will turn out like it always turns out, which is that his aunt once had a friend who knew the lady who cut Farrah Fawcett's hair.

Well, Trump is that kid, constantly making you write outrageous, stupid, impossible things he says into your notebook, accompanied by a scrawled *CHECK THIS!!!* But then—against all logic—most of them turn out to be true!

Like, of Trump National, Trump boasts, "This is the best course in New York! And it's not even mature yet!"

I nearly swallowed my tongue. Best course in New York? Do you know how many great courses are in New York? Winged Foot, Shinnecock, Oak Hill, and Bethpage (12 majors between those four alone), The National, Maidstone, Quaker Ridge, Deep Dale, and Garden City. I mean, give me a break. Except then you play it and you think, "Hmmm. Well, yes, this is possibly *that good*."

Then he says that his course in West Palm Beach, Florida, Trump International, is ranked No. 1 in Florida! Again, Florida is not a state that is just now getting golf. We're talking Seminole, Black Diamond, Doral, Lake Nona, Old Marsh, The Floridian, so many good ones. So you check into it and you find, well, yeah, it sort of *has* been ranked No. 1 in the state, by *Florida* magazine.

Why? Because Trump spends outrageous amounts of money to make the best golf holes he can possibly make. "Steve Wynn spent about $37 million on Shadow Creek [in Las Vegas], but I spent about $45 million on Trump International and $45 million here. [The price seems to have gone up in the last hour.] I learned a lot from Shadow Creek. Like, you know that waterfall behind 17 there? Well I made my waterfall three times bigger and four times wider."

You think he's full of it, until you actually *see* the waterfall. It's thunderous, preposterous, Trumpalicious. It's a kind of Viagra Falls—100 feet straight up, carved out of black granite, pumps 5,000 gallons a minute, *man-made*, and fueled by Trump testosterone all the way. Spielberg could easily film *Indiana Jones and the Temple of Trump* here someday.

"It's the largest man-made waterfall ever built on a golf course," he boasts. "Cost me $7 million." It's all the backdrop for a goose-pimply par 3 that requires a perfect 3-wood to be smashed over two lakes and God knows what else. And it is by far the loudest hole in golf. You find yourself yelling things that don't usually get yelled.

"WHADDYA SEE HERE? LEFT LIP???"

"WHAT?"

"YOU LIKE LEFT LIP HERE OR BALL OUT?"

"WHAT?"

"FORGET IT!!!"

IT IS DRIVING Trump nuts that he will have to wait to see how his chapter comes out. It's July and the book won't be out until May. "Screw the book!" he keeps yelling. "I really want you to write the back page [of *Sports Illustrated*] on me. C'mon! Why not? I can't wait a year for the book! I might be dead by then! I'm a guy who needs instant gratification."

And he turns to the ravishing Melania and says, "Right, Baby?"

Melania smiles at him a smile that could melt a Big Bertha.

Showoff.

HERE'S ONE: TRUMP says he won the club championship at Trump International. Now he is a very good player. He ain't no 3, as he's been listed in business magazines, but he's a good 6, and at 7, I'd take him all day for a partner, loser sweeps the streets of Baghdad for a year. I'd even say he is the best-playing billionaire I know. However, I just don't see him winning a club championship. But damned if it didn't check out: In the first year of the club, he won the match-play championship. The guy who lost to him in the final said, "I thought I should let him win the first year. I didn't want him to raise my dues."

Stuff like that torques Trump's rump. If he wins, they let him. If he loses, he's a big blowhard. "Guys call me all the time, they want to come beat me at golf. So I'll bet some guy and he'll beat me and he'll go back to his club and brag to everybody about how he whipped Donald Trump's ass. What he doesn't mention is the five shots a side I gave him."

Tycoons go to all lengths to try and beat Trump, including, one time, the visiting CEO who refused to play him a match at Trump International until he had his own clubs. So he sends his Gulfstream V from West Palm Beach, Florida, all the way back to San Francisco, just to get his clubs.

"But we'll give you whatever set you want out of the pro shop," Trump told him. The guy wouldn't budge. The jet went to San Francisco and back, just for a bag of metal. "I think the bet was like, $5,000," says Trump. "But you're talking $50,000 round trip to send his jet. I told him, 'You could have our pro shop order you 25 brand-new sets identical to yours for that. And you know what kind of clubs he played? Callaways, just like the set of Callaways we would've given him! And then he gets out there and what does he do? He makes a fucking 7 on the first hole."

Trump gambles every day of his life. He once bet a stockbroker a million dollars on the flip of a coin to settle a commission dispute. "The coin fell off the table and I jumped on it and hollered, 'Heads, I win!' " Trump recalls. "I never let him see it. He still doesn't know what it was to this day."

As a casino owner, he wins and loses millions in a single night, sometimes on a single player. "There's a guy named Roger King [of King World Syndicate] who bets $250,000 a hand, either on blackjack or baccarat, at one of my casinos," Trump says. "And he's a damn good gambler, too. He's a guy who can make you or break you in one night. I've lost $10 million to him in one night. But I love him to come around. He makes things exciting."

AND THEN THERE was the time Trump engaged in a fistfight on the 18th green at Winged Foot and got kicked out of the club, sort of. Well, everyone at Winged Foot tells you he did get in a fight and did get suspended—in the early 1980s—but everybody remembers it differently. This is the way Trump remembers it:

"It was this guy, this big handsome asshole," Trump begins, and you're pretty sure he's describing the *other guy*, "and he was just being a complete jerk! So I sink this putt on the ninth hole to win the match and then I turn and just coldcock him, just knock him out right there on the green! He's just laid out there, cold, and I walk off, Baby. They wanted to throw him out 'cause nobody liked him, but they ended up suspending both of us. I was back off suspension after two weeks and he never got back in."

And I'm sure that's *exactly* the way it happened.

YOU EXPECT TRUMP to be a cad. You expect him to have a new woman every weekend. But this is four years now I've seen him at fights and Super Bowls and galas with the same woman—the zipper-busting Miss Melania.

Here's a guy who owns a piece of the Miss Universe pageant and the Miss USA pageant—"I bought Miss Universe for $10 million," he says, unsolicited. "I've already made $100 million in ad revenue on it"—and yet he stays with the same woman. Why isn't *that* in *Guinness*? True, staying faithful to Miss Melania is like staying true to your Ferrari Testarossa, but still, think of the opportunities!

Why, Trump?

"Well, look at her!" he says as we watch her playing and laughing with Tiffany in the golf cart. "It's all real! My God, you should see her legs! The best! And breasts? Totally real! And she's so solid, so stable! Look how good she is with my daughter! Look how they're always holding each other! All the other girls I dated, Tiffany never said anything much about. But about Melania, she says, 'When are you going to marry her, Dad?' I usually get the flakes and the wackos, but not this one."

So, when are you gonna marry her, Trump?

"How 'bout this place, huh? Do you realize I spent $49 million on this place? Nobody in history—"

YOU CAN SEE why his ex-wives still sort of like him. The man is flamboyant, creative, energetic, unpredictable, fun, and nuts.

I mean, yes, everybody over the age of six sees how attention-needy he is, how full of himself he is, how if the conversation strays from him for 15 seconds, he lassoes it back around to himself. But you can also tell that at least half of him knows it and is chuckling right along with you. Yeah, he requires a lot of attention, but at least there's a lot to attend to. He's Big and Tasty—a complete whopper of a personality.

Plus, he doesn't hide his Croesus-like wealth. He's filthy and flaunts it. I mean, the man drives a blue Lamborghini. And isn't that how we'd behave if we could? And it's not like he doesn't have a heart. He opened the Wollman Rink in Central Park; helped redo Grand Central Station; helped restore the Jacob Javits Center; is on the board of the Police Athletic League; is cochair of the new Vietnam Vets Memorial Fund; and is trying to complete the construction of the Cathedral of St. John the Divine.

And last year, when Shaq and his brother needed a lift from New York to Florida, he took them in his 727.

So he's there, you know, for the needy.

YOU FORGET HOW much history we sports fans have with Trump. Remember? This is the man who nearly burgled the NFL.

His New Jersey Generals of the USFL were the first to sign Herschel Walker. He was also the first American owner to give Doug Flutie a chance. Not that he ever wanted the USFL to succeed.

"The play was always going to be: get into the league, sue the NFL on monopoly, win the lawsuit, and make them give us a team," Trump recalls. "And it was working perfectly." Teams folded and struggled and sued, until it wound up basically Trump vs. the NFL in an antitrust suit in a NY courtroom.

"The whole thing hinged on Howard Cosell," Trump said. "And we had them. Cosell was our next witness and he was gonna kill them. His testimony was going to be powerful. But then the judge calls lunch. So Cosell goes to lunch and comes back four martinis later, drunk. He starts ranting and raving! He's going, 'No! You listen to me!' He's insulting the jury, the lawyers, everybody! I just sat there and went, 'Oh, shit, there it goes, out the window.' They came back and found the NFL guilty and then they said, 'We award $1.' The damages had to be trebled, so that meant $3, which meant we didn't have jack. But for about 18 seconds there, I was in pig heaven."

WHEN A MAN exaggerates, stretches, and twists the truth into origami every other 30 seconds, you're pretty much expecting him to cheat like a monkey in golf. So, yeah, Trump fudges. And he pencils. And he smudges. But at least he does it openly. Nothing worse than a sneak cheat. For instance, on the par-5 16th hole, I hit it close for a birdie 4 and he was still off the green, pin high in 4. So he says, "Great birdie! This is good, right?" and scoops it up with his wedge.

First guy in history to give himself a chip-in.

But I know a lot of big-time, seven-figure-a-year businessmen who do this. You think messing with the bottom line stops in the budget reports? It's like *Atlanta Journal-Constitution* sports columnist Steve Hummer once wrote: "According to a recent survey, 82 percent of corporate execs cheat at golf. It can also be extrapolated that 18 percent cheat on surveys."

What are you going to do, call the marshal? It's his course, his club, his world. And besides, he fixed my driver swing. "You're coming over the top instead of under with that driver," he said. "Try it like this . . ." and he repaired my monster driver slice, just like that.

What's funny is what Trump does vs. what Trump says. "Make sure you write that I play my first ball," he says. "You don't get a second ball in this life." And that's true, except for on 1 and 13 and 17.

And he also says, "I don't like to take putts. That's not a true reflection of a man's score." And that's true, too, except for the putts he took on every other hole, plus the occasional chip-in, and, of course, the one time he said, "I made a 5, but give me a 4. I've got to take at least *one* newspaper 4 today."

Again, at least he's out front with it.

He shot 36-39–75. And thus you see how Trump's game is 80-proof.

Not that he wasn't good enough to beat me. I shot 45-38–83. Trump acted like I had just shot 59 at Pine Valley.

"I'm just so damn impressed!" he hollered. "You are the King! The way you hit it, you really ought to consider the Senior Tour!"

He is saying this as I'm paying him the $10 I lost to him.

IT'S 7 P.M. AND Trump says he and Melania are going to spend the rest of the night lying in bed, eating and watching TV and "whatever else comes up." And suddenly, I'm spit out on a Manhattan street corner.

Loved Trump. Loved the lies. Loved the truths. Loved the bullshit. Loved the beauty. But, as I collapse into a hotel room that is finally, blissfully quiet, I decide Trump was absolutely truthful about one thing.

One day *is* enough, Baby.

If the caddy says . . .

"We're match with Sergio and he looks at us and goes, 'Good-good?' And my man goes, 'Uh, there's still a little cum left on that dress, Señor.' And he goes all postal on us, but we're like, 'Sure, just brush that in.' And he puts this Vulcan thing on his wand and three-wiggles it! Then we make a camel ride on the next and stack it up on the one after that. So we torch him 4 and 3. Take a suck a that!"

He means . . .

"In a match-play tournament, our opponent, Sergio Garcia, asks us if we'll concede him a putt. We decline, saying, 'No, that's still a fairly lengthy putt.' And this makes our opponent angry, but we continue to insist he putt it in. And he grips his putter oddly and manages to miss the putt, which gives him three putts for the hole. On the next hole, we sink a very long putt to win the hole. And on the hole after that, we hit an iron shot very close to the flagstick, winning that hole as well. So we defeated him by being four holes ahead with only three holes to play. And this is very satisfying to us!"

4

TOM LEHMAN

By the Way, You're Fired

You are no kind of caddy until you have made it to The Show, Parnegie Hall, the PGA Tour. Not a pro-am, not a Monday Madness, not a two-day Cash-n-Dash. The straight-up Tiger Tour.

That was my pitch to Tom Lehman, the rumpled Dockers spokesman with the big bones, big heart, receding hairline, movie-star-blue eyes, and Jimmy Stewart decency about him. If Lehman isn't the nicest man in sports, he's at least in the photo. He's known to use a member's locker at a tournament and leave them three or four free shirts, a few dozen free balls, a few gloves, and a thank-you note. Unheard of—like a Crip stopping to fix a cop's flat tire. If Lehman didn't say yes, nobody would.

The good news was he said yes to letting me loop at The International. The bad news was he said yes to letting me loop at The International. Getting to caddy at The International in Castle Rock, Colorado, is the same as winning a week babysitting Bart Simpson. The International is to caddies what the Bermuda Triangle is to pilots. It's played at Castle Pines, the most mountainous, unwalkable, higher-than-a-mile course on tour.

Still, it was official money to Lehman, and official Ryder Cup points were on the line, with the Cup itself only a month away. This mattered. I started preparing. I went on daily long walks with a backpack full of encyclopedias, and 10-pound weights on my legs, hands, and belt. I looked like a Swedish tourist. I literally put bricks in my golf bag. I walked 36 one day.

But two weeks before the International, Lehman's wife, Melissa, delivered a stillborn child, Samuel, who would have been their fourth. Devastated, Lehman withdrew from The International and rescheduled me for the National Car Rental "Classic" at Disney World eight weeks later.

By the time he hit Orlando, Lehman had been through the wash, rinse, and tumble dry of life. Because he was such an emotional wreck, he missed three straight cuts after the British, including the PGA, and dropped from 9th to 11th in the Ryder Cup points standings, out of the automatic spots. Then somebody slipped U.S. Ryder Cup captain Curtis (Very) Strange a bottle of clueless pills and Strange didn't select Lehman with one of his two free choices, taking Scott Verplank and Paul Azinger instead.

Here was Lehman, 42, a man who has never lost a Ryder Cup singles match (3-0) in his life, a passionate team leader, a father who understandably wasn't within an area code of himself down the stretch, getting the pink slip for Verplank, a guy who'd never played in a single Ryder Cup or President's Cup, and Azinger, who hadn't played in a Ryder in almost 10 years.

Lehman was so cranked off about Strange's snub that he went out to the Las Vegas Invitational in his first tourney back and blew the joint up, starting 62-63 at the TPC at Summerlin to set an all-time two-day PGA Tour scoring record of 19-under. He wound up finishing second to Bob Estes, who went deeper than Jacques Cousteau all week, but Lehman still looked very much like a guy who wanted very badly to be back on the Ryder Cup team in 2004.

"I think Curtis just extended my career an extra three years," Lehman said.

The next week was Disney, and so it was that I was waiting at 6:30 that Wednesday morning outside the players' locker room. Right away the caddy gossip hawks were upon me. "Where's Andrew?" they said, meaning Andrew Martinez, Lehman's longtime caddy. Andrew had gone with Lehman as long as Laurel with Hardy or ketchup with mustard.

"Don't know," I said.

Davis Love's caddy, Cubby, said, "Andrew must have a case of the toos."

"Toos?" I asked.

"Yeah, he only skips when the tournament is *too* far or *too* hilly or has *too* many amateurs."

It *was* a wack format—play the first two days with two different amateurs over two very average resort courses (Palm and Magnolia). Then again, nobody comes to Disney for the golf. It's like going to Las Vegas for the art. They come here because their wives and kids *make* them come here. For tour wives with kids, it's the only major.

The perks could give you whiplash. Each player in the field, all 144, get a courtesy car. Not that they *need* a courtesy car, since an ever-waiting battalion of smiling, 60-ish courtesy drivers will take them anywhere they want in the Magic Kingdom. This allows the players and their families and friends to use up their unlimited free passes to any park their hearts should require. But first they should feel free to eat the gorgeous free breakfast and lunch buffets in the Polynesian Hotel, where, by the way, the room is damn near free. There's also free use of any of Disney's sailboats, pedal boats, water mice, canoeing, bicycling, horses, tennis courts. There's also babysitting, laundry, anything a player's wife can dream up.

Then there's the huge father-kid par-3 tournament, followed by a massive party with ridiculously huge graft for the tykes (the winner's trophy is actually bigger than the tournament winner's). All the Disney characters are there, but after a half hour, these ultra-advantaged kids are so wired and gift-whipped that they're whining to be taken on more rides and the characters can't get anybody's attention and mostly sit around and look at each other. "*Mommy, why are Goofy and Mickey slumped over in the corner, playing gin rummy?*"

Not only that, but Disney lately has let players *choose* who they want their pro playing partner to be. Lehman didn't know that, or he would've chosen Duffy Waldorf or Olin Browne or Loren Roberts, his three best pals on Tour. But the rest of the field knew. That's how you had Scott Verplank playing with Bob Tway; David Toms with Stewart Cink; Tiger with Mark O'Meara; Jeff Sluman with Love; Tom Pernice, Jr. with Kenny Perry; Robert Allenby with Stuart Appleby (hell on first-tee announcers); Azinger with Lee Janzen; Larry Mize with Mark McCumber; and Scott Hoch by himself. Hey, we kid.

It must seem like three lifetimes away from the golf life Lehman used to know, trying to scrape out a living in the bushest of the bush leagues, no money for a hotel room, sleeping in his car, driving all night. One time, driving from a nothing tournament in Montana to an even nothinger tournament in Idaho, Lehman could hardly stand the smell of himself. Just then came a monsoon of a rainstorm, an absolute Noah-floater. Lehman pulled the car behind a lonely closed gas station, jumped out, got his soap and shampoo out of his bag, stripped naked, and showered, right there and then.

There is almost no place on the globe Lehman hasn't been—trying to make a buck from golf. He was a club pro in California. He was a club pro in Minnesota. He came *thisclose* to taking the head golf coach job at the University of Minnesota, which included renting out cross-country skis from the pro shop in the winter. One entire wok-hot summer, he and his family zigzagged the country's minitours in an un-air-conditioned broken-down Volvo. He once found a dead man on his stoop in South Africa, tried to reason with women caddies in Japan, and had winner's checks bounce on him. "One time, first place was $6,500," he remembers. "It bounced. That would've set us up for three months!"

No wonder when a free week in Disney World comes around, with people shoving lobster in their mouths at every turn, the Lehmans never miss it. "It's the only tournament in the world," Lehman says, "where if you come home Friday night and tell your family you missed the cut, everybody goes, 'Yeaaahhhh! Now we can go to Blizzard Beach!' "

Of course, how would Lehman know, since he never *had* missed the cut at Disney, not in 10 tries? "Not once," I told the caddies. "Not since he started coming in 1984."

Suddenly there was this awful chill in the air. They all stared at me, no longer able to hold up the weight of their bottom jaws.

"Uh-oh," said Cubby.

"What?" I said.

"You just jinxed your man," said Cubby. The other caddies nodded in agreement.

"Now you've got no chance to make the cut," said Cubby.

There was this terrible silence.

"So, what you doin' this weekend?"

Gulp.

Just then Lehman came strolling out of the locker room, with a contraband banana, donut, and orange juice for me. Somehow, it was hard to picture, say, Nick Faldo doing this for his caddy.

His bag had just slightly enough junk in it to start a yard sale, including a Bible, a tin of Altoids, yardage books from all over the world, including tournaments more than two years old, God knows how many Band-Aids and tubes of sunblock and pieces of swing-weight tape and food and dozens of gloves and maybe four dozen balls and enough tees to pin down Gulliver.

"Don't blame me," Lehman said, laughing. "I never look in the bag. That's Andrew's department."

We played some practice holes with Lee Janzen and Chris Perry, two good touring pros. I noticed that they often talked through each other's swings, moved around during them, laughed, whistled, sang, whatever, right on their backswings, and it never bothered any of them. And yet if *you* were to so much as bat your eyelashes on one of their backswings, they'd throw you in Marion Federal Penitentiary.

Perry is the son of former major league pitcher Jim Perry and the nephew of former spitballer Gaylord Perry. I asked him if they'd given him any advice. "Yeah," he recalled. "One time my dad said, 'Stick with baseball. There's no money in golf.' " As of the end of the 2002 season, Perry had made over $7 million on tour, which, come to think of it, is about what a .230-hitting infielder makes in a year. Pops was right.

It didn't take me long to start screwing up. I managed to have the Magnolia yardage book out when we just happened to be playing the fourth hole of the Palm and therefore told Lehman the yardage was 187 when a blind hedgehog could see it was nothing but a damn sand wedge. It broke the players and caddies up. It reminded Janzen of the time Ray Floyd hit a shot in Florida that flew miles over the green. Floyd turned to his famous caddy, Golf Ball, and said, "Golf Ball, we ain't hittin' many greens today. What's goin' on?" And Golf Ball said, loud and clear, "Boss, I think I figured out why. I got last week's book."

Any more crap like that tomorrow from me and Lehman will be flying Andrew in.

IF THERE IS one man on tour who is nearly as nice as Lehman it was his playing partner for the first two days, German star Bernhard Langer, who had won in Europe the week before. They met on the way to the range Thursday morning, start of the tournament, and it was an instant Humble-off.

Tom: Hey, Bernhard! Great playing last week!

Bernhard: No, no! I was only lucky you weren't entered, Tom!

Tom: No, I don't think so, Bernhard!

Bernhard: And great playing by you last week in Las Vegas, Tom!

Tom: Thanks, Bernhard! I was lucky *you* weren't there!

Put it this way, it wasn't exactly Iverson v. Sprewell.

"I love Bernhard," Lehman said later. "I would trust him with my life. In fact, I'd trust him with my family. I could say, 'Bernhard, I'm going to war. You must live with my wife and kids for 10 years until I get back.' And Bernhard would say (Lehman goes into a thick, staccato German accent), 'I promise you, Tom, I will not even look at her in an immoral way.' And you *know* he wouldn't."

It's done in complete respect, but Lehman does the best Langer on tour. "The tone of Bernhard's voice never changes," Lehman says, "no matter what he's talking about. He'll be like (goes into relentless, deep, hammering cadence), 'Tom . . . I . . . vas . . . so . . . ve . . . ry . . . hap . . . py . . . I . . . could . . . hard . . . ly . . . con . . . tain . . . my . . . self.' "

The only thing is, Langer is without a doubt the slowest player in golf history. He is slower than the last day of school. He plays golf at the breakneck pace of a cold pot of honey tipped over. He doesn't realize it, but he is hell on caddies. He puts his peg in the ground and the caddies move to keep a respectful distance, then freeze, as we do for everybody. Then, *nope*, he scoops up the tee and ball and finds a new piece of the tee, much closer to us. So we have to suddenly scramble to move back, often tripping over the people who were freezing behind us—scorekeepers and sound guys and whoever—who suddenly have to start scrambling back, too. OK, we've all moved and frozen. Hit already. And he's ready to pull the trigger until—*nope*—he wants to retee again, even closer to you, and the scrambling and tripping and the freezing has to start over again. It's *Golf Groundhog Day*.

I asked Duffy Waldorf that night if it drives the players crazy, too. "Well, he does that and I always wonder, 'Is he changing his shot every time he retees? Does he start out wanting to hit a cut and then suddenly say to himself, "Nah, I think I'll move over here and hit a high draw"?' And then does he ditch that idea and go, 'Nah, I'll move over here and just blast it'? I don't know."

On the other hand, Langer hits wonderful golf shots, but not as many as my man hit on the front nine in that first round. One 7-iron on the 5th snuggled up to the length of a flagstick. And lo and behold, as I was trying to figure out a way to balance the bag, the towel, the putter cover, his water, my water, and my bag of puffed Cheetos, Lehman uttered these words: "Rick, what d'ya think this is gonna do?"

"Excuse me?" I said.

"Just take a look at this," he said.

Double gulp.

Here's a guy (me) whose worst part of his game is putting, who doesn't understand grain or drainage, giving one of the world's great players—and a golf architect, to boot—advice on a putt. I got down low and took a shot. "I'd say right lip," I mumbled.

"Me, too," he said.

And he stepped up, hit it on that line, and dunked it!

I *am* UberCaddy.

From then on, he asked my help on short putts, anything five or six feet and under. Together, we birdied 6, too, and made saving pars on 7 and 8 to finish the front nine at a respectable two-under 34. Hurrah! I am officially *part* of golf.

Unfortunately, he went Space Commando on the back nine, three-putting the 12th from 25 feet. (Never asked my help.) He was hot at himself. He slapped the putter face with his hand and yelled, "C'mon, Tom!" Note that he did not say, "Fuck, Tom!" or "Jesus Christ, Tom!" Just "C'mon, Tom!" It's as close to swearing as the man gets.

We wound up going 34-38–72, even par, which is flat-out awful at a bunny setup like Disney. It's like fighting to a draw with Dr. Ruth. We were seven shots behind the leader. If the field had been suddenly cut after one round instead of two, we would have missed it by a par 5.

"Dang, I hate missing cuts," he mumbled as we made our way back to the clubhouse. "I don't want to miss this cut! I hate missing cuts! Absolutely hate it!"

Triple gulp. The jinx rears its ugly head.

"You gonna hit balls?" I asked, knowing the answer would be yes. A pro as good as Lehman posts a score in the bottom fourth of the field, he'll hit balls until they have to drag him off with Clydesdales.

"Nah," he said. "Kids want to go to MGM tonight."

IF IT'S POSSIBLE, the pace got *slower* Friday, to that of geological plate-shifting, when Langer's amateur partner turned out to be a 26-handicap Munich banker who apparently learned everything he knew from watching Langer play on German TV: Study. Frown. Regrip. Retowel grips. Tee. Freeze. Back off. Retee. Study. Regrip. Retee. You could've dismantled and reassembled the *Luftwaffe* in less time.

This gave Lehman and me lots of time to talk. We'd be standing there, waiting for *somebody* to strike a golf ball with a metal implement, and I'd ask, *Why do you do that weird thing with your neck, where you lurch it out forward and then to the right, like a dog trying to scratch his ear on an unseen tree?* "I have this shoulder knot all the time," he said, doing it again. "That's where I carry my tension I guess. I can feel it pop when I do that."

I asked what he thinks when he sees his swing, which is more like a controlled crash, a violent shoulder-heave, like a man yanking out a stump with a chain. "I never look at videos of my swing," he said. "I don't like the way it looks. I always envision it looking like Ernie Els's, but it's not, is it? But, you know, I'm a feel player. The thing that makes me good is that I hit my irons the right distance. I don't think there's anybody much better than me about hitting it the right distance. (He led the Tour in Greens in Regulation in 1997 and 2001.) So, no, it's not pretty. It's not classical. But it's repeatable. That's the No. 1 thing."

And whose is prettiest?

"Oh, Tiger's, for sure."

By this time, Herr Rain Delay was finally ready to hit.

We parred our first hole (we started on Magnolia's 10th), then made a two-putt birdie on the 2nd to get back in red numbers for the week at one-under. On the 3rd, I made a mistake I'd been perfecting all week. I kept finding the yardage mark, pacing it off, then adding the yardage when I should've subtracted it, or, for variety's sake, subtracting it when I should've been adding it. I know it sounds Jell-O-brained—and it is—but I'll only say when you are trying to clean clubs, read yardage books, conduct interviews, take notes, make sly observations to yourself in those notes, sneak snacks and water, find the towel, and get the right distance, some things get dropped by the juggler. Unfortunately, it kept being the most important thing. For instance, I'd find, say, the 163 mark, pace off 11 behind it, and announce, proudly, "152," when it was no more 152 than it was 52. "You sure you don't mean 174?" Lehman would say, grinning. *Um, well, yes, that is exactly what I mean.* I must've done that three times in the first 27 holes.

"How'd you ever get through fifth grade?" he asked me.

As I walked along, humiliated, I wondered if Tiger was having the same trouble with his caddy that week. For the first time in all their years together, Tiger's caddy, Steve Williams, was going to miss a week with him. It's like being bikini-waxer to Halle Berry: It's just not a job where you call in sick much. Occasionally, Tiger will give Steve a week off so one of his friends can carry for him. He lets a kind of slide-ruleish high school buddy carry for him at San Diego sometimes as a way for the guy to earn college money. And by that, I mean money to purchase a college. Tiger's usually good for a top 2 there, which means about a $50,000 head start on books and cheeseburgers. This time, though, it was Steve's choice. He was opening a racetrack in his home New Zealand (only caddy on tour who *bought* the racetrack), so Tiger grabbed his old Stanford teammate and friend, Jerry Chang.

"He was pretty good out there today," Tiger said of Chang after Thursday's round. "He was excellent at raking traps and using the Pythagorean theorem to figure out yardages." Tiger's caddy was using the Pythagorean theorem; Lehman's still hadn't mastered subtraction.

So on our fourth hole, I was determined. I went out and got the yardage exactly right. Added when I should've added and had the number a good five seconds before him. I couldn't wait any longer.

"One forty-eight to the front, plus 17 to the hole, 165," I said, fairly bursting with excitement.

"Nice job," he said, looking at his yardage book. "Except that's Langer's ball."

WE MADE THE turn in two-under 34, which was good, but not good enough. We needed better. We needed to start "ripping some cloth" as they say on tour, start knocking down some pins, mount our charge, step on the gas. Unfortunately Herr Sun Dial was taking much of the afternoon plumb-bobbing a three-footer.

This allowed us time to contemplate the relaxing sounds of the Disney golf courses—screeching ghosts, howling wolves, and creaking doors. They were coming from the Haunted House next door. All day long, you hear the screaming. It's like living next door to Dennis Rodman. The last time I heard screaming like that at Disney was in 1996, when Tiger was just breaking out into a pheenom. He came to Disney as only the hottest rookie in Tour history and was in a battle with Payne Stewart on the back nine Sunday. There were thousands and thousands of people, easily the largest crowd I'd seen on any hole all year. Tiger was just about to tee off on the 14th when this lovely doe came bounding out of the woods. It was like Bambi had wandered onto the set of *Tin Cup*. With the gallery watching and laughing, the spooked doe went sprinting away toward the lake. It was bounding along the shore when suddenly this mammoth alligator sprang out of the water and took a huge chomp at it. The crowd gasped, women screamed, toddlers cried. You would've thought you were in the middle of Mutual of Omaha's *Wild Kingdom*. Bambi fairly flew down the fairway after that and disappeared into the woods up at the next hole, and the gator slunk back to his depths. Typical Disney happy ending.

I told Lehman my favorite Disney joke: Mickey is divorcing Minnie and the judge says, "Look, Mickey, I can't grant you a divorce just because Minnie is a little mentally unstable."

And Mickey goes, "I didn't say she was mentally unstable. I said she was fucking Goofy."

For his part, Lehman told jokes and did impressions the whole week. He's a God-fearing man and refuses to swear, but that doesn't mean he's a bore. When we weren't making golf shots, we were usually giggling. I asked him if he and Andrew talk this much out on the course.

"Andrew is one of my best friends in the world," he said, "but he's a different sort of dude. Like, every now and then we'll be trying to figure out a yardage and he'll say, 'Do you think God really wanted Abraham to sacrifice his son?' And I'm like, 'I don't know, Andrew, how far from that bush?' Or it'll be, 'Do you think man was meant to eat meat?' And I'm all, 'I don't know, Andrew. Do you think this one's outside the lip?' "

There's nobody out there like Andrew. He carried Johnny Miller during his best years and even though it's been eight years now that he's had Lehman, every now and then he'll say to him, "Johnny, do you think . . ." I asked Andrew once, if Tiger wanted him to leave Lehman and get on his bag—probably a salary increase of $1 million a year—would he do it? "No, I wouldn't," he said. "Don't get me wrong. I like Tiger. But we don't have the same philosophy of life. I'd rather be out there with a Christian brother. I don't care about the money."

That's fairly true on the Tour. Partyers tend to end up with partyers (Daly and The Mickster). Sports fanatics with sports fanatics (Faxon and Cubby all those years) and Born Agains with Born Agains (when Martinez isn't caddying for Lehman, he works for David Gossett, a devout Christian). In golf, opposites do *not* attract.

All we did on the back nine was throw a little 32 at the bastards.

A gorgeous wedge to five feet and sink it for birdie on 1. A two-putt birdie on 5, which included a wonderful six-footer for the bird. A birdie out of the sand on the 7th (he gets it up and down 55 percent of the time), and a 30-foot camel ride on the last to shoot 66 and get to six under, making the cut by one stinking shot. Langer made it right on the line at five under. Larry Mize shot four under and missed it completely. "Can you believe that?" Mize was muttering after the round. "Four under doesn't make the cut anymore? This is how it is out here now. There's so many good, young players. It used to be the rookies would come out and you'd see a few of them with kinda crazy swings on the range and you'd say to yourself, 'Ooops. That guy ain't gonna last.' Now the rookies come out and you see them on the range and you go, 'Ooops, that looks pretty good.' You know? Like Howell, Gossett, Kuchar. These guys all come out and get some exemptions and play their way into the top 125 *in their first year!* That never used to happen!"

One other stat from Friday's round. It took five hours and fifty minutes, or just longer than every Wagner opera put together.

TRAGEDY STRUCK US Saturday.

Lehman's friendship bracelet fell off.

It was the one tied on to him two years ago by his nine-year-old daughter, Holly. It fell off on drive impact on the 3rd hole and Lehman was thunderstruck. "Two years," he kept saying, looking at his wrist as though it had just been grafted on.

Unlike Michael Jordan, Lehman really *does* drive the carpool when he's home. He once swung his kids by their arms for so long at Bay Hill that he couldn't pick up a golf club for three days. As the defending champion at the British Open at Troon in 1997, he and the kids swung so often from a cable and into a river that he could only hit irons off the tee.

The next year, at the British Open at Birkdale, he was screwing around with his kids in a kind of human tube at an amusement park and slipped, falling on his shoulder, separating it. "That shoulder didn't just cost him the British Open," says Andrew. "It hurt him right through the PGA that year (at Shahalee), and he could've won there, too, the way he was playing." Once, on the Hogan Tour, he threw his kids up and down so many times that he could no longer swing. He shot 75 and missed the cut. At Disney he had a hint of a limp. "I was playing with Holly one day and she stomped on my foot. It still aches, six months later."

Do you have any idea how many tournaments this guy would've won if he'd been sterile?

Actually, it's probably better that he hasn't won more majors, considering what his kids to do his trophies. When you win the British, as he did at St. Anne's in 1996, you get the 137-year-old claret jug for a year. He kept it in the dining room on top of the buffet. One day, his youngest, Thomas, then three, was playing with the jug and one of his Ryder Cup trophies on the rug. "Thomas was pretending the trophies were guys," Lehman recalls. "Like, he's holding the claret jug and pretending it's an actual person and he goes, 'Hi, Billy, how are you?' And the Ryder Cup trophy goes, 'Hi, Frank. I'm gonna kick your butt!' And the claret jug goes, 'Oh yeah? Try it!' And Thomas just started banging the trophies together. The handle of the claret jug bent 45 degrees. I had to get a jeweler to fix it. Cost me a bundle. I mean, the thing had been in John Daly's possession for an entire year and now my kids go and ruin it."

Lehman didn't lose it at the kid. Lehman almost never loses it. Which is amazing, considering what he's been through in major golf championships. It's a wonder he doesn't bite a rake in half. Nobody since Greg Norman has come so agonizingly close to winning majors and not nailing them down.

There was the battle with Jose Maria Olazabal at Augusta in 1994, when he hit a 1-iron off the tee at the 18th on Sunday and into the bunker, earning criticism from CBS's Ken Venturi. "You're trying to win the Masters!" Venturi said. "You've got to go for it!" Says Lehman, "Looking back on it, I would. I would take driver and just kill it over that bunker."

Four times he has started Sunday in the final group at the U.S. Open and four times he has left without the trophy in his trunk. Once, at Oakland Hills in 1995, the winner, Steve Jones, gave credit for his victory to the calming things Lehman said to him throughout the match. One was on the very first tee. "NBC kind of rushed us so they could get our drives in before the commercial. We're walking off and he tells me he's a nervous wreck. I just gave him a little Joshua 1:9, you know, knowing God is with you. But I didn't know it would help him THAT much!"

How he lost that Open is Exhibit A at how the relationship between caddy and player can be torn asunder so easily. Lehman hit a driver on the 18th hole too far and into a bunker, which gave him no chance to go for the green, which led to a greenside bunker, which was good for a one-stroke loss. Andrew says he asked him to hit a 3-wood. "He'd been criticized by Venturi at the Masters for not going for the kill and I think that was on his mind," Andrew says. "I didn't like driver. I wanted 3-wood. I knew the course was drying out and the ball was really rolling. I knew that unless it was hit absolutely perfectly, it was going to roll into that bunker and we'd be dead."

Lehman's eyebrows went up when he heard that. "He says he wanted 3-wood? If that's true, I don't remember it. At least, he wasn't very strong about it. He *mentioned* 3-wood, but he didn't say that's what he *wanted*."

Andrew: "Well, things were happening too fast. There was so

much noise, people yelling and screaming, that I didn't really have time to state my case."

This is not to make trouble between player and caddy, but just to point out how, six years later, it is still a little pea under their player-caddy marriage bed at nights. And yet, that pea, and hundreds of others, have to be ignored—and have been—for man and loop to stay in bed together, figuratively speaking.

There have been so many others. There was the blown Open at Congressional when Lehman had to wait and wait and wait to hit his approach at the 17th hole because the persnickety Colin Montgomerie wouldn't putt up ahead of him. Monty wouldn't putt because the crowd at 18—an entirely different hole!—wouldn't all stand like statues for him. When Lehman finally got his chance, his iron spun back off into the water to sink his chances. Tried to the very edge of his rope, Lehman still did not punch a fan, push a rules cart into a pond, or take a divot out of Monty's butt. Not that he wouldn't have loved to.

"Being nice can get old," Lehman admits. "I frown once and people say, 'What's wrong, Tom? Are you OK?' "

Lehman hates only one person—really *hates* that person—and it's Alan Shipnuck, a particularly aggressive golf writer at *Sports Illustrated.* I happen to love the guy, but what are you going to do? The last time they spoke, it went like this.

Shipnuck: Can I talk to you?

Lehman: No.

Shipnuck: Why not?

Lehman: I don't like you.

Shipnuck: Oh.

Lehman: What do you want to talk about?

Shipnuck: (Tour pro) Joe Durant.

Lehman: Oh, OK. Here's my quote: Joe Durant is a great guy and if you rip him, I'll stick my fist down your throat and remove your heart.

Shipnuck: Oh.

WE RECOVERED HEROICALLY from the bracelet heartbreak. Playing with two achingly nice pros, Chris DiMarco and Skip Kendall—and no amateurs—the pace was brisk (three hours, forty minutes) and the play was fine. We parred the first three holes and then came to Magnolia's par-5 4th, his most hated hole in Orlando. On the practice day, he told me, "Your job on this hole is to remind me to put it in the right places. I always screw this hole up and it's not that hard." So, naturally, I forgot to warn him when we went through there the first time and I forgot again on Saturday. He hit his drive too far left, which meant he had to carry a 3-iron to reach in two, and since it is easier to stop a woman's tears than a 3-iron, it trickled off the back into a nasty bunker. In fact, it was up against the lip. He would have to hit the shot with one leg kneeling on the grass and his foot buried deep into the sand, gripping the club by the nub of the grip. Just before he hit, he gave me a look that would've withered titanium.

Gulp.

Somehow, he got it to six feet and curled in the birdie putt. As the crowd was clapping its approval, he walked over to me, handed me the putter, tipped his hat, and said, quietly, "By the way, you're fired."

We made two more beautiful birdies, so by the time we got to No. 9, where the crowds were getting big, I was pumped up and so was he. He stepped up to the 9th tee and just *crushed* one, and I yelled, "Man *was* meant to eat meat!"

At least Lehman got it.

Caddies get to give away used balls (if you call playing three holes "used"), so, naturally, I made a whole show of it. One time, as we were walking off a tee box, I announced to an eight-year-old kid, "Kid, for a free Tom Lehman golf ball, can you name the PGA Tour player who shot the lowest two consecutive rounds in history?"

The kid was stupefied, of course, until his dad quickly whispered something in his ear. Then the kid beamed and said, "Tom Lehman?"

"Right!!!" I said, flipping the kid the ball.

Then Lehman added, in full voice, "OK, 10-point bonus question. Did he win the tournament? No!"

Kendall seemed to like that one. For his size, Kendall was unbelievably long. The guy couldn't be bigger than 5–6, and yet he *mashes* the driver. I asked him how he managed to get such distance, besides his full extension and maximized arc. He said eating right and then he pointed to a drop-dead exotic brunette who was featuring prizewinning breasts in a leotard top in the gallery, "and that woman right there."

"She makes you longer?" I asked.

"No, you idiot!" he said. "That's my yoga instructor."

I can remember when guys used to be followed by the brunette from the all-night Scotch-a-rama the night before. Now they're followed by their yoga instructors. Whom they don't sleep with. And they eat right.

Something must've worked. Kendall shot 64, but we were right with him—another 66, for a tournament total of -12 after three days. We were only seven shots out of the lead. If we hadn't completely pissed away the first day, we might be leading this rodeo.

I checked a scoreboard to see how the pairings would be for the next day. We were at about the same score as Tiger, which meant it was possible we'd be in his group for the final day. Would that be interesting? After the new record he set for *Most No's Told to a Book Writer?*

Gee, T, I'm thinking it looks a little closed at the top.

Unfortunately, we missed him by one group—and on the wrong side. It was the worst place to be in golf—in the group *in front* of Tiger. All day long, people would be sprinting up to our tees and our greens to get a good spot for when Black Jesus came through one hole later.

I asked Lehman if he wanted to practice.

"Nah," he said. "Epcot."

Every night I went home and sat in the tub, exhausted. Every night, he went to another amusement park.

ON SUNDAY, I was nervous. Not only did we have a chance to win this thing, but Golf Channel was doing a little side bit on yours truly—Gagger Vance—and when the camera was on me I was a little more nervous than usual and put on my bib backward. I didn't appreciate the camera crew high-fiving their good fortune.

Lehman showed up when he always showed up, exactly 40 minutes before tee time, with my usual breakfast, only this time he was rolling his shoulders painfully.

"Today is going to be one of those days when I just have to work into it," he said.

Too much beer?

"Nah. We went to Epcot last night and I carried (six-year-old) Thomas on my shoulders all night. They're killing me."

There's a $3.4 million purse up for grabs—$612,000 for first place—and he's out turning into Quasimodo just for his son.

My kind of guy.

We were playing with the left-hander, Steve Flesch, and DiMarco again, and DiMarco did something I never thought I'd see. We were playing this little par 3, and the tee markers were just one yard behind the permanent yardage plate. And yet he stood between the markers, feet together, and *paced off* the one yard to the plate. One yard! Paced it off! Like he couldn't see it was about a yard? Like if it was only, say, two feet and eleven inches, it was going to change what club he hit?

"Chris?" I asked. "Did you just pace off *one yard*?"

It kind of startled him. The crowd around the tee box started to laugh. He got a grin on his face. "Well, you know what it says in those PGA ads. 'These guys are good.' "

Not that good. It reminded me of some of the stuff Greg Norman used to tell us during his heydey in the late 80s. One time, he lost a tournament on the final hole when his sand wedge from the fairway came up a little long and trickled down a bank to the bottom of a hill. "The shot was 103," Norman explained to us that day, "which is a perfect sand wedge for me. But it must've been a little bit of a hangin' lie and it went 104, then trickled off the back. But those are the breaks." A bunch of us sent up a muted groan in the pressroom. A buddy of mine quietly coughed: "Bullshit!" I mean, we know players would go to hell and back to keep from saying, "I just made a lousy shot there," or "I kinda skulled that one"—and especially Norman—but this was too much to swallow. He is *that* good that he can hit a sand wedge *exactly* 103? And the only thing that kept it from going *exactly* 103 is that it was a *hanging* lie?

Was that bullshit? I asked Lehman. "Well, I don't know about Greg, but for me it would matter if you told me the shot was 104 and it was 107. That much would make a difference. But one yard? I don't know. He *was* pretty hot then."

I think what happened with DiMarco is that pacing off the yardage on the tee box of a par 3 is part of his routine, and on the

PGA Tour, routine is king, shah, and emperor. Whether it's your preshot routine or drive-to-the-course routine or eat-your-Special-K routine, pros want to do things exactly the same every time, so that their swings, their thoughts, their *weeks* are repeatable. Repeatable is everything out there. Repeatable is more important than a trophy wife, a good coach, and a million-dollar hat deal, combined. You can't afford to waste a single stroke, and that stroke can be lost anywhere—a greasy towel, a mistimed burp, a stray doubt. That's why we get so many incredibly boring players now on tour. They hardly go out to dinner, they hardly go to the bars, they hardly do anything. It's a parade of guys in bent hats and Oakley sunglasses who are on the course from sunup to sundown, followed by room service, Bible study, and putting in the room. It's the Age of Beige.

The players love caddies who do the same thing every time, who will take their putter the same way, freeze the same way, clean the grooves the same way. They want caddies they can count on, which is exactly what I *wasn't* Sunday for Lehman as we set out to win the tournament. In fact, I believe I set a record, Most Mistakes on One Hole.

First, Lehman asked me to move our bag out of DiMarco's visual putting line, the line that extends from his ball to the hole and past on to infinity, apparently. I did that, came back to the green, and stood right in Flesch's extended line. Flesch had to tell me to beat it. Nice. Ashamed, I wanted to be sure to do something right on that hole, so as soon as Flesch putted out, I planted the flag hard, with a flourish, like Columbus planting the Spanish flag in the name of Queen Isabella. Unfortunately, DiMarco hadn't putted out yet. And the camera crew high-fived again.

Didn't bother my man. He parred 1 and 2, then hit his iron on the 3rd three inches from the hole. I'd never seen a guy hit his irons so accurately, Tiger included. I asked him how he manages to hit a little white ball to within a throw rug of the hole from hundreds of yards away, shot after shot after shot. "Well, I'm not *that* good," he said with a shrug. "I hit a couple fat this year."

Gee, a couple fat *this year?* You wonder how he stays on tour.

We followed that birdie with a two-putt birdie on the par-5 4th (lipped out for eagle). That put us in 7th place. When I read it on the board, I about swallowed my towel. I was thrilled, ecstatic, crazed. Lehman looked like he didn't even notice. I asked him later. He hadn't. Neither did the other caddies in our group. They kept looking behind us, amazed at how far a certain *Cablinasian* was crushing his drives, often rolling them right up to the green we were putting on.

"You see that?" they kept gesturing to each other. Just a little reminder of who was back there. Lehman didn't seemed bugged by the people running up to our green as we were putting, though. "If it's hard for us, imagine how hard it is for Tiger," he said. "I really feel for him sometimes. I remember once, he and I were driving somewhere, to Columbus, I think, and we pulled into a McDonald's in Akron. Now, there was nobody in there. It was empty. We ordered, got our food, and started to eat. In 10 minutes—10 minutes!—the place was packed. Filled up. The guy behind the counter must've called his friend on his cell and that friend called 10 friends and next thing you know, we were animals in a zoo, people looking in the window at us and everything."

I remembered how much Tiger seemed to like being with Lehman and the older guys at America's stirring 1999 Ryder Cup win. "We called him SuperKid," remembers Lehman. "Yeah, he's the greatest player in the world, but we still get to dog him. He's still a kid. So we'd have these meetings and say, 'OK, guys, this hole is going to be a driver and three-iron, except for you SuperKid. It'll probably be driver and 9-iron, 'cause you're young and on steroids.' He loved it."

We had to go nuts on the back nine to have a chance, but we got some cruel breaks. We missed the fairway by two lousy inches once and it settled down so deeply we had to chop it out. That was a bogey. By the time we got to the 12th hole, we were 15 under and our chances were slipping away.

And that's when a ghastly thing happened. We were on the 14th green. He'd left birdie putts on the last two holes right in the jaw, but short. So this time, he had an uphill 12-footer. We looked at it together and I said, "It's dead straight. Just don't be short." There was this awful hush all of a sudden. You could feel a clamminess come over the group. I'd broken a monster caddy rule: Never speak in the negative tense.

I'd mentioned something you *shouldn't* do instead of something you should. I'd cursed him. I'd put a negative thought in his head where there should be only positive. He blew it by the hole a good three feet and had to make a nasty downhill comebacker for par. He gave me that look again and said, "First mistake you've made all week."

Which was a lie, of course. We talked about it later. "Sometimes you can just tell when the caddy has said the wrong thing," he said, ever forgiving. "One time, before I had Andrew, I had this guy, a banker, who I gave a job to because he was out of work, and he really didn't know anything about golf. I mean, he tried, but he just didn't know a thing. So this one time I said to him, "What's on the right here?" And he answered, "Nothin' on the right, but there's a ton of water on the left."

Ugh.

I talked to Andrew about caddy semantics on the phone that

night. When I told him what I'd said, it was like I'd told him his dog had been run over by a train.

"You didn't," he said.

"I did," I said, morosely.

When he finally caught his breath, he tried to explain the way of getting your point across to your player without breaking the code. He said I could've tried, "Plenty uphill here" or "Just firm one up there" or "Kinda against the grain here" or "Nothin' quick about this one." He said that one time he was caddying for Bobby Clampett. They had a straight uphill putt and Andrew said, "No way you can miss this one." And, of course, he did. "And he gave me hell for it."

"One time, a friend of mine was caddying for George Archer," Andrew remembered. "It was a forecaddying hole with o.b. on the left, so before he took off to get down the fairway, he gave George his driver and an extra ball, just in case. George fired him at the end of the round."

Lucky for me, on the very next hole, Lehman nearly jarred it off the tee. This was actually even better than the one on No. 3. This one finished one inch short of the hole, the length of a Skittle, 13 blades of grass, Mini Me's pinky toe. It was becoming clear to me that this stuff was not just luck. It was such a privilege to work for someone who does something so freaking well. It was like standing next to a famous heart surgeon. You felt privileged just to hold his scalpel.

As we were walking to that green, I told him about two old brothers at the muni I grew up playing. They'd play every day together, each hole for one dollar, instant pay. You win the hole, the guy has to give you a dollar bill. Whenever this one would beat the other, he'd snatch the bill and say, in his stutter, "Tttttake a sssssssuck a that!" So when Lehman approached the gallery, he lifted his hat and smiled and said, under his breath, "Tttttake a ssssuck a that, Curtis!"

As we were walking up to it, that ball just hanging on the lip, I gave him his driver, as a joke, instead of his putter. But he took it! So, with great flair and panache, I yanked the driver cover off and the crowd went crazy. He then putted it in with the driver. "You know," he said. "If I were in the press tent, and they asked me what I hit on 15, I'd have to say, 6-iron, driver."

We closed with birdies on 16 and 17, and parred the last to shoot 72, 66, 66, 67–271, 17 under par, 13th place, six shots behind Argentinian rookie Jose Coceres, who would make a six-footer on the last hole to win. We beat both of Strange's Ryder Cup picks—Azinger and Verplank. But the thing Lehman was pumped about was something different.

"We beat Tiger!" he said, looking at the board, sure that it was a typo. "I can't remember the last time I beat Tiger!"

"You mean here?" I asked.

"No, anywhere. Any tournament. Anywhere in the world. It's just hard to beat Tiger."

SuperKid rules.

There was one other little item. "What do I owe you?" he said. We made $65,000 and Lehman was determined that I have 7 percent ($4,550), plus the standard fee he would've paid Andrew ($1,800)—a total of $6,350. But the deal was always that I wouldn't take money, that the player could either: a) keep it, or b) give it to his caddy anyway. But Lehman wouldn't hear of it. This was messing with his routine, his karma, his golf gods. "I *have* to pay somebody," he said. "I *can't* keep it. It would be bad luck."

Finally, we agreed on c) he'd give it to the Professional Tour Caddies' charity arm, which usually helps down-and-out caddies, which is a whole hell of a lot of guys. Not that helping caddies is anything new for Lehman. He has a mole caddy on tour he sneaks $500 checks to quite often. "I know if I give him $500, he's going to keep $100 and give away $400 to other guys. If I give him 20 shirts, he's going to keep two and give 18 away. I know because caddies will come up to me and say, 'Hey, thanks for the shirt!' But don't write that."

Of course not.

Then it was time for the dreaded critique.

"Nothing terrible," he said. "You read greens pretty well. It was fun to talk about something besides theology and philosophy out there. But never—never!—say, 'Don't be short.' "

I promised I never would. Even to me.

I had one last thing to ask him. "You're such a family man. You're crazy about your family and your family is crazy about you. And yet I never saw them out on the course this week, watching you. Not once."

"Hey," he said. "It's Disney Week. You were lucky *I* showed up."

He was right. I did feel lucky.

If the caddy says . . .

"Oh, man, we had to chase balata with some nasty chops today. These guys were sprayin' Vin Scullies everywhere, knockin' it Oscar Bravo, checkin' into the Hosel Hilton. It was about as much fun as a chapped shooter."

He means . . .

"Oh, friend, we played in the traditional pro-am tournament today with some golfers who were not very good at all. These players continually hit only the top half of the ball, and hit the ball out-of-bounds quite often, and hit many shots on the hosel of the club instead of the face itself. It was about as much fun as a chapped anal opening."

5

DAVID DUVAL

The Maniac Behind the Shades

It would take a tank of gas to drive the distance between David Duval's brooding public image and what he's really like.

You learn that in the first 10 minutes as his caddy.

"Rule No. 1," he declared as we boarded his rent-a-jet. "*Never* lose my dip."

He was grinning. But he meant it.

Dip is Copenhagen snuff and he's got one buried in his bottom lip much of the livelong day. A dip to Duval is what a cigar was to Groucho. Duval had one in then, as we took off from a private airfield outside Denver, after he'd finished 24th at The International in Castle Rock, Colorado. We were boarding with Duval's caddy, Mitch (Fort) Knox, so named because Duval has made him slightly richer than Kuwait. Give you an idea: Mitch collects sports cars. Right now his driving choice is his BMW M3, though sometimes he likes his 1965 Shelby AC Cobra.

Telling you, kids, this caddy thing is *the* career choice of the future.

Nobody else was on the plane. Nine-seat cabin and just three of us. Usually, it's just two. Duval likes to have plenty of room for his: a) round-the-world gin game with Fort, b) books, and c) dip. And

Fort is ever ready with the dip. "Every bird he makes," Mitch says to me. "He likes a new dip, got it?" One would think we were working for an Alabama quail hunter.

Oh, and Duval never starts his golfing day without a giant full-strength Starbuck's coffee, in the handy keg size. The rest of the day, he knocks back Diet Cokes like he got the John Daly starter kit for Christmas. Then, during dinners, iced teas. The man has more caffeine in him than Juan Valdez. And he wonders why he doesn't sleep well on the road. "It's my curse," he says. "My mind just races." He tries to get the top floor in any hotel so he doesn't hear the footsteps above him, but it really doesn't help. *Gee, Boss, you think it could be the vats of Joe thumping in your veins?*

We were about to go wheels-up when the big, hayseed captain of the leased jet came back and gave us the big greeting. "Hey, Day-vid!" he bellowed. "How you doin'? 'Preciate meetin' you! I used to fly Payne Stewart a lot! Helluva guy! Well, you ready to go?"

Yeah, that's *exactly* what you want to hear before you take off in your leased private jet: Your pilot flew Payne Stewart a lot, who died in a jet just like this. Helluva guy.

We were on our way to play in the Fred Meyer Challenge in Portland, Peter Jacobsen's two-day two-ball golfapalooza that draws some of the best players on tour. It's not a Tour event, but it's got a better field than a lot of them. It's 24 guys and most of them stars. This year, Duval would be playing with an entirely new partner, one he'd never teamed with before in a pro event—his dad, Bob Duval, the Senior Tour regular.

If you had 100 men in front of you and you had to guess which one was David Duval's father, Bob would be your 100th guess. Bob is all tan and smiles, gregarious, a chain-smoker, 10 on the Fun Meter, a laugher and a backslapper, a flirter and a partyer. David is a librarian on the outside and a Sex Pistols concert on the inside.

On the inside, Bob Duval, a club pro his whole life, hides a gaping sorrow—the death of David's 12-year-old brother Brent in 1982. It kept him from moving on with his career, trying out his talent, hitting the road a little. He finally went for it in 1997 as a 50-year-old divorcé at the urging of, well, David. "When you gonna stop talking about how you could be playing on the Senior Tour and just go do it?" Bob recalls David saying in Bob's book *Letters to a Young Golfer.*

And he became a wild success. In fact, in 1999, the Duvals became the first father-son team to win on the Tour and the Senior Tour on the same day. On a March Sunday in 1999, Bob won the Emerald Coast Classic and Duval won the Players Championship. If that ever happens again in history, I'll come to your garage and eat your snow tires.

Set against Bob, David looks adopted. He's quiet, pale-skinned, seemingly more serious. He does not let the public through. Literally, that's true. He wears wraparound sunglasses for an eye astigmatism that causes sensitivity to light, but they hide what little expression he gives. His dad doesn't wear any sunglasses at all. David's a hungry reader, so much so that he owns an *Oxford English Dictionary.* His favorite book is Ayn Rand's *The Fountainhead.* Most pro golfers' reading begins and ends at The Sprinklerhead.

So they would finally play together on one team and David seemed pumped up for it, as pumped as a David Duval can seem. Even chock-full of nukes, Duval still had all the wild unbridled enthusiasm of Perry Como on Quaaludes.

Still, I'd caught him at a great time. Two weeks before, he'd won the 2001 British Open at Royal Lytham St. Anne's. He'd done it heroically, slashing a monstrous 6-iron on the 15th out of calf-high gunch 210 yards onto the green and saving par to seal the deal.

"I can tell you've been lifting," I said, "the way you mashed that thing."

"Nah," said Duval, throwing another card on the gin pile as we jetted northwest. "I'd just put a new chew in. Man, I swung so hard, I nearly swallowed it!"

They laughed at that, the two of them. All the pressure was off them now. He'd won his major and the golf world only cares about majors. You could never get another top 10 your whole life, but you win a major, and hey, your career is complete by us. Never mind that Duval had already played possibly the greatest Sunday round in PGA history—his 59 that won the 1999 Bob Hope Chrysler Classic by a single shot. Never mind his 13 wins in his first 9 years. All golf wants is a major, and as soon as you feed it one, the beast is satisfied. Until then, you are branded a choke, a wimp, a gag. (See: Mickelson, Phil.)

"Amazing how everything changes," Duval said with a grin, holding up a card. "I used to get beat up all the time for coming so close at the Masters, but not winning it. Now they all go, 'He's won the British Open and gee, look how close he's been at Augusta!' All of a sudden, your close calls are trotted out as a good thing, not a rip."

And it was one of those rips that caused his breakthrough at the British. "I was walking off the 10th green and somebody in the crowd said, 'Don't worry, David, you still have plenty of time to botch it!' And I said to myself, 'Not today. Today's my day.' It sort of galvanized me. All the people were screaming and yelling. It was boisterous and crazy. And I thought, 'This is just a game. All this over a game.' And I just stayed calm."

And when he hit his final approach to 18 with his three-shot lead, he and Mitch had one of the coolest experiences in sports—engulfed by thousands of fans running madly for a spot on the green's fringe, as over 130 years of tradition dictates.

"That was a little scary," Duval said. "Several times I couldn't move. I got my arm pinned behind me once. I could see Mitch in front of me, with all the people banging him and the clubs. And I thought, What happens if they break the heads off? What if the driver gets bent?"

Typical pro golfer. Not "What happens if I get trampled?" Not "What happens if somebody dies?" No, it's, "What about my graphites?"

Not to worry. Within a few hours the only things bent were he and Mitch. "We had a little fun on that plane ride home, didn't we?" Mitch drawled. Yes, they did. Armed with the claret jug, they drank champagne out of it, Colt 45, and, for the capper, a $4,500 bottle of Chandon. Is the life of a caddy decent or what?

It is until it comes time to unload Duval's Hannibal-like load of luggage. If you travel with Duval, get a truss. Nobody this side of Madonna carries this much baggage. Here is what he took with him to Portland—albeit one stop in a four-week trip—and I know because I lifted every ounce of it:

- a blue bag with three pairs of golf shoes, one pair of running shoes, and at least four dozen balls.
- a Ziploc bag full of at least a dozen sunglasses.
- a long, narrow bag full of nothing but hats. Fifteen hats. Why you need so many damn hats? "Hey, they get salt-stained!" he yelled. "I can't go out there with a shitass-looking hat!"
- another Ziploc with protein bars (he eats two a round), vitamins, and medications. (He's got chronic sinusitis. It's an infection. "My sinuses are never clear," he laments.)
- a movable closet of perfectly ironed shirts and pants and jackets, which he hand-carries around on hangers like some door-to-door brush salesman who has a clothes bar suspended in his backseat.

- a huge, monstrous, evil black trunk (much like the one Kate Winslet brought aboard *Titanic*) full of more clothes.
- the golf bag itself (with 23 clubs in it, two umbrellas, and four extra-heavy warmup clubs).
- a black leather backpack containing his CD holder (two Limp Bizkits, eight REM, and two Pearl Jams), books (a John Irving, a Nick Hornby, a Flannery O'Connor, and one by Billy Graham's wife, Ruth. Duval says he'd like to own a bookstore someday). Also workout magazines and four decks of cards.

When we landed, Mitch and I had to pile all that into his hotel suite, which was naturally on the top floor of a two-story walk-up. We were ready for a beer. Duval, of course, went to work out.

At one time Duval used to be just slightly fatter than Spanky of Our Gang. This is what you get when your dad works at a country club and you have signing rights for snacks. "And I loved 'em," he admits. His first few years on Tour, he was a chub. Now he's a calorie-counter and a pill-swallower and an obsessive body-shaper. Welcome to the post-Tiger golf world.

"Years ago, I'd have probably ordered a pizza right now." Instead he spent the next 40 hard minutes at the health club doing box jumps, step-ups, lunges (hates those the most), leg extensions, toe presses, standing calf-raises, seated calf-raises, ab exercises, incline reverse crunches with weights on his feet, and declining oblique crunches with weights. Thus, what was once a 37-inch waist is now a 32. What were once 226 pounds are now 180. What once held rolls now holds the claret jug.

He works out so fast and with so little eye contact that people generally stay away, which is just how he likes it. Duval and fame are not especially friendly. In fact, he barely tolerates it. As an interview, he will only spark if you ask him a question that does not bore him so badly he'd like to fake his own death. He does not like to be recognized. When he is, he does not give you the big hello to make the moment less awkward. He *wants* it to be awkward.

When we arrived in Portland, for instance, we were picked up by a "host" in a sedan. It took a shoehorn and a lot of sweat to get all of his crap into the thing, and the whole way the "host" was nervous, flop-sweating, nearly killing us with his driving he was so excited. He kept trying to small-talk Duval on subjects Duval would sooner jump into moving traffic than discuss. In caddy parlance, this man would be considered a "headcover." As in the caddy sentence, "This total fucking headcover came up and we couldn't get away from him for 15 minutes."

At one point the headcover pulls over to fiddle with the trunk and Duval curses. "Can't they just give us the damn car and we can drive ourselves?"

He is one of the world's worst schmoozers. In Ponte Vedra, Florida, he lives across the street from former Jacksonville Jaguars coach Tom Coughlin and yet has never spoken to him. He likes to be alone more than Garbo, which is why he spends a lot of time at his house in Sun Valley, Idaho, snowboarding and fishing. He especially loves snowboarding. With the goggles, the helmet, and the baggy clothes, he looks like everybody else. In the summer he goes there and fishes for weeks at a time. "The best part about fishing," he grins, "is fishermen *want* to be somewhere where nobody else is." Which is why he nearly swallowed his bait the day the mayor of nearby Ketchum, Idaho, hung a banner in his honor—"Home of David Duval"—and strung it across the main drag.

He is not the kind of guy who will punch your shoulder or embrace you in a drunken stupor and bawl, "I love you, man." It bugs him to surf e-Bay and see stuff for sale with his own forged signature on it. Despite winning the British, he hasn't suddenly started cash-ing in on the IMG gravy train the way so many have. He's pretty much got all he can spend. He's that rare thing in pro sports—happy.

This might be why Tiger and he have become pals. They play practical jokes on each other, send needling text messages to each other's phones, fish and golf together. "I think he knows I don't want anything from him," Duval says. "Nothing. And when he knows that, he lets down. He's a more happy-go-lucky guy than people think. He's fun-loving. It's just that his situation demands so much of him."

That was said while downing his fourth iced tea over dinner, and so, naturally, it was time for bed and a good, long stare at the ceiling. As his caddy, I retired to prepare the dip.

THE FRED MEYER Challenge involves 12 two-man teams playing best-ball at The Reserve Vineyards and Golf Club outside Portland in a town called Aloha. (Gee, you think developers had anything to do with it?) It also involves more freebies than you could load home in a semi. Even the caddies load up. First thing I was given was a free Tommy Bahama shirt. Cool. Then I noticed every caddy there was wearing the shirt, too. We were all suddenly waiters at a Jamaican Denny's. Very cool!

Saw Joe LaCava, Freddy Couples' longtime caddy. He said, "Hey, with you on the bag, I think Duval could get a top 12 finish here," knowing full well there are only 12 teams. Funny.

While Duval ate breakfast with the players, Mitch started yelling at me. Had I marked his balls yet? Uh, no. (Duval plays a Nike Tour Accuracy DD—for you know who—and he likes the swooshes highlighted with a yellow marker.)

Had I cleaned the grips yet? Uh, no.

Did I know his club yardages? Uh, is that important?

So Mitch made me write down Duval's exact yardages with each iron. I list them now, along with mine (at altitude) for illustration purposes:

2-iron . . . Him: 243. Me: Don't own one.
3-iron . . . Him: 230. Me: Never heard of one.
4-iron . . . Him: 217. Me: We're not speaking.
5-iron . . . Him: 205. Me: 200, if not hooked hideously.
6-iron . . . Him: 192. Me: 190, one time out of five.
7-iron . . . Him: 179. Me: 175 when the planets align.
8-iron . . . Him: 167. Me: 167!
9-iron . . . Him: 153. Me: 155. Take that!
Pitching wedge . . . Him: 140. Me: 135.
Sand wedge . . . Him: 127. Me: 115. (He gets that much out of a sand wedge?)
60-degree wedge . . . Him: 110. Me: 105 when I do not feel an incurable set of the shanks coming on.
Don't even ask about the driver and 3-wood. He hits them hideously long.

Suddenly it was time to go and I swung the bag around in the locker room and goosed Craig Stadler with the umbrella handle. He said he enjoyed it. That's what kind of week the Fred Meyer is.

Next came a skills challenge, with Jack Nicklaus and Arnie picking teams from among the 24 players. It'd be like, "OK, bunker shot. Jack, who do you want?" And Nicklaus would survey the 22 fantastic golfers arrayed in front of him, as if he were a schoolyard kid picking his kickball team, and go, "I'll take Billy Andrade."

Problem was, Arnie was having a kind of Senior Moment. He couldn't remember some of the players' names. He'd look at Stewart Cink and say, "I'll take the big fella." He'd look at Jean Van de

Velde and say, "The guy in the red sweater." Poor guy. It will happen to all of us someday. After a while, it was clear that Nicklaus was just taking guys he was pretty sure Arnie wouldn't know in order to save Arnie the embarrassment. After all, the man is still The King.

The pros kept hollering out, "Take the kid! Take the kid!" The kid, of course, was Sergio Garcia, then 21. The pros all like The Kid and a lot of them feel sorry for him, because of the omnipresence of his golf-pro dad. He is a nice man, but he hangs around too much, hovers over him, hounds him. "That guy needs to back off so The Kid can go out and get laid like every other 21-year-old," one longtime Tour star muttered to another that day. And every time a reporter or a p.r. person or an official came looking for The Kid, I'd see him tucked in a back room in the locker room, playing Nintendo.

The clinic was hilarious. Jacobsen said squat Tour pro Ed Fiori is the only guy who can iron his pants in a toaster. Cink hit a shot out of a hospitality tent—and *spun* it! Phil Mickelson placed Sign Boy—the Foot-Joy ad character played by a young L.A. comedian—three feet in front him, and then took a full swing with a lob wedge right in his face. Sign Boy closed his eyes tight, held his nuts, and grimaced. The ball popped straight up in the air 15 feet and landed at Sign Boy's feet, soft as left-out butter. Said a pale-white Sign Boy afterward, "Dude, I was scared to death!"

Mickelson did that once to the ex-ABC reporter Bob Rosberg. Only he had Rosberg face away from him and cup his hands out in front of him, like he was carrying water. Mickelson took a full swing and plopped it over his head and into his hands, *voila.* Then he had Rosberg face away from him again. Secretly, he put down the lob wedge, picked up a 1-iron, and hit it thru Rosberg's legs.

Change of underwear, Rossi?

It's a funny thing about Mickelson. The pros are all amazed at what he can do, but a lot of them think he's a phony. They think his immaculately polite behavior and methodical answers in press conferences come off as Eddie Haskell from *Leave It to Beaver*. "My, Mrs. Cleaver. That's a beautiful divot you made!" But what they don't get is, the whole family is really like that. Phil's younger sister Tina, a 2 handicap, is achingly sweet and polite, too. She speaks like a preschool teacher, too. "Well, Rick," she will say in measured tones. "I have very much enjoyed getting acquainted with you." And she will mean it. So does Phil.

Anyway, when it was time to play, who did we draw in our pairing? Jack and Gary Nicklaus is all. Jack Goddamn Nicklaus himself. G.P.T.E.L.: Greatest Player to Ever Live, to most. And Gary, Heir to the Bear, Son of Greatest Player to Ever Live, to most. Son who finally got his Tour card the year before after 10 years of trying.

A certain caddy gulped.

These two golf families had crossed swingpaths before. Jack and Bob were once in the final pairing at a U.S Senior Open. And Nicklaus once took David out for a practice round at the 1992 U.S. Open and taught him a lesson about golf management. They were standing on the tee box at the famous 18th when Nicklaus said, "How do you plan on playing this one?" David said he'd probably just bomb a driver off the tee and try to reach the green in two. Nicklaus shook his head. "Too risky," he said. "There's a sprinkler out there that reads 102 yards. You need to play this hole so that your third shot comes from right near that sprinkler head. Whatever two shots get you there, whether it's a 3-wood and a 6-iron or two 4-irons, whatever, get there." Duval says it made him start thinking about the idea of playing a hole backward to get the most out of it.

So off we went, Nicklaus, the old god, with Duval, god-in-training. Duval seemed totally at ease with the situation. Me, I was a mental pretzel. I've interviewed Nicklaus for 15 years, and he's always been one of the best and most generous quotes I've ever known. But being on the course with him? It was even better.

For one thing, he was funny. One time, on the 2nd hole, Bob hit a tee shot that hooked nasty left into severe spinach.

"What's over there?" Bob asked his caddy.

"Your ball," Nicklaus cracked out of the side of his mouth.

One time Nicklaus hit a drive that was headed for a fairway bunker. "That's close, Jack," said his caddy.

"Close?" said Nicklaus, disgusted. "The only thing that's close to is us."

The whole day Nicklaus was goggle-eyed and drooling over David's distance. On the first hole, for instance, a 346-yard par 4, I paced off the distance David had left to the green: 5 yards. Nicklaus's eyes bugged. On the fifth, a 305-yard par 4, we had to hit *3-wood* or we'd fly the green. It rolled into the greenside bunker, but all we did then was hole the damn thing. I high-fived him as he emerged victoriously from the bunker. And I'm thinking, "SportsCenter, here we come!" Didn't happen.

Meanwhile, the Nicklaus boys couldn't light a match with a flamethrower. Nothing happened for them. Zilch. Nada. Nicklaus just kept looking at us like a hungry kid with his nose pressed to the window of a McDonald's. We made birdie after eagle and birdie.

We were going so good, I just had to ask the ultimate question as we marched down a fairway: "David, is it all right if I put my mouth on your ball?"

He looked at me as if I'd just sneezed in his ball pouch.

"No, Dude, use the towel."

"No," I explained. "What I meant is, can I speak to your ball as it's flying?"

He thought about that for a minute and said, "Don't. You might jinx it."

As deliberate and methodical as Duval looks, he actually is very quick out of the box and almost impossible to keep up with, much less get ahead of to get the mark and the number. He could sense I was constantly lagging, and he kept looking at somebody in the crowd and touching his right wrist. Finally I got up the nerve to ask, "Who are you looking at in the crowd and what does that mean when you touch your right wrist?"

"I'm signaling Mitch," he said, pointing to Mitch, who was walking along outside the ropes. "I want him to bring in the reliever."

That, of course, would be Mitch himself. To replace me. Duval grinned larcenously.

The day was a joy. Duval was funny, talkative, loose. Come to think of it, so was the whole damn group. One of the other caddies had a line when Duval smashed another driver 340 down the middle. "There's some heat on *that* toast."

Now that's pure caddy. I *really* need to come up with my own. I thought of a few . . .

Close the shutters, Granny, it's hailin' balata! Or . . .

Oooh. They felt that one at the FACTORY! Or . . .

Damn! That makes me slightly moist!

Still no good.

I had one line that Bob thought was halfway funny. He hit a great 5-wood to knock it on a par 5 in two and I said, "*That's* why you've been named Father of the Year seven years in a row."

At the turn, the hilarious on-again, off-again Tour player Charlie Rymer was interviewing all the players for some ESPN package. He'd been Duval's roommate in college and had occasionally caddied himself. I asked him if he had any advice for me.

"When you're a caddy, there's three tried-and-true responses that'll keep you out of trouble: They are . . . 1) 'Good shot!'; 2) 'Sorry, my fault; and, 3) 'You got fucked.' " By the 14th hole we were a jaw-dropping 10-under and had the freaking lead.

Imagine that. Jam Boy, in the lead.

Then Bob eagled the par-5 16th hole to get us to 12 under. Meanwhile, the poor Nicklaus boys were on their way to a top 12, still at 1-under, last place. I thought about all the other father-son teams in history. Raymond Floyd and Ray, Jr.; Dave Stockton and Dave Stockton, Jr.; Arnold and Deacon Palmer. But I couldn't imagine a team that could've beaten these two, can you? Bob and David looked at each other and thought about it and then Bob said, "Well, honestly? No." And they both laughed.

It's been a long, strange trip back for the two of them from that day when Brent Duval was 12 and the doctor told them what was wrong. Brent was usually so energetic and funny, but suddenly he started losing zip. You could see it when he played on the Little League team with his nine-year-old brother, David. Turns out, Brent had aplastic anemia. Basically, his bone marrow had stopped working. Next thing you knew, they were in Cleveland, testing the whole family for possible bone marrow donors. There was one match: David. In his book, Bob recalls, "David took it terribly." He'd seen the huge needles they used on his brother. It was going to be painful and he knew it.

But David did it. And they brought the bags of marrow in to Brent and stuck the needles into him and fed him the very essence of his own brother. And right away, it seemed to heal Brent from the inside out. It seemed as if David had saved his life. A few days later they all went out to lunch, Brent's first trip out of the hospital in months. But when they got back to the hospital, Brent threw up the lunch. Brent was rejecting the transplant. He immediately started getting worse. They took David in to see him once, near the end, and David screamed, "That's not my brother!" and ran out. He never saw him again.

The Little League team served as Brent's pallbearers. David hates talking about it, but his father says, "David blamed himself for Brent's death. And I blamed myself, too."

For years after, Bob felt hollow, miserable, useless. A country-club pro—just as his own father was—he hated having to fake a good mood when he gave the members lessons, so he found that good mood in liquor. The booze and the grief made for a very tense house. Finally he got a divorce, deciding that he had to take care of himself, "if I was going to take care of my kids."

At first, David hated his father for walking out on his mother. He holed up inside himself to keep from having to talk about it, but as he grew up, he learned to understand how thickly webbed the situation was. He began to open up to his father again. Began to see him as a man who'd been through the same sorrow he knew so well himself. Brent changed them both. They don't speak much about him, but they never forget him. As Bob wrote, "The scar remains but the wound has healed."

Now, father and son are buddies again. In fact, Bob and new wife Shari live near him. Most of the time, Bob comes to David's house by boat. Then they go fishing together. Or hit balls. Or just shoot the breeze.

And tomorrow, they would try to win their first pro tournament together in their very first try, if their doofus caddy didn't blow it.

As David said, "How cool is this?"

We wound up the day at 12-under 60 and tied for the lead with Brad Faxon and Billy Andrade, who are best friends and who tend to take home the coveted "denim jackets" the winners get at this thing. Faxon had won it four times already and Andrade two. Boys, how about sharing a little?

Not a caddy for even one year and I was already playing in the final group. I dumped the bag in the locker room, cleaned up, and headed upstairs to the pressroom. For once, I was going to know more about the rounds of the leaders than maybe the leaders themselves. I kept imagining the questions from the press.

Media Member: *Uh, David. How invaluable was your caddy today in forging out this crucial halfway lead?*

Duval: *Well, it was just a delight to be with him today. He's forgotten more about golf than I'll ever know. He kept my swing on plane, my head screwed on right, and, most important, always had my dip ready.*

Instead, Duval never showed up. In fact, nobody showed up in the pressroom to be interviewed. Not a single player. The press was well and truly screwed. But Duval was the one they were most pissed about. The coleader, the recent British Open champion, wasn't coming in to talk to about 40 press members who happened to be on deadline.

I went down to the player lounge and just casually asked Duval why he wasn't going up to the pressroom. "Well," he said, "the press guy asked me if I wanted to come up there. And I said, 'Do I want to? No, I don't *want* to.' He seemed all right with that answer, so I didn't." And neither did anybody else.

I understand where Duval comes from with the press. They mostly want to ask him why nobody's risen up and stopped Tiger. But you're talking about a force never before seen in golf. It's like saying, *Why doesn't anybody do anything about the damn hurricane?* Duval will go down in history as the guy who was the last No. 1 in the world before Tiger took it over and stuck it in his back pocket for the next—well—God knows how many years. But for Duval, overcoming what he has—his shyness, his weight, and his own family sorrows—gives him plenty satisfaction enough. He is a reader and a thinker, and golf is only one part of his complex life. He was never meant to be Tiger. And even if he were as good as Tiger, he couldn't/wouldn't handle the klieg lights pouring on his face at all times. The sunglasses shield only so much. But nobody wants to hear all that, so he goes to the pressroom only when somebody says, "You *have* to."

But if I were that p.r. guy, I'd have had his butt up there.

THE NEXT MORNING I got to the course early. Wanted to be ready this time. Wanted to clean the grips early. Get the dip lined up. Get the swoosh outlined real neat and nice. Problem was, I couldn't find the bag.

Uh-oh.

I'd left it overnight in the locker room with all the other bags. I knew Mitch said that was a cardinal sin, but I checked with the rent-a-cop in the locker room and he said there was going to be somebody stationed in there around the clock. So I figured, why lug it back to the hotel? I went to dinner with a bunch of the caddies and David and Bob went out with some Nike people and everything was not only hunky but dory as well.

Until that morning. Ever wreck your dad's car? This is how it felt inside, times 10. I'd lost the clubs that won the British Open, shot the 59, and were leading the Fred Meyer Challenge. I'd lost Picasso's brushes, Coltrane's sax, Rosie O'Donnell's fork. I sat on a bench, whitefaced. I could've cried.

Suddenly I saw Mitch and Duval, peering around the corner of some lockers, snickering at me. Behind them was the bag. Bastards. They'd taken it back to the room with them the night before.

"Cardinal sin," Mitch said. "We never—*ever*—leave the bag. Nowhere. No how."

We went to the range. Despite the gallon or so of caffeine he'd already gulped, Duval carries himself with such grace, élan, and patience, you'd think he was on beta-blockers. There doesn't seem to be the slightest strain in his game. Even his swing, so fluid and beautiful, ends up leaving him straight as a two-by-four, not contorted or bent. He warms up without a target, too. "I just swing down my body line," he says. "And work on tempo."

And, my God, is his tempo sweet. Bob says he may have learned that tempo through the range games the two of them played when he was small. They tried to see if he could hit a 5-iron to every green on the range—90 yards, 120, 150, 170. He bet him he couldn't hit high shots with a 4-iron, punch shots with a sand wedge, big sweeping cuts and low darting hooks, punches and floaters and sailers and screamers. And now those shots are all there when he needs them.

Same with putting. Duval is so still when he putts that he purposely rests his sand wedge against his left leg as he practices putts. It never even wobbles. And he only putts a few long ones and a few short ones. Most pros have a Marquis de Sade approach to putting practice. They'll force themselves to stay out there until they've made 25 four-footers in a row. Or 10 three-footers, 10 four-footers, and 10 five-footers, all in a row. Cink once told me how he never ends a practice session until he makes 40 four-footers in a row, all in a circle around the cup. Maybe he should've practiced two-footers, because that's the length he missed on the 72nd hole at Southern Hills to blow his spot in the playoff at the 2001 U.S. Open. But Duval doesn't practice the short ones over and over. In fact, he doesn't really care if he misses them. He barely watches. "You miss 'em, you miss 'em. You're only human."

And you wonder if Brent taught him that, too.

As soon as we started on No. 1, the very likable Mr. Faxon started knifing us in the back. And in the front. And in the sides. He and the world's greatest putting stroke started making everything. It was useless—10 feet, 40 feet, 75 feet—he canned them all. It was like his ball was allergic to daylight. We weren't playing badly, but by the 9th hole, we were four behind.

What was weird is that Faxon kept asking Andrade for advice on putts. Or he'd ask his caddy Tom (Chop) Lamb. Finally, after he'd poured in another putt just slightly longer than Highway One, I stuck the flag in the hole and said, "Faxxy, you've made everything you've looked at. Why the *hell* are you still asking people for advice?"

And Faxon looked at me with a grin and said, "Because we're on TV, you idiot!"

I have *so* much to learn.

Chop got a good line off on 10. I was anxious to reach a green at least once before Duval, so maybe I started moving a hair quicker than appropriate as Faxon was through the ball. And Chop said, "You trying to quick-trigger my man?"

Another great caddy gloss.

Could be used in other facets of life, too. *Honey, last night in bed . . . were you tryin' to quick-trigger me?*

We were getting hopelessly thumped by Faxon's putter, but I still had my moment of glory. It was on 13. Andrade was coming out of the rough on the left 30 yards behind us. After he hit his shot, the big crowd kept walking, not realizing Duval was about to play his shot. He stood over it in the noise and then backed off.

"STAND STILL, PLEASE!!!" I bellowed, holding my arm up. I was loud, forceful, and authoritative. I could easily have been mistaken for Gen. George Patton. Or at least Knute Rockne. Three hundred people froze in their tracks. They damn well better. It's one thing for a marshal to say it, a whole 'nother thing to hear it from a caddy. In a game of Stratego, players would be 1, caddies 2, and marshals 8. I was feeling very powerful and satisfied.

In perfect silence, Duval hit a great shot and, in the middle of the big roar, said to me out of the corner of his mouth, "You've wanted to say that your whole life, haven't you?"

"Honestly?" I said. "Yes."

As we came up 18, the throngs were huge: bleachers and packed tents and thousands of people. It was a thrill. I asked Duval if he thought his dad enjoyed the two days. "Oh, man," he said, looking at all the people. "He ran a pro shop for 30 years. How good is this?"

Bob was loving it. He was going in for shoulder surgery the next week so this would be his last taste of golf for six good months. We were going to finish with a 63 and third place, but it didn't matter a lick. "I never dreamed I'd be here," he said. "I never thought I'd be playing with my son in front of 30,000 people. It's like a dream."

And, for just a second there, I got to thinking about my dad. And I got to thinking how great it would've been to play in just one tournament with him. But even after he stopped drinking, I was still angry at him and, underneath that, scared of him, too. And when I finally stopped being scared of him, he was too old to play anymore. Too bad, too. He was good. He shot a 63 once on sand greens. He was always coming home with some Elks Club championship trophy under his arm or Moose Lodge championship plaque in his trunk. I always wanted to go with him, but he never took me. Maybe I never asked.

Watching the Duvals and the Nicklauses, it made me pine to go back and rethink some of those years. I'd love to go back and see my dad as just a guy, just like me, with his goodnesses and his faults. I'd love to play just one two-man best ball with him. I think we'd be right in it, too.

We'd come down to the final hole, with a chance to win it, and maybe we'd both think, "How good is this?"

If the caddy says . . .

"What'd we post? How's eight sound? Man, we had the beast singin'. All day, we were drawin' steel and rippin' cloth. We keep rakin' like this and I'm gonna be winner-winner-chicken-dinner!"

He means . . .

"What score did my player shoot? How does eight-under-par sound to you? Sir, he was really hitting his driver well. The entire round we were taking our irons out of the bag and hitting the ball very, very close to the flagstick. If we continue to play this well, I will be buying my hotel roommates dinner, as it is customary for the winning caddy to do this."

6

DEWEY TOMKO

Just a Lil' Ol' $50,000 Nassau

The leading money winner in golf may not be Tiger Woods.

It might just be a former kindergarten teacher with 38 clubs in his bag, Vaseline on all the faces, and a gambling jones that could fuel the state of Nevada.

His name is Dewey Tomko. He's 55, built like a newspaper stand, and wears a crew cut that sticks up like a garden rake. He putts between his legs, and will shake your hand only with the ends of his fingers, in case you've been sent to break his knuckles.

You can only pray to Jesus you never meet him on the first tee.

Nick Price won't bet him. "I'm scared of you," Price tells him. PGA Tour pro Danny Ellis won't either. "I'll play *with* him, but never for money," he says. "He's too good. He's *way* too good."

Tomko is the world's biggest golf gambler. He plays $50,000 Nassaus (in which there are three separate bets: the front 9, the back 9, and the entire 18), two-down automatics, sometimes with three and four guys at once. He has won more than a million dollars in one round and dropped more than a million in one round. He will bet on anything, anytime, with anyone. He once bet $100,000 he could make more free throws wearing cowboy boots and a sportcoat than another man wearing a sweat suit. And won. He once bet $10,000 that two raindrops making their way down a windowpane would collide. And lost. He once bet a man $300,000 he couldn't lose 100 pounds in a year. "And we had a rule," Dewey says. "Any body part he cut off, we had to weigh." He let the guy buy out for half.

Of course, the only thing dumber than betting Dewey Tomko on the golf course is trying to make it up afterward in cards. Dewey is one of America's most dangerous poker players, having finished second twice in Binion's World Series of Poker. He also happens to be one of the world's largest sports bettors, and one of the few that actually makes money from it.

But you know what proves he's the biggest gambler of all?

The fact that he agreed to let an accident-prone caddy anywhere near him in the first place.

BEFORE HE'D GIVE me his bag, Dewey insisted I understand gamblers' golf rules.

- "First off, no out of bounds," Dewey says. That means if you can find it, hit it. If it's in the halfway house, hit it. If it's in the bank drive-thru, hit it. If it's in the backseat of somebody's Honda, hit it.
- "No gimmes. Never." That's cost guys a few thou, slapping it away from the hole toward their cart and hearing Dewey go, "Dang, Pards, that's gonna be a tough three-jack from there."
- "No free drops, anywhere, anytime." No drops from drains, flower gardens, plugs, rodent holes, ground under repair, women's purses. Nothing.
- "Don't even lean over like you *might* touch it," Dewey says. "Don't even lean over to tie your shoe." In Dewey's world, if you're in the rough and you bend over and they can't quite see what you're doing, you lose the hole.

- Well, OK, you can move it off a sprinkler head, Dewey says, but only because they were ruining too many sprinkler heads, and Dewey *owns* the course where some of the biggest action in the nation happens. He bought it with his World Series of Poker winnings. It's called Southern Dunes, in Hanes City, Florida. If you're not willing to lose five or ten Large, don't get within a par 5 of it.
- "We tap down all the damn spike marks we want."
- No 14-club rule. With these boys, you can take as many as your bag will hold. When I picked up Dewey's huge pro bag, I wanted to call my chiropractor. He's got 38 clubs, including seven wedges, one for every five yards. "That way I got no half shots," he says. He also carries two putters—"in case one goes bad." He carries metal woods 1 through 11, including a 2 ½. He carries a left-handed tree club, a tiny left-handed club (for tight spots), and a tiny right-handed club. He might use them only once a year, but they might save him $50,000 some days. Some guys carry smooth-faced clubs with no grooves. Some guys carry clubs with a special groove that makes it cut every time and stop on a dime. It's a very sporty little crowd.
- There's no same-ball rule, either. For very windy holes, for instance, Dewey carries the smaller English balls, to bore through the hawk. If he's playing a hole where you need distance, he might switch to a Top Flite. Hell, if he's got a cut going, he might play a Polaris. One time Dewey was playing Davis Love and Dewey blew it 70 yards by him with a greased, hookface driver and "a little rocket ball" he happened to have around.
- Grease up. Use Vaseline, KY Jelly, even Chapstick. If it works in porn, it works in this game. Dewey let me hit a few drivers with grease and I've never hit the ball farther or straighter. I

was 50 yards longer and 30 yards straighter than I'd ever been. I kept looking for my slice and never saw it. "Problem is," says Dewey, "you get addicted. Pretty soon, you're goin' greased from 80 yards. You can't stop." The other problem: It's completely illegal in any other game.

- No bolting. "You can cuss. You can spit. You can take your pants off and play. You just cain't leave," he says. If you do, you pay all bets all ways through the nine, or the equivalent of a large four-bedroom ranch.
- No handicaps. Gamblers don't have handicaps. "Never had one in my life," Dewey says. (I'd guess about a 5.) "I never turned in a score in my life. Handicaps are for guys to cheat with. They don't turn in the good ones and only turn in the bad ones. Why do I need a handicap? I ain't gonna cheat you. 'Cuz if I cheat you, I get a bad rep. And once you get a bad rep, you'll never get a game again. Who wants that?

  "People don't believe it, but there's honor in gambling. You take Pug (a.k.a. Puggy-Wuggy, a longtime poker legend and golf gambler). With Pug, you know he's gonna cheat at golf. You know he's gonna drop (balls secretly out of his pocket when his original is lost) and improve (his lie) and pull his cart over your ball in the rough (so you can't find it). You figure it in to the bet."

  In fact, some of the cheating that goes on is sort of admired. There was once a bulbous man named Jack Strauss, whose best skill was getting low in a bunker, swinging with his left hand, and throwing the ball out with his right. "Nobody better at that, ever," Dewey says with admiration.
- No strokes, either. At Dewey's joint, nobody gets pops but the caddies. "We give spots," he says, meaning they give head starts. For instance, Dewey might play from the backs and you

> get the ladies' tees. Or Dewey might play from the whites and you get to start from the 150-yard markers. Or maybe you get to foozle it everywhere. Or never take a penalty stroke. Stuff like that.

Sometimes they'll give a "reverse spot," which is your opponent gets to take any three clubs out of your bag. For instance, he might take your 3-wood, your pitching wedge, and your putter. Suddenly you're putting with your 4-iron. Or they might make you play with all woods and no irons. Not easy to blast out of a greenside bunker with a 5-wood.

Sometimes you think of a good spot and it backfires on you. Dewey once bet three-time World Series of Poker champ Stewie Unger $100,000 that he couldn't beat him even with Stewie teeing up from the 150s and getting to use a tee anytime, anywhere. Problem is, the next day Stewie shows up with every length of tee known to man. Some are six inches, some are a foot, some are three feet. He looked like a carpenter. If his ball was in the tall rough, Stewie would tee it up and suddenly be above the crap. If he had a sidehill lie, Stewie was even again. One time Stewie chunked one into the edge of a pond, used the three-foot tee, and suddenly he had a nice, dry shot. "Some lessons you learn cost more than others," Dewey shrugs.

When Dewey plays touring pros—and he's taken hellajack off Love, David Frost, Robert Damron, Paul Azinger, Andy Bean, Fulton Allem, and Denis Watson, among others—he's got a standard bet: The pro has to play from the back tees and Dewey plays from the next set up (that's 7,200 vs. 6,800). And get this: They completely skip the par 5s. "They're too good on the 5s, so we don't play 'em. Then I figure I'm even (odds) to beat 'em from the 150s in, 'cause I can putt lights out. And I can get to the 150 marker a lot easier than they can. They gotta hook it around trees and lakes and shit and I don't."

Plus, the greens at Southern Dunes are among the slickest in the world. "If you got any choke in you, it'll come out on those greens, buddy. One time this big-time player-manager came down and this guy really had the nuts. (He could really play.) But those greens drove him crazy. Finally they just broke him. He had a two-footer and he couldn't pull the trigger (bring himself to putt it). And he started to cry. Right then and there. Our greens made a man cry!

"One time I took Frosty to play 7 guys in a 7-on-2 deal. Our best ball vs. their best ball. Frosty shot 62. I gave him a free 10 percent roll (Frosty was entitled to 10 percent of Dewey's winnings and none of his losses). At the end of the day I won a hundred (thousand dollars) and he won ten (thousand dollars). He couldn't believe it. He had no idea we were playing for that much. That's why I didn't tell him. He might not have been able to breathe.

"See, we hit shots the pros can't. We know how to hit it out of a 2-inch plug. Nobody else practices that shot. I can spin the shit out of it off a cart path, and they can't, 'cause they never have to do it. Buddy, there ain't a pro alive that can beat me. You know Phil (Mickelson) and Tiger, right? Well, you tell 'em, they ain't barred from my place. They're welcome anytime. They want to play fifty (thousand dollars) a hole? I'll play it. They wouldn't bust 68 at my place first time out."

Now *that* I'd like to cover.

WITH DEWEY YOU go in style, and so it was I became the first caddy in history to travel to the golf course in the back of a silver stretch limo.

It was sent by Shadow Creek Golf Club, Steve Wynn's mind-bending masterpiece 20 minutes outside of town, a Xanadu that sits in the middle of desolation and yet is as lush as Vermont. It's as though God dropped a green hanky in the middle of the desert.

What you had here in the backseat was: a) Dewey; b) another character called Hill Street, or "Hilly" (Dewey and Hilly are permanent partners. They might be on opposite teams some days, but no matter what, day after day, they share the wins and losses, 50/50); c) a rotund, red-faced Alabama boy named Billy Mac, who looks like he could've been kin to Azar's Big Boy; and, d) Phil, one of the largest bookies in the country, a frenetic Easterner who was occupying one of the largest suites at the Mirage. Phil is known far and wide as the best tipper in Las Vegas. If he shakes your hand, you'll usually find $300 in it afterward. At Stefano's Italian restaurant at the Golden Nugget, if a waiter comes up and sings a good song to Phil's girlfriend, that waiter will suddenly find himself $500 richer. In fact, the best fights in Vegas do not involve Don King. They involve the caddies at Shadow Creek, fighting for Phil's bag.

Oh, and: e) Me with exactly $67 in my pocket. The four of them began settling up yesterday's action.

"You owe me six," Dewey said to Billy Mac, the big Southerner.

"Six?"

"Six."

Six, of course, means $60,000, so Billy Mac pulled them out of his pocket in tight rolls of $100 bills, rubber-banded at $10,000 each, and flipped Dewey six. He flipped them like a barmaid flips drink coasters.

"Same bet today?" said Billy Mac.

"You got it," said Dewey.

Dewey stuck them in his pocket and Hilly said to Dewey, "Don't lose those, now." Then he said to me, "He's always leavin' money places." It's true. One time Dewey left $40,000 in a brown paper bag at a TCBY. He left $30,000 in the trunk of a car once. "I'm constantly finding 10s ($10,000 rolls) in coat pockets and the bottoms of luggage."

Reminder to self: Check rental car for possible Dewey droppings.

"That's nothin'," Dewey said, then told how his mentor, two-time World Series of Poker champ and legendary golf hustler Doyle Brunson, once moved without ever finding the $300,000 in gold Krugerrands he buried in his backyard.

Dewey is better, but Hilly's damn clutch. He's one of these bastards that starts the day 6-7-6 and finishes 4-2-3, when everything's tripled. Although the other day, Dewey was about to board a flight for London to play in a poker tournament when his cellphone rang. It was Hilly, going, "I'm down 280 [$280,000] after two days." Dewey changed his flight and flew to California to help him. "He gets all turned around," Dewey explained. Still, Dewey trusts him. "I know he ain't gonna parkin' lot me [pretend he's my partner, then lose on purpose and split the winnings with the opponents]."

These kinds of boys never write checks. Not for anything. "If you don't got cash, then I don't wanna be paid," says Hill Street. The legendary gambler Amarillo Slim, who is playing in the World Series a table or two away from Dewey, says the same thing that night. "I'd rather have a gambler's word than any businessman's check. I got shoe boxes full of bounced businessmen's checks. Gamblers pay in cash."

Dewey's gang doesn't much go for dealing with businessmen anyhow. "I won't play Square Johns [businessmen]," says Dewey. "You beat 'em and they say 'You hustled me,' or 'You conned me,' or 'You set me up.' I don't need it. I don't play pigeons [players who are easy pickings], neither. Everybody thinks we're out here conning people. We ain't! We're playing each other! I don't play poor people and I don't play Square Johns. They'll bet millions on a stock but you gotta get a court order to get some of them nits [people who don't bet] up to 100 [dollars] a hole. I play gamblers. Gamblers understand losing. They lose every day!"

Dewey was imploring me to understand, gesturing with his arms.

"See, a guy's got to have the gamble [the innate desire to gamble] in him," Dewey continued. "He's got to be the kind of guy who will go you 50 [thousand] on a flip of a coin. Some guys don't have the gamble in 'em, see? They wouldn't go fifty on a flip of a coin if you gave them 3-to-1 odds."

Some of their ilk come in silk, such as Bill McBeth, an immaculately handsome and elegantly dressed man who happens to be president of the Mirage and of Shadow Creek. He looks like he should be in a Polo catalog, not trying to make three-foot gaggers for $100,000. "You have to love to bet," says McBeth. "I know guys worth $4 billion who wouldn't bet a truckload of flour could make two biscuits."

All four in the limo agreed that even though they were friends, they were gonna bet each other high that day. In fact, if they didn't, it'd be an insult. "Hell, you're in Vegas," says Dewey. "Everything is air-conditioned. The food is good and free. They got the game on to bet. And they're playin' poker! It's heaven, man! You gotta make it worth a guy's while to go out there and sweat." Besides, as Hill Street points out, "You got to bet your friends, 'cause your enemies don't come around."

When we arrived at Shadow Creek, The Boys found it to be a bit crowded. It was 10 A.M. and already two other groups had gone off that day. Everything was free, of course—the golf, the food, sweaters in the pro shop, the carts—because of the Monopoly cash they drop at the tables.

All of a sudden, out on the first tee box we had a sixsome, so it would be Indys (individual bets, as opposed to team). Dewey explained his strategy (hope you like brackets): "Everybody thinks it's all done on 1 [the first tee]," Dewey cautioned. "But it ain't. You might give the guy the best of it [the advantage in the setting up of the bet] in order to get it back later. You can give him the best of it, but only if he plays higher [for more money] than he's comfortable with, you know? Or you give him the best of it and then get him to double [double the bets later], or get him to readjust [take fewer strokes on the back nine]. He'll find a way to lose. Trust me. I used to be a goose [the easy loser]. But I learned. I know now when I got the nuts [the decided advantage]."

Dewey decides to go a little light on the bets, hoping to set up Phil for bigger action tomorrow. He arranged $20,000 two-down automatics with Phil, $5,000s with Hilly, and $5,000s with Azar's Big Boy. He bet a lousy dime ($1,000) with some nit named Dave, an L.A. CEO in miles over his head, and finding the number of oxygen molecules in Las Vegas a little low at the moment.

Since we weren't at Dewey's course, everything was decided with shots. Dewey gave everybody a few shots, plus he gave Billy Mac a spot: letting him tee off from the front of the front tee box. One time Dewey gave a guy 100 feet from the front of the women's tee box, but the guy kept walking way too far before he'd tee off. The next day Dewey brought a 100-foot rope. "A man can lie," he says, "but a rope cain't."

(And they do lie. One time Dewey came to the clubhouse and met his opponent for the first time. Guy said he hadn't played for six months. That's when Dewey noticed the perfect tan line across his left hand. You don't get that playin' softball, pal.)

Dewey's also bet $5,000s with a young stud hoss named Ty, who actually is a greeter/facilitator at the course but wants nothing more than to be Dewey when he grows up.

"Hey, Dewey," he said. "I nearly got to Bean Valley the other day." (Bean Valley is gamblese for losing $100,000 in a single day.) He seemed proud of it, like a young race driver telling his dad, "Finally hit the wall in turn 3 the other day, Pops!" And the dad proudly going, "Yeah? It ain't soft, is it, boy?" And so Dewey said wistfully to Ty, "Hell, yeah, I remember my first trip to Bean Valley."

So off we went, six players, six carts. These are gamblers. You think they're going to *share* carts? Plus, three other sweats (people watching the match) and a Shadow Creek buddy with an injury. On the fender of each cart, each player has globbed a pile of Vaseline or KY Jelly, ever ready. They do it to smooth the grooves on the faces of their clubs, so absolutely no spin is imparted on the shots. Ty went first and bombed one 360 right down the sprinkling system. Everybody else was dead straight, too, and not one of them less than 250, many 300. Telling you, grease is the word.

In the cart, Dewey explained that he "wouldn't mind" losing money on the front nine to set up bigger bets on the back nine, and again tomorrow. "Now look, I wanna win, but I don't wanna show too much. I wanna kinda squeak it out, you know?" For that reason, he wasn't going to putt between his legs until he needed it, hoping the boys might double the bets and then he could bring out his secret weapon. He'd done pretty much the same thing two days before with a guy named Ricky who'd sat next to him the night before at the poker tournament. The guy complained that there wasn't a damn thing to do during the day. That's when Dewey's eyebrows raised a little. "Well, want to come out tomorrow and play a little golf with me?" As far as invitations go, it's the equivalent of the wolf asking the sheep to dinner.

Dewey fleeced the guy for $65,000. "It wasn't high," Dewey said. "But it was somethin' to do."

Dewey has a lot of ways to come out the winner. One good one is to catch the guy just off the jet. Give him the best of it, because he'll be too stiff to play. The second is to catch a guy just coming off a lesson. Dewey used to bring guys down to Grenelefe, in Florida, and, just as a show of friendship, set them up with a lesson with the famed teacher David Leadbetter. As with any lesson, they'd come out as twisted as a corkscrew. "Then I'd take them out and bust their ass for 36 holes."

One thing Dewey never does, it turns out, is take a caddy. He only took me, I have a suspicion, to immortalize himself and his buddies in literature. "I don't like caddies 'cuz when you're playin' high, you don't wanna depend on nobody but yourself. And I don't want to be able to blame anybody but myself."

Why?

" 'Cuz when you can blame somebody else, you're makin' excuses. And when you're makin' excuses, you're settin' yourself up to be the goose next time, too."

Still, I tried to get him yardages and pin positions and hand him clubs, but he was getting everything himself anyway, and all I was doing was bumping into him all the time. Pretty soon, I was going to hurt him, and hurt or not, in gambler's rules, you pay off through nine.

"Why don't you just stay in the cart?" he said, kindly.

Benched after one-and-a-half holes.

And yet I still managed to screw up.

It was the third hole and Billy Mac hit an approach that looked pretty good in the air. "Nice shot," I said. I realized it was the first time anybody had complimented anybody's shot the first three holes.

"Better not say anything," Dewey gently scolded. "You might say 'nice lag' to a guy when he was tryin' to make it for $10,000. They don't wanna hear 'nice lag', 'nice putt', nothin'."

It ain't exactly like playing with your wife. Nobody even pretends to look for anybody's ball, except Dewey looks for Hilly's and Hilly looks for Dewey's. Hilly played better than Dewey on the front nine, which is good, since Dewey shot 41 and lost $27,000. He didn't seem torqued about it, though. And he still hadn't putted between his legs. Sadly, Phil didn't want to raise the stakes on the back, so Dewey was stuck playing low. He looked like a kid who just found out Christmas will be postponed indefinitely.

At one point on the back nine, Ty, who goes about 6-5 and looks like he ought to be on a Wheaties box, had about $20,000 on the line. He was waiting his turn to hit when I asked him why he risks this kind of money, when he certainly can't be making the kind of monster bills Dewey pulls down.

"I used to be a college jock, you know?" he said. "Football, baseball. But this right here, this is how I get my rocks off now."

Ty bets the high rollers and the jocks when they come to town. He'd just finished a few days with Atlanta pitcher John Smoltz and apparently took much more than he gave in $5,000 Nassaus. He tangles with Michael Jordan when he comes to town, giving him two and a half a side, though he won't say who wins what. A gambler I know at Atlanta's famously high-betting club, Hawk's Ridge, says Jordan tends to lose more than he wins. "He came down and got me for $100,000 last month," the guy said, "but I got him for $200,000 the last trip." Could be lying, though.

I also checked in with the CEO from L.A., to see how his lungs were working. "Man," he said on the 10th hole, "I'm ruined for member-guests at my own club and $20 games. You can't get it up for them once you had the adrenaline of these babies pumping through you. It teaches you discipline of the mind. If you start thinkin' of what you could lose, you wanna go slit your throat."

But why bring reality into this? At Shadow Creek, reality is only an option. It's hard to tell whether you're in Oregon, Colorado, or one of Steve Wynn's lobbies. Once you're inside, there's no seeing out, and yet you can't resist. Sometimes I'd pull the cart over, pull apart a section of the 10-foot-high hedge that surrounds the place, and peer out into the very real, flat, barren desert all around us. It's like looking behind the background jungle scenery at Paramount and seeing only cardboard boxes and union guys eating out of their lunchboxes.

The gamblers are not interested in the beauty of the course, or its fantasy, or each other's family lives. They are only interested in the bets and Dewey is losing exactly on the right schedule. He shoots another 41 on the back nine—perhaps helped by Phil's quick-triggering him on 12 tee. This time he wins $26,000 on the back nine bets. For the whole day, though, he loses $21,000, which he probably has in the seat cushions of his rental car.

You got the feeling he didn't mind, on account of his partner, Hilly, was doing a very good impression of Tom Watson. He made back-to-back birdies, then aced the par-3 17th. That's not a bad hole to have an ace on, either—an incredible par-3 17th, the majestic waterfall hole at Shadow Creek that is missing only Acapulco cliff divers. Hilly shot 75 for the day, despite the fact that he says he's "about a 10." Hey, Hilly, would you be free for a member-guest?

Young Ty said he ended up pocketing $5,000. The CEO lost $10,000. Good ol' Hilly won $68,000 on the day, and since $58,000 of that was from people other than Dewey, Dewey's cut is $29,000. And since Hilly covers half his $21,000 loss, Dewey really lost only $10,500. So, the $10,500 he lost, plus the $29,000 he won on Hilly's half, minus the $10,000 he lost straight-up to Hilly, means he wound up ahead $8,500 for the day.

"That's OK," Dewey said, scratching those straight-up hair bristles of his. "This ain't no one-day event. This is a lifetime deal. It don't hurt to lose. I don't mind showin' him [Phil] I can play bad. Then when the stakes are higher, I might just get lucky and wind up playin' good."

Imagine that.

ELEPHANTS EAT 20 hours a day. Sharks must keep moving to live. And Dewey Tomko must have action every waking hour or he'll die. That's why even though he only had one hour sleep last night and we've already had a late, huge Italian meal and I need chopsticks to keep my lids apart, Dewey says now we must go see what kind of dollars are to be had at the poker tables.

He has always been like this, even when he taught migrant kids in kindergarten in Polk County, Florida. He'd play poker all night—from 9 P.M. until 6 A.M.—then hightail it for the classroom, usually smelling like smoke and other people's whiskey and old pizza.

Hey, kids, can you spell Advil?

When naptime came, Dewey would lie right down on a mat with the rest of the five-year-olds. Problem was, sometimes the kids couldn't wake Dewey up. The parents would just tiptoe in, take their children home, and Dewey would wake up about 5:30, then head for the poker game again.

He knew it was time to quit when he had $98,000 in his jeans, two pigeons at the table, but had to leave for his $5,400-a-year job. He left for Vegas the next day.

"Buddy, I cain't change a lightbulb," he says. "Cain't hammer a nail. Cain't do one damn thing real well in the world except play poker."

By 1982, Dewey became the No. 1–ranked poker player in the world. "I just know how to read people," he explains. Take, for instance, a favorite pigeon who used to fly up from Florida to play him. "I had this tell on this ol' boy that couldn't miss. [A "tell" is a "read" on a player that gives away what kind of cards he has]. See, every time he had the nuts (the good cards), he had to have some water out of his bottle. If he didn't go to the water, it meant he was petrified and didn't have the cards, so he'd try to just sit very still and not give away how scared he was to be bluffing. That ol' boy paid off like a slot machine."

Figuring out a good "tell" isn't cheating, though Dewey has seen every kind of cheating there is. "Guys putting in their call [bet] and sliding money back out as they bring their hands back," Dewey says. "Or guys using a tiny mirror on their fingernail to see the card as they deal." He's also seen marked cards. Sleeved cards. Stoolies across the table tipping cards.

And still, the only way to beat him was usually with a gun. He used to play cards now and again against a bodyguard for a big-time mobbed-up Vegas guy. This thug had been indicted 21 times for murder but never convicted. It was the weirdest coincidence—all the witnesses kept showing up in coffins. "One time we had this real high game and it was him against me," Dewey recalls. "I was bluffing, but he couldn't tell. Real high money on the line. And he looks right at me and says, 'Dewey, if you're bluffin', I'll kill you.' And every time I'd raise him, he'd say it again. He'd look real hard at me before he'd call me, and he'd go, 'Dewey, you better not be bluffin', else I'll kill you.' I was so scared! It came down to the final bet and he looked at me one last time and folded. And I threw my cards in before he could see 'em. And he stands up, real mad, and says, 'Well, did you have them cards or not?' And I said, 'Acourse, I had 'em!' And I was sweatin' so much I nearly ruined the deck."

Ma'am, would you happen to have a change of underwear handy?

It's not as bad as the time Dewey was at a game when a rough kind of character tapped out, broke, but stayed around to sweat the game. One of the leading players left for a moment to take a dump, taking his money with him. The poor sap was in the stall when he saw a gloved hand holding a Glock revolver come under the door. "Give me that money," said a voice. The man handed it over. Well, under. When he came out, the bent-nose was suddenly back in the game and our hero was suddenly sweating the game himself.

Tomko won so much money from one of his World Series of Poker second-place finishes that he went home and bought Southern Dunes with the cash. It's a British-style links course. Naturally, Dewey changed the names of the holes. Now they're called, among others, "Ante Up," "Dealer's Choice," and "Dewey's Double Down."

And that was the first drip of money that would soon flow like it was coming out of a firehose. "Everybody to me looked like a piece of chocolate cake," he says. All that cake bought orange groves, real estate, and part of a Costa Rican casino.

Then again, God knows how much he'd own if he wasn't so damn stupid with his money. Dewey has lost millions in schemes you couldn't trick an Alzheimer's patient into. He lost piles searching for the Titanic, processing gold in El Paso, processing gold in South America, rescuing gold doubloons from a ship sunk off Venezuela, backing a Christian radio station that had no antenna. That's the problem with gamblers—they don't know when to stop.

"One time, years ago, I won $10,000 off Steve Wynn. When he handed it to me, he said, 'Put this in stock in the Golden Nugget.' That was his first hotel in Vegas. The stock was $4. But no, I wouldn't do it. Instead, I went and blew it somewhere. I still can't remember what I did with it. I figured out the other day, that $10,000 would've been worth $20 million now."

For a few years, any money Dewey made on the poker tables, he'd lose right back on the golf course, most of it to the redoubtable Doyle Brunson, the place where all rookie gambling money goes to die. Brunson, of Fort Worth, Texas, is a FedEx truck of a man, over

400 pounds, and arguably the greatest poker player in history. He may be the only man alive who has won more money gambling golf than Dewey.

Naturally, we meet Doyle at a steakhouse. Even though he's got a diet bet going—if he can lose 100 pounds in the next six months, he wins $200,000—he orders food like he's going to the electric chair in the morning. So far, he says he's lost, well, 20 pounds. He'll probably just pay the guy the $100,000 settlement and never miss a bite.

Losing weight is the only thing Brunson can't do. He's as tough as a bus-station steak and smarter than NPR. A wise guy once mentioned that he'd put a dozen ice picks in Brunson if he didn't start cheating in a certain poker game and cutting the wise guy half. Brunson refused, then showed up the next night with his own wise guy. It was a wise guy standoff.

Brunson once played poker for five days and five nights without sleep. He's been jailed 50 times for playing poker. He's seen four guys drop dead at the poker table, one of old age, one of a heart attack, one of mysterious circumstances, and one shot by a jealous husband. "He came flying in, firing, and we all went flying out the back door, money in our fists. We dove in the river and swam."

A devout Christian, Brunson is not big on showing mercy to his vanquished. "I won't take money off a milkman making $20,000 a year," he says. "But I'll damn sure take it off a gambler." Once, playing pool, he took everything off a man, right down to his skivvies. The man even lost his car to Brunson. He said he'd walk home, get the car, and bring it to the back door. It was 10 years before Brunson saw the guy again. Said Brunson, unsmiling, "You gave me *just enough* time to cool down."

His only equal in American gambling history may be the legendary hustler Titanic Thompson, whom he knew well. "I saw him pitch a key into a keyhole once," Brunson recalls. "I lost money to him playing horseshoes once. He just threw ringer after ringer. Damndest thing I ever saw. I once lost a bet to him that he couldn't throw an acorn over a building. Damn thing had a BB in it."

Brunson's trick for winning on the golf course was "takin' the worst of it [in the bet setup], but makin' them bet for a helluva lot more than they were comfortable. They always choke."

And for the first few years, that choker was Dewey. "My first trip to Vegas," Dewey remembers, "I had $95,000 to bet with him. He sent me home on the plane with nothin'. He was the best I ever saw. I'd win a bunch more, come back out, and lose it all to him again."

But he learned. He went from a goose to goose-slayer. Brunson stopped betting against him and started taking some of his action. He had a standing $100,000 bet that nobody could whip Dewey in a putting contest, providing Dewey could putt between his legs, of course.

Dewey's will became diamond-plated. He used to play hit men and drug dealers. "I wasn't scared," he remembers. "They weren't gonna kill me. They just needed the gamble. I'd clean 'em out and they'd leave town and come back the next week with $50,000 more. Sometimes they'd pay you with money that was all singed or smoky, like they blew up a safe or something for it. I didn't know. I never asked."

He and Brunson won so much money it was comical. "We used to pick up the paper and laugh at the leading money winners on tour," Dewey says with a grin. "Hell, sometimes Doyle'd make more in one day than the leader would make in a whole year."

Square Johns tried to hire Dewey to run casinos and whatnot, but Dewey never took the jobs. "I had to ask a friend of mine once, 'They're offerin' me $200,000 a year. Is that a good salary?' I mean, I just didn't know." And he never took the job either.

"Why should I ever take a job? I never have to do anything I don't wanna. I eat the best food. I stay at the best hotels. I get up in the morning and say, 'Well, what'll I play today? Maybe a football game? Maybe go to the pool hall? Maybe play golf? Maybe go shoot some free throws for money? Man, this gamblin' life is the best."

But you wonder. He is the father of three boys who he rarely gets to see. His marriage is troubled. He never allowed cards at home and warned his boys against becoming gamblers. There must be something he hated about it. And yet, his boys have become gamblers anyway. One of his boys was in Vegas at the same time as us, staying at the same hotel, and yet Dewey rarely saw him. No wonder a kind of loneliness settles into Dewey sometimes. Here it was, way time to call it a night, and he couldn't help himself. He just had to wander back over to Binion's and jump back in a game, knowing he would be flipping cards again all night, his earplugs in to keep out the distractions, not particularly talking to anybody, not particularly laughing much. He'd just end up winning or losing another $100,000 that will end up meaning no more in his life than a pocketful of lint will mean in yours.

From what I saw, he's an addict. Clean, well-dressed, perfectly polite, handsome, funny, richer than Croesus, and absolutely trapped by a disease known as Action. Each day, each hour, each minute, he feeds the beast and yet it only makes the beast hungrier.

Before I left him to find my pillow, he said that at 8 tomorrow morning, we would feed the beast again.

IN THE LIMO ride this morning, the talk is of Big Al. Dewey would dearly love a piece of Big Al because mostly Big Al is the biggest goose of Christmas. Word is, Big Al won $260,000 on the craps tables last night and Dewey would very much like to relieve him of all the headaches that come with such a windfall, i.e., taxation, financial planning, and the dizzying number of investment choices.

In fact, Dewey nearly needs a napkin he is salivating so much over Big Al. This will give you an idea how much of a chop Big Al is: The last time Big Al was in Vegas, he and Phil were going high—$60,000 Nassaus. They were playing the very difficult 18th at Shadow Creek as though they were wearing boxing gloves and using snow shovels. One was on one side of the green, seemingly permanently bunkered, and the other was having a chunkathon with his lob wedge. Finally, Phil was about to attempt a two-footer.

"What's that for?" Big Al hollered across from the bunker.

"Thirteen," hollered Phil.

"Pick it up," Big Al yelled. "I can't beat that."

You don't get a goose like Big Al every day, but they do come along. The late Stewie Unger was that way. If Dewey is a 10 out of 10 on the gambling addiction scale, Stewie was a 23. One time Dewey bet Stewie $400,000 he couldn't break 120. Stewie got up on the first tee, with about 30 guys sweating the bet, and whiffed his first eight swings. Stewie threw down his club, spun around, and said, "Which one of you motherfuckers bent my clubs?!"

Former *Welcome Back, Kotter* star Gabe Kaplan is the Spruce Goose of geese. A rabid poker player, gambler, and golf-action hound, Kaplan once bet a friend $1 million that he'd break 90 in his lifetime. Kaplan still hasn't done it. My question is, how does the friend collect?

"The minute Gabe gets it, he loses it," says Dewey. "But hell, I ain't worried about Gabe. He's set. He got two stock tips when he was a young man that made him $30 million. He can fuck around all he wants. It's just that, some guys always find a way to win, like Doyle, and some guys always find a way to lose, like Gabe."

And if the geese don't know the way, Dewey will find it for them. One time Dewey and former Boston Red Sox star Ken (Hawk) Harrelson were in a huge three-day game at Isleworth, the creamy Orlando resort where Tiger, Ken Griffey, and Arnold Palmer live. They were playing a very evil game called backgammon, wherein a cube sits in a cart. Each team has the right to turn the cube to double the bet, then double again, then double again, until the cube collapses from exhaustion. They were playing $40,000 a hole before the cube had been turned a single time. After the first night, it hit Dewey that a team could easily lose $600,000. So the next morning, Dewey showed up at the first tee with a clear, plastic bag containing $600,000 in $100s. He held it up in front of their opponents and said, "You boys ready to lose *this* much?" Shortly thereafter, "they started gaggin'."

To his undying credit, Big A1 wants no part of Dewey today. There is nothing Dewey can say to be part of the group. Hell, it would only be an eightsome, Dewey argues. But Big A1 looks to me like a man who would no sooner want to bet Dewey in golf than he would like to fill a cavity on a sick crocodile. Now you see why Dewey is spending more and more time lately in Costa Rica. The geese are running from the axe.

This so seems to disgust Dewey that he dispatches his very own caddy. "I'm staking you in a game against Ty," he says. "Thousand dollar Nassau. I want you to clean him out."

He says this laughing. Dewey no more cares about a $1,000 Nassau than he cares about the new Paris fashions. He just wants me out of his hair. Secretly, I think he blames yours truly for his losing the day before. He'll play with three others in the group behind Big Al, hoping he can get them into something worth leaving the air-conditioning for. As for me, I'm bad luck, a distraction, an excuse waiting to be used, and Dewey just doesn't do excuses.

So, dressed in sneakers, using borrowed clubs, and nervous as Barney Fife, I play for 10 times the amount I've ever bet. Ty has scorecard bets with everybody all over the course, so I'm no more than a gnat buzzing near his knee. For me it's scary, but not palm-sweating scary. I know Dewey has more than I could possibly lose stuck in his shoe bag.

Still, I win the front nine and $1,000. My mistake is telling Ty I've beaten him, which reminds him he has a bet with me at all, which propels him to whomping my gluteus on the back nine to win that bet plus the 18.

Dewey comes back to the ranch about 20 Gs richer, minus the news I'm about to give him.

"Uh, we lost $1,000 all day, Dewey," I say, timidly.

And he says, "Whaddya mean, 'we'?"

If the caddy says . . .

"Could you even believe the hawk today? It was blowin' brass monkeys! We had to tie Woozy to a tree! Guys were out there making, like, Frosties and Bo Dereks. I think Carnac made Malcolm on 11. We were in the Brillo so much I shoulda wore waders."

He means . . .

"Could you believe how hard the wind was blowing on the golf course today? It was blowing very, very hard. It was so windy, in fact, we had to tie Welsh pro Ian Woosnam, who is only 5-foot-5, to a tree, or he would've blown away. Of course, I am only speaking figuratively, not literally. Many players were making 8s on holes, and even 10s. I think Jack Nicklaus made an 'X' on the 11th hole, which is to say I'm not sure he ever finished the hole at all. My player and I were in the rough so often I should've worn rubber fishing pants to protect my pant legs, though, again, I do not mean this literally."

7

JACK NICKLAUS

We'll Always Have Vail

Perhaps the lowest moment in your life was unwittingly dragging eight feet of toilet paper by your heel through the entire Nobel Peace Prize procession.

Or maybe you accidentally served your new Amish in-laws pornographic fortune cookies.

Or chances are you sneezed a hocker into the sultan's soup.

For me, it was when Jack Nicklaus's umbrella suddenly collapsed hideously upward, causing me to lurch to save it, causing me to dump nearly all his golf clubs out of the bag onto the sopping turf, just as he was asking me for a new ball, many of which were starting to run down a slope toward an unfathomable cavern.

This was not just the lowest moment of my life. It would be the lowest moment of a mole's life. It would be the lowest moment of Shirley MacLaine's lives.

After all, I had convinced the greatest golfer in history that I could do this, that I was a real caddy who wouldn't mess up, wouldn't be a bother, and most of all, wouldn't embarrass him. Which was true, sort of. I wound up embarrassing only myself.

. . .

THIS WAS A moment that actually surpassed in sheer agony the first day I met Nicklaus. This was 15 years before, the Wednesday of the 1986 Masters, the one that some people, including me, believe is the greatest Masters ever played, the one where Nicklaus came from five down with nine to play, shot 30 on the back, and won his sixth green jacket, at age 46, with his son Jackie on the bag, no less. That win is still the single largest cause of goosebumps since freon.

It was not just my first Masters, it was my first golf tournament as a *Sports Illustrated* writer. I was 28, had a lump of Spam for a brain, and was charged with writing the lead, a job once filled by not just Herbert Warren Wind but the great Dan Jenkins as well. The rumor was that Nicklaus—six years removed from his last major win—was in financial trouble. Word was he'd overextended himself on some golf-course projects and was up to his famous blond bangs in debt. The editor said I had to ask the legend about it. I said I wasn't sure he'd be able to hear me over my knocking knees.

I kept trying to ask Nicklaus, but things kept getting in the way, like the apple in my throat. Finally, on Wednesday, just as the famed man was about to walk into the famed Champion's Locker Room on the famed second floor of the famed Augusta National clubhouse, I said, timidly, "Uh, Mr. Nicklaus, can I ask you a question?"

Suddenly my personal golf god was smiling at *me*, and waiting for *my* question. And that's when I heard myself utter, "Uh, well, Mr. Nicklaus, we hear you're broke."

He stopped and stared a hole through my forehead. I really was hoping the old wooden floor beneath me would give way and suck me to a sudden and satisfying death. Instead, Nicklaus smiled, took my shoulder in his hand, and said, "Now, son, where did you say you were from?"

Nicklaus gave me a very good interview that day. Said he was just overextended is all. Which he was. And he's still a good interview. Of all the thousands of athletes I've interviewed, Jack William Nicklaus is the most helpful, the most giving, and the most thoughtful. The man just never dodges a question. He answers every one, whether you're from *60 Minutes* or the *Toledo Blade.*

Some players drippingly call Nicklaus "Carnac," because "he's got all the answers." But I disagree. It's just that Nicklaus gives such *good* answers, and answers *every* question, that writers go to him on every subject under the sun, and then quote him liberally. For instance, when Tiger Woods shot 74 on the first day of the 1997 U.S. Open at Congressional—after coming in on a monster hype machine—he refused to come into the interview tent. He just blew past a gaggle of 25 reporters like we were a Stuckey's on I-80. He'd been doing that a lot that year and I finally asked Nicklaus, "Jack, did you ever do that?"

And Nicklaus said something that was picked up all over the country. "Well," he said, "I just always thought if you fellas thought enough of me to wait around after my round and ask me a question, I ought to stop and answer it. I figured it was part of my job and part of yours." And I noticed Tiger never blew off the media at a major again.

So I begged Nicklaus for a caddy job. Any tournament, anywhere, anytime. But he always said no. "The kids have too much fun doing it."

Stupid kids.

Nicklaus, now 63, is nuts about his four boys and one girl. He and Barbara used to bring all five of them to tournaments in their old station wagon and stay in one room. Today, every playing father brings along a nanny and some that don't have kids bring one along, too, right, Tiger? The Nicklauses never had a nanny in their lives. Nicklaus used to skip important tournaments just to watch one of his son's high school football games. When he won the 1980 U.S. Open at Baltusrol, the victory dinner was at McDonald's, because that's where his six-year-old, Michael, deemed it should be held.

Unable to stand me groveling anymore, Nicklaus finally granted me a one-day job carrying for him at the grand opening of a new course he designed in Vail, Colorado, called The Summit at Cordillera. He said he would play the Fred Meyer deal in Portland that Monday and Tuesday, then do Vail on Wednesday. I said I was going to be at the Meyer, too. "Great," he said, "I'll give you a lift."

It took me a few seconds before I realized he was offering to fly me on Air Bear, his Gulfstream III, from Portland to Vail.

Will there be a meal?

OF ALL THE friends a guy might like to have, Nicklaus would be 1 through 10, if only just for the tickets he has. He has 12 season tickets to the Miami Dolphins (and went to one game the previous season). He has season tickets to the Florida Marlins (and has been to one game, total). Has season tickets to the Florida Panthers of the NHL (and has yet to go). Has season tickets to his favorite team—the Miami Heat (and had been to one and a half games so far that year).

Same goes for his many homes. He's got one at Reynolds Plantation, outside Atlanta. He's got one at Muirfield Village, outside Columbus. He would end up buying one at Vail at Cordillera, where I'd be caddying. He's got one on the edge of a game preserve in South Africa. "I've shot every kind of big game you can see—except leopard—from my back porch." *Hey! One-stop dropping.*

He spends most of his nonroad nights at his home in North Palm Beach, Florida. One hundred and sixty two nights a year, though, on average, he's on the road, building golf courses, at $2 million plus expenses each, usually.

It's not a bad name to have on the front of your scorecard: J. W. Nicklaus: 2 U.S. Amateur titles, 70 Tour wins, six Masters, four U.S. Opens, five PGAs, three British, 19 *seconds* in majors, 48 top threes in majors, eight times the leading money winner, dominant fat, dominant skinny, dominant crew cut, dominant mod, dominant hated, dominant loved, Fat Jack, Golden Bear, Golfer of the Damned Century.

But Nicklaus hasn't just left his handwriting on *how* the game is played at its best, but *where* it's played at its best. Someday he may be more remembered for building golf courses than demolishing them. By Father's Day, 2003, Nicklaus will have designed 222 courses, many of them the finest in the world. Over the years, 36 of his courses have made various top 100 national and international lists.

Not that he cares.

"Course ratings is all politics," he says. "It's flat-out who's best at kissing the ass of the course raters." Fact is, at the one club he owns—The Bear Club in Florida—Nicklaus has refused to let the raters come. So has The Honors Course in Tennessee and so has Shadow Creek.

He has built courses on six continents now and 28 countries, including Guam. He built one in Brunei to go with a hotel of the sultan's. Problem was, the first time the sultan's nephew, Prince Hakeem, played it, he told Nicklaus, "I like this one. Build another one for the hotel and I'll keep this one." Then he added, "Oh, and put lights on it, will you?"

So Nicklaus built them another one and flew over for the opening. "I remember the prince was going to come," Nicklaus says, "and they laid out 54 pairs of pants for him to choose from. And they told me they have 4,500 cars in the royal family. When I was there, Jaguar had just come out with this incredible model, like an $800,000 one. The prince had one in every color. It's the same with the Gulf-streams. He has this thing about them. He had three G-3s, four G-4s, and five G-5s. I saw a friend of mine from Gulfstream afterward and I told him, 'You guys should've come out with the G-12.' "

For an overseas course, Nicklaus's company gets $1.5 million and Nicklaus visits twice. Sometimes two visits is more than enough. "They have these official dinners," Nicklaus says. "And it can get pretty weird. My guys have had to eat monkey brain. They get the monkey to pop up and they lop its head off and hand you a spoon." Enjoy!

If you sign up for a team project—Jack and his son Jackie, or Jack and Gary—the fee is $1.1 million. For Jack and Michael it's $800,000, and all business dinners must be held at McDonald's, of course.

Nicklaus's standard $2 million is the fattest in the industry. Tom Fazio and Greg Norman each get $1.2 million and Arnold Palmer gets an even $1 million, though "he'll do one for $750,000," says Nicklaus.

But if you pay full boat you get Jack's full attention—and exactly eight visits. "I used to go fifteen times," he admits, "but my guys (he's got 10 designers) are so good now, eight is all I need."

On the first visit, he flies over your property in a chopper and takes a look. (For The Summit, they took a Snowcat.) On the second visit, he gets down on the ground and walks it, figures out the routing and the center line. On the third, he checks out how the clearing is going. On the fourth, he approves the rough grading. On the fifth, he approves the fine grading. On the sixth, the finish grading. On the seventh, the greens. And on the eighth, he plays it. In this way, he's built some of the greatest courses in history: Glen Abbey, Muirfield Village, Castle Pines, Shoal Creek, Valhalla, Harbour Town, Colleton River, Desert Mountain, PGA West, and Cabo del Sol.

"My designs have changed dramatically," he says. "I think my finished work is so much better now than it used to be. Muirfield Village, Shoal Creek, Glen Abbey, those are all great, but they're all part of your education."

His best hole? "Probably 3B at Punta Mita."

I agree. It's an incredible, unfathomable, goddess of a hole just outside of Puerto Vallarta, Mexico. It's a par 3 that, when the tide is up, requires a six-wheeled amphibious vehicle (and operator) to drive you or boat you out to the green. You tee off from the beach in the general direction of Hawaii to a natural island backed by a natural rock formation. It's like playing to Alcatraz and back. Pelicans rest on the green. Waves crash. Dolphins bark. And to think it was the 19th hole he designed there. The original third is a helluva good hole along the beach, but during his opening round, Nicklaus realized what he'd missed. So, at Punta Mita, you get to play two No. 3s. It may be the greatest 19th hole since the Tavern Room at Pebble Beach.

"What kills me is how many *bad* designers are out there," Nicklaus says. "I mean, who *isn't* designing courses? Absolutely horrible players are designing courses. Sergio [Garcia] is 21 years old (now 23) and he's designing courses!"

When they're finally ready, Nicklaus plays them, usually with the head pro and maybe the owner. Then he'll get an assistant pro or maybe some freaked-out member to caddy for him. One time, a nervous type who'd begged for the privilege was standing next to Nicklaus as he addressed the huge crowd. Jack held out his right hand, waiting for the guy to hand him a golf ball. Instead, the guy shook his hand.

WHEN WE LANDED in Vail, he invited me to dinner with his staff, many of whom had flown in for the opening. And he lit up for it.

Nicklaus was funny. Nicklaus was engaging. Nicklaus was open. Nicklaus was frank. Nicklaus was slightly tipsy. Naturally, this was a perfect time to ply him with controversial questions.

Do you get pissed when people call Tiger the greatest golfer in history? I asked.

"Well, I do think all of you are crowning him too early," Nicklaus said. "He's only 25 years old [then]. To crown him today as the best of all time, it's too early. You can say he's the best at this age in history. But the trick is to keep it up. And will he WANT to keep it up? It's not easy. Will he want to keep it up just to break my record [of 18 majors]? And what happens when he gets married and has kids? That changes you. I hope he gets married and has kids, but kids are a whole new world. There were plenty of times I didn't prepare like I should have because I felt there were more important things I could be doing—like being with my kids.

"I think he's going to want to get married some day, I really do. After all, it's gonna get old going back to the hotel room and saying, 'Hey, Butch [Harmon, then Tiger's coach], I did it again!' He has to have someone to play for."

I happen to think he's right. Nicklaus didn't just have 70 Tour wins, and 18 majors, he's also had 43 years of marriage, five kids, 12 grandkids, all of whom live within a mile or so of him in Florida. What does Tiger have? (I mean, besides $150 million and a 12-car-pileup Swedish girlfriend?) Just the golf.

"And what about injuries?" Nicklaus continued. "Nobody talks about what injuries he'll have. I hurt my hip when I was 23. At 25, I used to get cortisone injections in it, three days a week for 10 weeks. Tell me that didn't hurt. I remember on the 18th hole in San Francisco once, I hit an 8-iron and all of a sudden, I couldn't walk. I limped in, missed the cut. So they gave me some injections. Today, they wouldn't have done it. Injections destroy the capsule of cartilage in the hip." (Ironically, the next year Tiger would have knee surgery.)

There is also Nicklaus's contention that the players Tiger is whipping aren't within a par 5 of the guys he beat. "I had a bunch of guys who knew how to win," he once told *USA Today*. "I mean, his best players are all fighting for the category, Best Player Never to Have Won a Major. I had guys who'd won six, seven, eight majors—Arnold, Gary, Trevino, Watson." He pointed to Mickelson's zero majors, Duval's one, Colin Montgomerie's zero, Sergio Garcia's zero.

I happen to think he's wrong. Sure, Mickelson's, Montgomerie's, and Duval's numbers don't equal Palmer's, Player's, and Trevino's, but then again, maybe it's Woods that's *keeping* them from becoming Palmer, Player, and Trevino. If they didn't have the bad luck to be born in the era of Tiger, might they have three or four each?

It drives the current Tour players bonkers when Nicklaus gets on this rant. "If Nicklaus had to play against Tiger," Brad Faxon said, "he wouldn't have any 18 majors."

And, as long as Nicklaus was ranting, he took on the ball Tiger plays. "Do you realize Tiger never hit it in a bunker at St. Andrews [in winning the 2000 British Open]? If that doesn't tell you everything you need to know about the equipment today! The bunkers weren't in play for him! He drove over ALL of them!"

It bugs Nicklaus that he's being considered a short hitter compared to Tiger. "I played a ball that wasn't anything *remotely* like the ones they're playing now." Nicklaus played the MacGregor, known far and wide as one of the worst pieces of shit in history. "I remember once, a USGA guy had one in his hand and said to me, 'How you ever won a golf tournament with that thing, I'll never know.' " (MacGregor is out of business now.)

Earlier that day, Nicklaus's p.r. guy, Scott Tolley, handed him a press release from the Masters announcing the increase in length of many of Augusta National's holes. Some were increased by 60 yards. Nicklaus just kept shaking his head as he read the release. "Augusta stood the test of time for 60 years, right? Now they're having to tear it up, because of the ball. I mean, you look out there, there's no par 5s for these guys anymore. No more. Anywhere. It's not the same game. It's ridiculous.

"I mean, this course here, it's 7,600 yards. This course will be obsolete when they bring out the next ball, whatever it is. Wouldn't it be simpler and cheaper to change the *ball* rather than all these great courses?"

I asked Nicklaus to rate The Summit. "This course tomorrow is probably 'OK,' because of the nature of the land and the expense to move the dirt. I just felt like it wasn't worth the costs, so we didn't do a lot."

Wow, that's some endorsement. Can't you see them printing that on the scorecard? *The Summit Course: "It's probably OK!"—Jack Nicklaus.*

YOU FEEL STUPID caddying for Jack Nicklaus, really.

I mean, what is the point of standing on a tee box and telling him, "OK, this is a little 389-yard dogleg with a pond guarding the green left," when he *DESIGNED AND BUILT* the freaking thing?

"Jack will want *exact* yardages," his man warned me a week before. "But he *hates* to be clubbed. So don't say, 'It's about a 7-iron.' He just wants the yardage to the front, yardage from the front to the pin, and, sometimes, yardage from the pin to the back. He'll pick the club."

Really? History's winningest player doesn't want you to tell him what club to hit? Hard to believe.

They handed me a pair of white overalls and a hat. I asked them where the "NICKLAUS" was for the back of the overalls and the green No. 1.

They just stared at me.

I said that was the famous caddy bib that Nicklaus's Masters caddy got to wear every year Nicklaus was defending one of his six titles. The caddy of the defending champion always gets No. 1.

They just stared at me some more.

Too bad. I *really* was going to steal that NICKLAUS.

Jack showed up, beaming. He loves opening days. "If we open 10 courses this year, those will be 10 of the most enjoyable days of my year," he said, rifling through his bag. "This is the fruit of all your work. All the construction, the designing, everything. You finally get to see it."

He'd been working on this thing for almost two years, but he'd never really seen the finished product. It would be like painting a canvas from 3,000 miles away over the phone. You want to finally see what the picture looks like.

There was a whole rigamarole on the first tee, in which former President Gerald Ford showed up. The two chatted about their wives warmly. Very nice. Ford looked good—old, but he seemed taller and thinner than he used to. Then Mr. Felix showed up and made a little speech you could hardly hear, then Nicklaus took over and proceeded to entertain the 300 or so people following us for the next four hours.

A huge speaker followed us down the fairway, so the 300 could hear his every thought on anything that came up. And plenty did. On one hole, Nicklaus said, "If you want to drive this green, I'd suggest using a cart."

Another time, his playing partner, head pro Pente Tofferi, outdrove him, and Nicklaus didn't know it. He walked to the ball of

Tofferi, even though I was standing perfectly still back at his own ball. He saw me and his shoulders sagged.

"You know what the longest walk in the world is?" he asked me, the crowd hanging on the question. "The walk *back* to your ball."

You could see on the very first green that The Summit, the highest private course in the country at 9,040 feet, had a unique problem. Herds of migrating elk tear up the greens and bunkers. So many elk, in fact, they had to fence off the greens. Elk vandalism is not a big issue at, say, Lubbock Country Club.

Understand, as he's trying to entertain the crowd I'm trying to caddy and get stuff for the book and not choke from nervousness. So, when he was answering my questions, the whole crowd was hearing them, which put a lot of pressure on Caddy/Journalist Boy.

"Has there ever been a better lag putter than you?" I asked after he cozied up a 50-footer on one hole for a nice par.

"Hard to say," he replied, though you knew it wasn't going to be hard to say at all. "Sometimes I'd go into May or June without a single three-putt. One time I went clear to the British before I had a three-putt."

This, of course, is patently unbelievable and the largest whopper ever told. But it speaks to the man's confidence in himself. I honestly believe Nicklaus believed it, because Nicklaus's mind is so strong it wouldn't *register* a three-putt. Had to be a spike mark or a sloppy hole cut or a camera click. And if it was, he didn't count it. He was famous for that kind of stuff. Like, sometimes, if he'd hit a bad shot into a green, he'd go fix a ballmark right near the pin, shaking his head and saying something like, "These damn greens won't hold *anything*," even though you and he and everybody around the green knew his ballmark wasn't anywhere *near* the pin. It's the kind of unshakable belief system you have to have in yourself to win 70 tournaments, I suppose.

"Noooo!" he protested. "It's true! See, I don't make a lot of putts. I just don't miss a lot."

Huh?

He went on to explain that he's not the kind of player who makes a ton of gaggers—like a Phil Mickelson when he gets hot. It's just that he doesn't miss a lot of three- and four-footers—like a Mickelson when he gets cold. "That's just how I was taught," he said. "If you just concentrate on trying to get it up there close for your two-putt, you'll be money ahead."

I asked him if he'd ever had the yips.

"Never," he said. "And I think if you look at the guys who got the yips and you look at some of their nighttime habits [read: drinking], you'll notice a correlation." That's cold and nasty and probably accurate. Watson knew his way around a wine list with the best of them and got a terrible case of yips. Lloyd Mangrum was an aficionado of the grape and got them. A contemporary of Nicklaus, Larry Mowry, once told me, "You don't know how hard it is to make putts when your hands are shaking from the night before."

Nicklaus also said his putting these days isn't near as good as it used to be. "I don't have the nerve anymore to challenge the hole. I'm not that bold."

Still, he turned the front 9 in 33, although Tofferi was giving him anything shorter than Shaq's arm. For some reason, they held a press conference between 9 and 10 and somebody asked Nicklaus toward the end how his caddy was doing.

"Not bad," said Nicklaus. "He's only cost me two shots so far."

All the legends in the world and I have to get a comic.

The truth was, I'm sure it's not easy playing with somebody grilling you between every shot. "Nah," he said. "Remember, I played with Trevino. In fact, one time, we met on the first tee and I said, 'Lee, I don't want to talk today.' And Lee said, 'You don't have to talk, Jack. You only have to listen.' "

I was always amazed at Nicklaus's memory for stories and golf shots. I was telling Tofferi, "This man can remember every shot he's hit in competition for his entire career. He can tell you what club he hit into the 13th hole in the third round at the Pensacola Open in 1962."

"That's a lie," Nicklaus rebutted. "I didn't play Pensacola in '62. I played it for the first time in 1965. And in the third round, I hit 7-iron into the 13th hole. I shot 67. I finished second."

I checked it out. He's right. Show-off.

The crowds were loving all of this. It's hard to underestimate what Jack Nicklaus means to Americans. If you have ever once struck a golf ball and happen to be between 25 and 95 years old, Nicklaus is a little part of your life, a little joy you had, all those years. The name Jack Nicklaus *meant* golf. It became a brand for golf. For a time he was one of the three most famous people in the world. The actor Jack Nicholson once told me, "Do you know how sick I am of little old ladies asking me how to hit a 3-iron?"

And so all those people think that because Nicklaus was part of their life, they simply *must* have been part of his. They will come up to him wide-eyed and open-handed and say, "Jack, I don't know if you remember me, but you signed my visor after the Cincinnati Pro-Am in 1962."

And Nicklaus always says, "How could I forget?" And the guy laughs, not sure if he's serious or not, but happy either way.

Someday, Tiger may get comfortable with being a god, the way Nicklaus and Arnie did, but he's nowhere near them yet. Jack and Arnie didn't take as long as Tiger is taking, but then, no golfer in history has had the kind of worldwide onslaught Tiger has. Still, he could be, should be, needs to be, better. Nicklaus and Palmer have a way of going into a room where *every single person* wants to meet them and remaining relaxed, nonchalant, unhurried. Their whole carriage hints that, yeah, they might meet everybody and actually enjoy it and hell, isn't the world of golf *fun?* On the other hand, Tiger's whole carriage hints that if he doesn't get out of this room in the next 10 seconds, somebody's going to get a 5-iron through the cerebellum. Of course he'd have somebody that *does* that for him.

But being open and unintimidated has meant a lifetime of people busting the hell out of Nicklaus's personal bubble. That's one reason Nicklaus took so fanatically to fishing and the outdoors. And even then, there was still no place on earth for escape. "One time we were fishing this New Zealand wilderness area. I mean, this place was *totally* remote. We hadn't seen anybody for days. We were crossing this rickety old rope bridge over this huge cavern. It was just pouring down rain. I mean buckets. I had on a hat, glasses, slicker, big boots. Suddenly we see this old couple at the other end of the bridge as we start to cross. Now the lady starts running toward me! Running! I'm thinking, what the hell? What's chasing her? I'm scared. I start backing up, but she keeps coming. She opens her arms, jumps on me, and screams, 'Jack Nicklaus! My favorite golfer in the world!' "

Speaking of rain, it had been raining off and on most of the day in Vail and that, combined with trying to caddy and interview, plus the ridiculous distances between green and tee (OK, so we took a cart sometimes), plus the altitude, plus the three bottles of wine the night before, started to chip away at my looping skills.

And that's about when it happened.

We were on 15 and the rain was coming in almost sideways and the wind was done practicing and starting to get serious. At this point in the day, Nicklaus's umbrella and I were not on speaking terms. It had been a pill all day. It kept trying to blow away when I set it down, or poke me in the eye, or fake a "click," making me believe it was locked open and then collapsing nearly on Jack's head. But this time it went too far.

Jack was giving the folks a little chipping lesson and I was standing on a hill while trying to write and not realizing I had the bag a little upside down and also trying to make damn sure the umbrella really "clicked" and was not just conning me and so perhaps I forced it too hard and suddenly it folded up the wrong way, like a contortionist bending back through her own legs. Three hundred people gasped, then laughed. I felt like Mary Poppins' crackhead sister. And as I looked at horror on that, the bag toppled over backward, sending some of the clubs out, and, unfortunately, some of the balls out of the unzipped ball pouch just as Nicklaus asked me for another ball to chip.

Busted.

Nicklaus looked at me, amid the guffaws, waited a while for the laughter to die down, and then said, "Don't quit your regular job."

Still, on the bright side, once I'd picked everything up, it left an opening. "Who's the worst caddy you ever had?"

"Present company excepted?"

Funny.

"I had one caddy named Four-to-One," Nicklaus recalled. "All he wanted to do was shoot craps. I remember once at Memphis, on the 7th hole, I had about a 20-footer for birdie. He was tending the pin. I hit the putt and he lifts the pin and the entire cup comes with it. It hits the cup and ends up an inch short. So instead of a 2, I make a 5. I end up losing in a playoff."

He must've felt that he wasn't getting much of a caddy in 1963 in Palm Springs when he was assigned one he'd never met, a Las Vegas cabdriver with a huge blond Afro named Angelo Argea, who was Fluff before Fluff was Fluff. All they did was stick together for the better part of three decades and win more tournaments than some touring pros will *play*. "How could I let him go?" Nicklaus said. "I got him at the Desert Classic and I won. I took him to the Tournament of Champions and I won. I took him at Sahara and I won. I won the first six tournaments he caddied for me [Aha! It was actually five of the first six!] How you gonna let a guy like that go?"

Not that it changed Angelo. He was still an unrepentant gambler, unashamed partyer, and unconscionable self-promoter. "Hell, half the time he was out nights promoting his book," Nicklaus remembers.

"I remember one time I won the Sahara Classic [in Las Vegas], I gave him his check," Nicklaus said. "He'd been asking me to go to the craps table with him for years, so I finally went. I had a bunch of money with me and Angelo had $40. Well, I never got the dice. Angelo got so hot, he wound up making $25,000. I did pretty well, too, I have to admit. So I said, 'Angelo, give me the money.' He did. Now, this is a guy who'd never saved a dime. He had debts all over the place. I said, 'Angelo, how much would it take to pay off all your debts?' He said, '$3,000.' I said, 'OK, here's $3,000 to pay off your debts.' Then he goes, 'Can I have $3,000 to send my mother?' So I gave him another $3,000. So I said, 'I'm taking this $19,000 and I'm setting up a trust fund for you. This is going to be money for you to start your retirement on. You have to have an absolutely, drop-dead, fantastic reason to get any of it out, OK?' He said we had a deal. Within six months it was all gone."

Since Angelo saved zippo, he's still working for Nicklaus. Angelo still does all the yardage books at every Nicklaus course. In fact, I was looking at one of his numbers now on the par-5 17th as Nicklaus prepared what I thought was an absolutely Spam-brained shot. He wanted to hit a 3-wood that would have to go over a cliff, cross a cavern, and navigate some trees guarding the green. He would have to hit it 285—carry 260. Even at this altitude, you had to be wearing a stupid patch to even try it.

"Give me the 3-wood," he said.

"That's pure nuts," I said.

He is Jack Nicklaus.

I am Pencil Boy.

He proceeded to hit the greatest 3-wood I've ever seen, over the cliff, over the cavern, between two trees, rolling up to five feet from the hole. Then we missed the putt for eagle. Lousy read by the caddy.

Finally, the day was about over. He had a 25-footer for birdie on 18 and said, "Do you know I've never missed a birdie putt on any of my 18th holes in any of my course openings in my entire career?"

"That sounds like the biggest lie since 'I did not have sex with that woman,' " I thought.

"Nope," he said. "It's absolutely true. And this is why . . ."

And he drew his putter back and slapped the ball directly to a kid who'd walked all 18 holes through the wind and rain and crackhead sister act.

". . . Because I always do that."

He shot 35 on the back for a highly suspect four-under 68, the course record. Of course, every round he plays at an opening is a course record. He's guaranteed to set about 15 course records a year, even at 63 years old. Must be fun.

That night, I was in the lobby of the hotel playing the six torch songs I know on the piano: "As Time Goes By," slow stuff like that. And who should suddenly be leaning on the piano, listening, but J. W. Nicklaus himself.

He started singing along. Had a nice voice, too, and it was my rare privilege to accompany him that night, as it had been that memorable day.

If the caddy says . . .

"Damn, I'm hot for Keep On's bag. Kid just nuts it. I mean, he just flat torches his lumber. The guy is longer than Dirk Diggler. Too bad I'm stuck with Deane Beman Boy. My guy gets in the hunt and right away, it's gargle time. We either Meet the Hendersons or bombs go off in our hands. Wanna swap?"

He means . . .

"Honestly, I would love to caddy for young Tour pro Ty Tryon, who is known sometimes to us caddies as Keep On Tryon. He hits the ball a very long way with his driver. Very long. Unfortunately, I'm stuck with a player who hits it very short, in the manner of former Tour player Deane Beman. Anytime my player comes close to the lead in the tournament, he tends to perform badly under the pressure. We either hit it out-of-bounds into people's yards or we lose our touch with the putter and putt the ball far past the hole. Would you care to exchange players?"

8

DEEPAK CHOPRA

The Seven Spiritual Laws of Double Bogey

I knew I was in for a different kind of loop when I asked my man—mystic, healer, and self-help author Deepak Chopra—why he was wearing only a golf shirt in the 45-degree *brrrrr.*

I had on a sweater *and* a windjacket. So did his instructor. So did everybody at Meadows Del Mar Golf Club in northern San Diego this chilly morning in January. But there stood the 55-year-old Indian svengali—the man who has had Bill Clinton, Michael Jackson, and Madonna worship at his sandals—in a cotton golf shirt that barely covered his brown biceps.

"Aren't you cold?" I asked.

"Oh, no!" he said in his distinctive New Delhi accent. "Don't you know I'm a trained guru? I maintain my own body temperature. I was trained to do this twenty years ago."

Really? How?

"It's very simple, really," he said, looking up with a beatific smile on his face. "You simply imagine a bonfire in your rectum."

Oh.

Guess that would do it.

"So," I asked, "how do you keep yourself cool on a really hot day?"

"This is also simple," he said. "You simply imagine an icicle in your rectum."

You figure this is how he got the name Deepak?

"It is common in the East," he said. "Tibetan yogis can sit in a pile of snow and within minutes, the snow will have melted around them."

This, to me, did not seem like such a great skill. I've known guys who can do the same thing after eating the Smothered Burrito Special at Chubby's Mexican Café.

Anyway, we began walking to the first tee, and I couldn't get my mind off it. I imagined what other possible things it might be helpful to imagine in that cavity during a round. If it's rainy, do you imagine an umbrella? If you're hungry, do you imagine a kielbasa? If you're on your last golf ball, do you imagine a sleeve? It was a very weird day already and it was only 8:30.

I should've known it was going to be bizarre because it was an idea given to me by one of the most bizarre people in the history of golf—the brilliant Swedish Tour star Jesper Parnevik. I once spent a week with Parnevik for a feature story for *Sports Illustrated.* In that week with him, I ate volcanic dust, tried to solve his amazing card tricks, and spent too much time discussing the vial of his blood kept by a healer in Sweden, who would call him with blood readings like, "Be careful. Today you could get sick." And, "This would be a very good day to make brave shots."

Before I left, he handed me Chopra's six-part audiotape series, *Magical Mind, Magical Body*, and it boggled my brain. Since then, I've read many of his books, including *Grow Younger, Live Longer*, which I finished a week from this coming Thursday.

So when I heard he'd taken up the game of golf six months before and was coming out with a book called *Golf for Enlightenment: Playing the Game in the Garden of Eden*, I called to see if he might want a free caddy for a day, somebody to kind of *enlighten* the load.

I mean, could the same principles he uses to help people find peace, love, and happiness help their short game? Dr. Chopra's teachings have helped people heal their hearts, banish disease, and approach nirvana, but could they do something *truly* meaningful, like teach you to hit a 1-iron?

I sincerely doubted it. Golf just doesn't usually give a rat's ass about the "infinite organizing power of your cells," does it? Golf just wants to yank down your pants in front of the Ladies Senior Auxiliary Luncheon and slap you in the face a few times.

Look, it's all well and good to teach people that "the world is as it should be," as Chopra has written many times, but try telling it to some guy who's just paid $185 at The Bridges of Osprey Sanctuary to shoot 121 and is now so torqued off he's making long scrapes in his rented Taurus with his spikes? And, sure, it's easy for him to write, "Do not see obstacles." But has he ever played the island par 3 at TPC?

And why would a man who reportedly can levitate be fascinated by lob wedges, anyway?

So I called. You wouldn't believe who called back—Tina Mickelson, Phil's sister and the editor of his book.

She looks remarkably like Phil. She's two years younger. Same eyes and chin, except blond, beautiful, and skinny as a 2-iron. A four handicap herself, she edits books, has a syndicated "Golf Tips with Tina Mickelson" column, and suffers every day being endlessly compared to Phil.

"It never fails," she says. "Like the other day, I met this nice guy and he asked me out. So we go to dinner. The meal hadn't even arrived yet—hasn't even *arrived*—and he goes, 'So, when do I get to meet your brother?'

"That made me *so* mad. I was *fuming*. So I said, 'Oh, you mean Tim [Phil's younger brother]? You want to meet Tim? I can arrange that.' And I never went out with him again."

Suddenly and quietly, in walked the prophet himself, Chopra. He was short and stocky, handsome and dark, with a bit of a Buddha's gut and a smile that warms you from the spleen out. He was wearing khakis, an untucked blue golf shirt, and brown golf shoes. When he introduced himself and looked at me with those bottomless eyes, my knees nearly buckled.

It reminded me of the story of a woman who went with a friend to his Chopra Center for Well-Being to take a cooking class. When they were ready to leave, she found a black Mercedes blocking her car. So she went inside and asked if someone could please move it so she could get out. Sure enough, Deepak Chopra himself came out. Her girlfriend, Heather, was awestruck in his presence, but recovered in time to ask him to sign the book she'd bought in the gift shop. He did. As they drove away, the girlfriend opened the book to read the inscription: "To Heather, love and enlightenment, Deepak."

She was beside herself in amazement. "He knew my name!" Heather gushed. "Can you believe he knew my name? That is the most amazing thing I've ever seen! The man is a mystic!"

And her friend goes, "Heather, you still have your name tag on from the cooking class."

He must have been talking to me for a good 30 seconds before I realized it. "I had seen people playing this silly game and it seemed odd to me," he was saying. "Guys hitting a ball and chasing it and taking all day to do it. I had no interest. I was a cricket player." But after his first hour on the range, he declared, "I'm never giving this up. I'm going to play this the rest of my life."

Golf. It even sucks in the gurus.

First, we went to the range. He'd been custom-fitted for a set of Taylor-Mades, but they hadn't arrived yet, so he was using Tina's. I checked them out as we walked: Driver, 3-wood, 5-wood, 7-wood, 9-wood, 5-iron, 7-iron, 8-iron, 9-iron, three wedges, and a putter. Your typical 30-handicap rental bag.

He introduced me to his coach, former LPGA touring pro Wendy Werley. Only I'd met her before. She taught *me* for a time at a club I belonged to in Littleton, Colorado. "I remember you," she said. "You were too long and too quick." Said to you by a woman, that's a little unsettling.

Werley was also blond and attractive and plagued by men. "You meet these guys and you know there's only one thing on their mind," she said.

Right, I thought to myself, *Sex*.

"Lessons!" she said. "Lessons! First date, every time! 'So, can you help me with my driver? Or my wedge game?' They're so transparent! The last guy I dated, I found out it was all about the golf lessons. That's the only reason he was taking me out. He kept begging me for it, so after a few dates, I gave in. We went out to the range, but he wouldn't listen to me. He kept doing the same things wrong, over and over again, but he wouldn't listen to my advice. He was sure he knew better. So I finally said, 'Either listen to me or let's go home.' We broke up. Now, I don't give golf lessons to anyone I date."

Werley came to Chopra in hopes of curing her killer migraines. She was living in Atlanta at the time. "I was a total achiever," she says. "I was totally attached to outcome." Not only did she play on the LPGA Tour, but she competed in the Olympics at 16 years old—in tennis. She came from a hard-driving family and lived with the pressure of a relentlessly demanding dad. She won seven state tennis titles. She played No. 1 on the boys' golf team at Columbine High School in Littleton. She was a debutante. She had straight A's.

She played the LPGA from '90 to '94 and on the Japanese golf tour after that.

But the more she achieved, the more she felt she wasn't getting accomplished, and all that lack makes a head ache. The migraines were stopping her cold for days at a time. Chopra first taught her to meditate. Then he taught her during meditation to concentrate on feeling her hands gorge with blood, making their temperature rise, making them tingle. To do this, blood must be transported from the head and when that happens, the migraines disappear. "I lost my migraines!"

She was so overcome, she moved to La Jolla just to be part of his work. Before long, she was convincing him to try the ultimate mind challenge—golf. "Deepak has the best concentration of any student I've ever had," she told me. "You'll see. It's amazing. I've played golf for 31 years and he understands it so deeply in six months. I'm amazed. God, I wish I'd known him when I was out on tour."

He set up over a rockpile and took his stance, Wendy watching every move. His stance seemed way too wide. Perhaps he *did* have goods stored in certain cavities. And his head was too far hunched over. But suddenly, before he'd hit one, he was rising again, with a smile on his face like he'd slept with a hanger in his mouth.

"I love golf," he said, wistfully, in that peaceful tone, "because it has brought me back to my childhood. It's play. When I am playing golf, I don't have a worry in the world." He'd played cricket as a boy and was captain of the cricket team at medical school. "The greens are like the pitch of the cricket field."

He went back to that awful stance, took it back slowly and calmly, then whipped it through the zone as if he were late for his next reincarnation. Most of the ones he hit were skanks or heel jobs. I started peppering him with questions.

"You're known for your incredible mind," I asked. "What is your swing thought?"

"Nothing," he said. "Nothingness."

And then he swung and the ball went off 70 degrees sideways, thus proving it.

You have written that to be happy, one must not attach oneself to outcome, I said. *But how can you do that in golf, which is totally based on outcome?*

"One should play golf the way one plays the game of life," he said, lining up a 5-iron. "You can't get caught up in the ego."

The shot dribbled off the tee and went 30 yards. It would not even have made a decent googlie.

"Damn!" he said, under his breath.

OK, so he's still a little attached to the outcome thing.

We walked to the first tee. I asked him if he'd ever had a caddy before. He said only in India. "There, you get three caddies," he said. "One walks with you and two ahead of you. The two ahead look for the balls. Balls are very expensive in India, more than 100 rupees each, or about $2. That's a lot there." He said the courses aren't nearly as good, but they do have something U.S. courses don't have: "Peacock Crossing" signs.

Meadows Del Mar is one of these achingly ritzy joints where they hand you a mango-scented towel on the fifth tee and hound you with "player assistants" (grouchy marshals) and want you to pay $40 to frame your first divot as a souvenir. Ten years ago, it would have just been Del Mar Meadows. Twenty years ago, it would have just been Del Mar Golf Course and Deli. But it was gorgeous—a private inland course about 20 minutes from La Jolla, and we pretty much had it to ourselves.

He hit a leaky drive to the right on the first tee box and was pleased, then took two mulligans from the fairway. "I don't keep score," he said, happily. "But I think that was about a six."

I used to know a guy in New York who insisted that he *never* kept score, had no idea what he might have shot that day, and, furthermore, didn't care. "For me, golf is just about the purity of the shots," he'd sniff. "Not score." I asked him once, "What do you *guess* your handicap would be—and I'm well aware that you don't keep score—but just roughly, guessing, what do you think it would be? Like, about 10, about 20, what?"

And he thought about it and said, "Right now?"

"Yeah."

"I'd say I'm about a 5.4."

Not that he keeps track, of course.

Is cheating in golf wrong? I asked Chopra.

"Yes," he said, "and also it is bad for your game. Because when you cheat, you feel guilty. Karma is in play. And as you're swinging on a ball that you've cheated with, you're worrying about the other person finding out you've cheated. And you often hit a bad shot."

Admit it. He's right.

I asked him if he's played *with* any other golfers yet. Like, in a real round. He said he'd recently taken his son, Gotham, a Bostonite who was once named one of *People*'s 50 Most Beautiful People, to Palm Desert, California, to play. It was Chopra's first time playing with others.

"We were put in a group with a man named Jim," he recalled. "And as this man, Jim, hits the ball on the first tee, he begins talking to the ball. He says, 'Come left! Come left!' And to my amazement, it did come left! And I thought, 'What a mystic this man is! He can control inanimate objects with merely his will!' Furthermore, he kept referring to himself in the third person. He would say, 'Aww, Jim, what are you thinking?' Or, 'Nice shot, Jim. Nice fucking shot.' And I thought, 'This man has attained what nobody else but the great mystic Shankara-charya has attained.' Shankara-charya has attained total loss of ego, so that he himself doesn't feel pain or wetness or wind, only the vessel he lives in feels these things. He will say only, 'This body is hungry' but he will never say 'I am hungry.' And this Western man Jim had attained such enlightenment already!"

Does that mean the mooks in my Saturday morning group are mystics, too?

On the second hole, another par 4, he smother-toed one sort of left, then Wendy had him hit his 5-wood over and over, until he got one in bounds. When he did, it was a beauty, with a little rise in it and straight as Billy Graham.

Is golf spiritual? I asked.

He paused a moment before he spoke. (This was a day with much pausing.)

"Golf, I think, can be spiritual," he announced. "I mean, look around us. So green, so many trees, beautiful water, beautiful sky. Does this not bring you back to the Garden of Eden?"

Don't know. Is it a Weiskopf design?

"But it is also transportive," he added. "It is the stuff of dreams. I play tennis, yet I could never hit a tennis shot like Rod Laver, or a cricket shot like Murali. But once in a blue moon, I can hit a shot like Tiger Woods."

This dude put the "chop" in Chopra, but I love the way he talks.

He gave himself a 7 on the hole. Not that he was keeping score.

He did nothing without asking Wendy first. It's unusual to see a man who has mastered quantum physics, who was one of the country's foremost endocrinologists, whom spiritual leaders run to for wisdom, afraid to choose a club without his 5-foot-3-inch coach.

"How's my grip, Wendy?"

"How's my stance, Wendy?"

"How's my clubface, Wendy?"

And when he hit a lousy shot, he would turn to her and say, ashamedly, "I am so very sorry, Wendy."

At night, he said he was reading not Stephen Hawking, but *Golf for Dummies.* At home, he is not contemplating the world's sorrows but standing in front of his mirror looking at his backswing. Hours he used to spend understanding neurological science are now spent watching the Buick Classic.

And they say golf isn't an addictive substance.

On the 3rd, a par 5, he was near the green in three, but then skulled a few chips, then chili-dipped a few, then foozled the rest. He was frustrated. While Wendy was chasing balls down, I took the liberty of showing him a little no-wrist chip shot, played off the back foot, that's easy to hit solid most every time. He tried it a couple times and hit them both much better. "This shot feels good in every cell of your body," he said.

Not sure I've ever heard those words uttered on a golf course before.

He butchered No. 4, unleashing a few swear words along the way. You just don't expect to hear a man of infinite peace, a man who has lifted himself above worldly desires and avoidances, a man who has freed himself from ego and envy, say "Goddamn piece of shit" under his breath. He looked like a man who at any minute might break all his clubs over a camel's head and quit the game forever.

But then, just as quickly, he actually *parred* the fifth hole, with a decent drive into the first cut of rough, a lovely, high 9-iron to 20 feet, and a rare and totally legit two-putt. Suddenly the wisdom was flowing again. And he really did have an uncanny understanding of the game for a guy who can't play dead in a cowboy movie.

For instance, he kept talking about Karma. He wrote once, "The

Law of Karma says no debt in the universe shall go unpaid." Now, right away, I know Karma has never met my golf buddy Two Down O'Connor. But now he was saying Karma is not necessarily a good thing in the game of golf.

Say what? I said.

"You see, there are two kinds of action. Karma and *kriya.* Karma action is a present action influenced by a past action" (e.g., you pretended somebody else's Titleist Pro VI was actually yours last week. Somebody hit your new Lexus with one this week.) "*Kriya* action is totally *independent* of the past. So, if I'm not influenced by the last shot, then it's spontaneous action, that is: *kriya* action. *Kriya* means that each shot should be hit as though it's for the first time."

I felt I had all the intelligence of Britney Spears until it suddenly hit me.

"Ohhhhh," I said. "You mean: 'Play each shot one at a time!' "

"Exactly!" he beamed.

The touring pro Nick Price says that was the single thing that changed for him during his monster year in 1994, when he won the British Open, the PGA, seven tournaments around the world, and Player of the Year. In the middle of his freakishly good run, I asked him, "Nick, what gives with you lately?" And he said, "For the first time in my life, I'm able to play each shot for its own value, its own worth. I'm playing each shot absolutely by itself, without anything attached to it, without thinking, 'OK, this is big. I've *got* to have this.' Or, 'I just bogeyed that last hole, I've got to hit this close.' Or, 'I need three birdies in a row here to win.' And I'm doing it whether it's a practice round or the last round of a major."

So Deepak Chopra, a 36 handicap on his best day, already understood what it took Nick Price his whole career to learn.

"Now," said Deepak. "Imagine if you lived your life like that!"

Whoa. Live every hour just for that hour's value? Not wasting it away pining for the bigger house I'll get someday or the better job or the fancier car?

"Precisely!" he raved.

So, I got that goin' for me. Which is nice.

We walked to the next tee box, me pumped up about how "present" my life was going to be from here on in, him pumped up about his par (not that he was attaching himself to outcome or anything). "Golf, I think," he said, glowing, "can be quite a lot like sex. When golf is very good, there becomes a loss of ego. There is a timeless awareness. It's authentic. And there's a spiritual expansion inside your soul."

This is true. And when your Maxfli hits a sprinkler head and bounces over the green and into the hot-dog stand, golf can also be quite a lot like sex in that you feel well and truly fucked. But this was merely a private thought.

In his famous *The Seven Spiritual Laws of Success* he wrote, "True success is the experience of the miraculous." On the 6th hole, he proved it. It was a tiny par 3, maybe 70 yards long from the forward tees we were playing. He hit his wedge high and long and then canned a 75-foot putt for a birdie! He was now one-under for the last two holes, making him low prophet. He beamed like Siddhartha. There was something preposterous going on.

Are there golf gods? I asked, planting the flag back in the hole.

"Oh, I think there are absolutely," he said, "in the sense that you are sending out negative or positive energy that can be returned to you. For instance, when I'm playing, I want the other person to hit a good shot, because, then, it inspires you. Any flicker of a negative thought can make you fall apart."

Two Down often says the same. "Never hope your opponent gags. The golf gods will get you."

You write often of how meditation has changed your life. (He med-

itates one hour every morning and one half hour every evening.) Would it help to meditate on the golf course?

"Golf can be kind of a meditation in itself. As you walk, you should be aware of all that surrounds you. As you walk, be aware that you're breathing."

But then, on the 7th tee box, a par 5, he drilled more skulls than a neurosurgeon. He topped one, two, three straight drives into some nasty weeds. At that point he didn't look like a guy playing the front nine at Garden of Eden. He looked like a guy who could melt a lot of snow with the red ass. He was about to let rip like Billy Bob Thornton with a sling blade when Wendy gently chastised him.

Wendy: Deepak, can you tell me the one thing you're forgetting to do?

His head sank.

Deepak: Yes.

Wendy: What is it?

Deepak: I'm forgetting to breathe.

Wendy: Exactly. You're forgetting to breathe.

Now, if golf is so hard it makes *Deepak Chopra* forget to breathe, a man who thinks of nothing but his breath one-and-a-half hours a day, what chance do the rest of us have?

On No. 8 tee box he said, "I must not slice it here, Wendy. I dream about slicing here. It torments me."

Again came the icy rebuke.

Wendy: Deepak, what have we said about negative thoughts before we swing?

Deepak: Not to let them creep into my head before I swing.

Wendy: Exactly.

Man's written 20 books about the human mind and a lady golf pro is telling him what to think.

He went on to make a mess of that hole, too. His own mother would've given him no better than a 7. He was a little discouraged.

You write about golf requiring "supreme effortlessness," I asked. *But isn't golf too hard for that?*

"No," he said after a pause. "Understand that in your body are 100 trillion cells. And each one of those cells is doing six trillion things per second. The body is a miracle. It has infinite organizing power. Your soul has infinite organizing power. Your soul animates your body. Your intention has the ability to connect instantaneously all parts of your body. Thus, when you swing, it is a miracle of orchestrated action. It's a wonder. A miracle."

And I'm thinking, *If a normal, simple golf swing is a miracle, what would he think of Jim Furyk's swing?*

On 9, he was triumphantly on the green in two, but his first putt climbed halfway up a hill then back down to him, past his feet, and off the green. He tried it again and the same thing happened. On his third try, he blew it up the hill, past the hole, and off the green the other way. Generally speaking, golf will kick intelligence's butt every time. He Gretzky-ed it in from there.

Overall, my man played two holes like Tiger Woods, two holes like Earl Woods, and five holes like a bear in the woods. He looked like he wanted to bite his putter in half.

Doesn't golf just suck sometimes? I asked.

"It's true that in golf, one never leaves feeling completely content," he said, smiling happily again. "There is always something you could've done better. But that is fine. Discontent is divine, too."

Tell it to Tina's brother.

I started taking his bag to the 10th tee box, but he said his day was done. "Nine holes is all I usually play." He was off to a seminar where people had paid $6,000 each to meditate with him. "Amazing things happen," says Tina. "People levitate. Deepak calls it 'lifting off.' He said that one time, so many people were lifting off it looked like a popcorn popper."

Before he left, the mystic gave me a stack of signed books and one of those looks, eye-to-eye, that makes you think you're staring straight into the cosmos.

"I hope you enjoy my book," he said. (The book, as it turned out, was kind of a mixed bag, full of great little spiritual tips—"Stop trying to steer the river"—and stuff so stupid you wouldn't wish it on Colin Montgomerie—"He swung the driver and . . . distant galaxies trembled.")

But as he left, I couldn't help wondering what he was doing letting himself mess with this maddening game. Here's a man who has written 25 books (translated into 35 languages), produced over 100 audio- and videotapes, starred in five public television shows, delivered countless lectures (at $55,000 per), and helped hundreds of thousands of people save themselves from their wretched lives. To think that he was suddenly saying to his secretary, "Screw world peace. I gotta work on my short game," seemed wasteful somehow.

Golf is so hard and such a time gobbler, I said. *Wouldn't your talents be used better somewhere else?*

Pause.

"Well," he said, "for me, personally, it's kind of like I've been there done that . . . My goal now is to be less than a 10 handicap within the year."

And I think he can do it.

If he doesn't keep score.

If the caddy says . . .

"This blows. Why'd I ever take Vijay anyway? I got this Betty waitin' for me with some cones that are about 13 on the Stimpmeter. And where are we goin'? Back to the blister box, as usual. Dude is totally dialed in. Why do we gotta live at Fungoland? He's just gonna stack 'em up on top of each other out there anyway."

He means . . .

"This is disappointing. Why do I caddy for Vijay Singh anyway? I have this very beautiful young girl waiting for me and she has some breasts that are very large. But where am I going instead? Back to the practice grounds. My player is playing excellently. Why must he spend so much time at the practice grounds? He's only going to hit all his balls so perfectly that they end up in a pile on the other end of the range, anyway." (This, too, is an exaggeration.)

9

CASEY MARTIN

Hell on Wheels

I'll be honest. Part of the reason I asked Casey Martin if I could caddy for him was selfish. I wanted to ride in that cart. An entire week off for the dogs? Blister heaven. I was looking forward to it the way Roseanne looks forward to the Sizzler buffet.

"You don't look like a loop!" Martin hollered at me when we met in front of the Richmond, Virginia, Residence Inn.

And he didn't look like one of the most controversial figures in golf. He looked more like he might sing tenor in the high school choir or live next door to the Cleavers—clean-cut, button-down shirt, no facial hair.

Out of blind luck, the week I was to caddy for Martin on the Buy.com Tour happened to be the same week the United States Supreme Court decision on him was supposed to come down. Martin has a rare leg disorder that makes it impossible for him to walk two holes, much less 72, and he had sued under the Americans with Disabilities Act for the right to ride a golf cart. The PGA Tour howled that it had the right to make its own rules, that walking was "integral" to the game, and that if they let Martin ride, they'd have to do the same for every pro who had bursitis or swollen arches. He won in Oregon, won on appeal, and now it was in the hands of the Supreme Court.

It was a golfing *Roe v. Wade.* People either were passionately for the kid or vehemently against.

Those for him saw a devoutly Christian, good-looking, piano-playing American—part of Stanford's 1994 NCAA championship team—who had somehow fought his way to the PGA Tour on a leg and a half, being treated like he was the visiting pro from Kabul. They felt what PGA Tour commissioner Tim Finchem should've done was welcome the kid as the million-to-one winner that he was. It was the p.r. equivalent of coming out against puppies.

Just from a marketing point of view, it seemed completely Cream-of-Wheat-brained to me. Did the Tour think there were thousands of golfers out there who could break 70 with disabilities—*real* disabilities that would qualify them for a handicap parking placard, not just old guys with sore backs and knees? There hadn't been before and there probably won't be again.

Besides, walking has never been "integral" to the game. The PGA Tour itself uses carts on the Senior Tour, and at the Tour qualifying school and in certain tournaments to ferry players from certain greens to tees. Jack Nicklaus howled in protest about Martin's cart, then used one on the Senior Tour when he hurt his hip. Arnold Palmer preached about the sanctity of the rules, then publicly endorsed an illegal Callaway driver. When's the last time you heard a fan go, "Hey, let's go out to 13 and see Tiger walk!" Any tiny advantage Martin might have from riding in a cart would be offset 100 times by his disability.

I think most people—not the golfing elite, but most people—thought this was golf trying to pretend it's a rigorous sport instead of a polished skill. It isn't. It's outdoor billiards. And the sharks who play it (gotten a load of John Daly's waistline lately?) are no more fit athletes than Minnesota Fats. Wasn't "we want to make our own rules" the excuse the Tour used to keep blacks off the Tour in the 1950s?

Anyway, Martin was Dorothy in the twister, the subject of one thousand arguments and columns, and each day there was a new rumor that the ruling was about to be announced.

"There's been so many teasers," he said in the hallway outside his room, leaning this way and that against the wall, trying to keep pressure off that brittle leg. "We were told it was coming two weeks ago. I called my family and told them, 'Get ready.' I prepared myself mentally for it. Then one morning they said it was coming out for certain by noon. They said they'd come out and get me. I'm trying to play golf and my heart is racing. Every hole, I'm waiting for somebody to come up and say, 'You won. Your career can go on.' Or, 'You lost. Your career is over.' "

But the ruling still hadn't come. "Last week, a ruling did come down," he said, "but it was on the marijuana thing, not me."

Drag. Bumped by doobies.

"Anyway, maybe this week," he said.

He looked beat, so I asked him a few quick questions: What time tomorrow? Anything special he requires? And how do we do the bag on the cart, just belt it into the back or should I keep it loose between us?

"Yeah, right," he laughed.

Pause.

"Excuse me?" I said, confused.

"Buddy, you're not allowed to *touch* the cart," he said. "You have to *carry* the bag. You can't put so much as a *towel* on the cart."

I felt like suing.

. . .

THE BUY.COM TOUR is to the PGA Tour what the Toledo Mud Hens are to the New York Yankees. Nice players, just not quite there yet or been there once and fell off. Nice courses, but nothing to bring a tear to your eye. This one was the Stonehenge Golf and Country Club in Richmond, Virginia. A respectable course, but shaggy, like Cary Grant with a hangover. And very few fans. If there were 1,000 fans there the whole week, I'll eat your divot. A big first-place check on the Buy.com is $100,000 and last place money is $1,500. It's not the Ritz, it's the Red Roof Inn.

The caddy money gets shrunk, too. Instead of $700 a week, they get $400. And 5 percent of $100,000 is a helluva lot less than 5 percent of a million. But the quality of the caddies is still first-rate. Lots of Tour caddies were in Richmond that week—like Mike Carrick, who carried Tom Kite for 19 years. Guys like Carrick would rather tongue-bathe Osama bin Laden than give up caddying.

In fact, Martin's playing partners that Tuesday for the practice round of this 2001 Richmond Open were two familiar faces—Morris Hatalsky and Don Pooley, both longtime Tour vets, playing on the Buy.com's 49-year-old exemption you can use to get ready for the Senior Tour. "I wanna see what I can learn," Martin told me that morning. He needed some kind of change. He'd made only two cuts in seven tries.

Still, Martin was unfathomably nice. And he kept being nice, even after the 1st hole, when I was standing off the green, hands held behind me, in the *perfect* position to advance to the next tee, when I noticed him waving me over. I set the bag down on its side (Tommy Aaron, take note) and sprinted over to his side.

"Is there any possible way," he whispered, "I could have my putter?"

Oops.

And he was *still* nice on 4, when I'd given him his putter, had my hands held behind me, and was in perfect position to go to the next tee, and noticed him waving at me. I motioned to him that he already *had* his putter. But he was still waving me over, so, bag on its side, I sprinted over.

"Is there any possible way," he whispered again, "I could have my ball?"

Oops. I'd taken his ball to wash it, got excited about a rare chance to take the flag out of the hole, cleaned his pitching wedge, had a laugh with another caddy, and lost track of giving it back to him.

If it were Aaron, I'd be trying to dislodge a 5-iron from an orifice by now.

The stupid cart was a bit tricky, too. I kept thinking I could put stuff in it, but I couldn't. And I kept thinking I could drive it ahead for him, but I couldn't. That's the thing about the freaking cart. The PGA Tour had slapped more rules on it than radioactive material, for instance:

- No carts with roofs. And it seems that Casey is the only one who knows this rule, so half the time, the head pro sets out a cart for him with a roof and he has to scramble to find one without. In fact, for the 1998 U.S. Open at Olympic, they not only didn't give him a regular cart, they gave him a one-seater, three-wheeled job with a bar instead of a steering wheel and little shopping cart wheels. It looked like something you'd see in a Shriners' parade. "I remember, I'm playing a practice round with Tiger and there's 22,000 people following us, and these guys are walking down the fairway, looking cool," remembers Martin, "and there I am, weaving in and out of them on my little tricycle. It was Tiger and this crippled kid." Worse, it had almost no brakes, so he'd have to take his foot off the gas 50 yards ahead of where he wanted to stop. Worst, it lurched, causing him to nearly roll it once. He found USGA president David Fay that day and *made* him take a ride in it. Fay did, then got out and announced, "Somebody's gonna get killed in that thing," and put him in a regular cart.

- Martin cannot carry any of his personal stuff on the cart, up to and including a tee he might stick in the little tee holder or a water bottle in the cup holder.
- Martin may not ride ahead of the walking players. Again, the implication being he would somehow cheat, I guess.
- No ads on the cart. (Though people offered him bazillions. "Not that we would've taken it," says his agent, Chris Murray.)

Riding a cart during a tournament is more dangerous than being in Gerald Ford's gallery. A golf course is a complicated thing. There are all kinds of ropes and galleries and tents and TV towers and Häagen-Dazs carts and Martin has to find his way through all of them. Every hole he's going in and out under the ropes in order to get the cart through everything. He'll be going along at 5 miles per hour and reach out for the rope to grab it and pull it over his head without stopping. Only some fan, trying to be nice, will pull it up for him the instant before he grabs it, which means he misses the rope and it catches him in the face instead.

"At Houston, I nearly got decapitated," he said. Sometimes it will get him in the neck. He's actually got a rope scar on his neck from a well-meaning fan at The International.

Or sometimes he'll be driving along and not realize he's caught a 2-iron or the little basket on the rope. Now the tension on the rope is so great that something has to give, which is when the rope stakes will rip out of the ground and come zinging toward him and the stupid cart. "That really scares me," he says. "Some guy in Japan got impaled that way once. Killed him."

Another thing that sucks about the cart is that when you walk playing golf, you get a tempo going. You have a sense of where you are on the hole—how far you've walked and how far you have to go. In a cart, you have no sense of that. Ask any guy who plays for money on any tour, anywhere, whether they'd rather walk or ride and they'd say, "Walk."

I also noticed that when Martin hit a wild shot, he'd get mad and leadfoot it off to his ball—against the rules—leaving his poor caddy and the other players well behind. "I hate when I do that," he admitted. "The last thing I want is to get up there and look at my shot for five minutes." And try as he might to slow down the cart, Martin is a go-go guy, which means he was always at his ball miles before his 43-year-old bad-backed caddy, which made his poor caddy have to jog with a 40-pound bag on his back, which made the caddy wish he'd done a book on strippers instead.

The thing that bugs Martin the most about the cart, though, is that it makes him so purplishly different from his colleagues. "I despise being different," he said that night at dinner, his leg stuck out on a side chair to keep the pain down. "I resent always being the center of attention, always being special. I just want to walk. I'm sick of having to humble myself to play golf."

That's the thing. He can *really* play golf. I had him for a 5-under 67 that practice day. He was trying out a new belly putter—the butt end of the putter is anchored against your belly button—and he made everything. Not that they were long putts. Everything was ten feet and in. He struck his irons so perfectly, Pooley and Hatalsky were amazed.

That night we were in his room, talking about stuff we'd still like to do in life, and I mentioned running with the bulls in Pamplona, Spain.

And he said, "Hey, that sounds fun! Do they allow carts?"

It'd be hilarious if it weren't so sad.

Anyway, he looked like he was dreading another night alone and we had a late tee time the next day, so I finally got up the courage to ask.

"Casey, would it be possible for me to *see* the leg?"

He looked at me.

"Sure," he said. He almost seemed relieved to show it to somebody.

His agent warned me that it's a bit much to take, especially if you've just eaten. I thought I was prepared, but I wasn't.

He stood up, took off his pants, then took off two nylon restraining stockings that run up his leg and keep the swelling down. What was underneath looked like a baseball bat some kid had hit a thousand rocks with—long and skinny and full of lumps.

"Watch the blood drain into it," he said. And, over the next two minutes, that bony stick of a leg started turning purple and globby and marbled right in front of my eyes, bloating to twice its size. Grotesque pools of blood gathered everywhere—groin, knee, and ankle. It looked like a science project somebody left in the refrigerator two years ago.

"Run your hand over it," he said. That was about the last thing I wanted to do, but I did it anyway. He took my hand and gingerly ran it along his shin, which felt like a long, fat, Glad sandwich bag filled with spaghetti and meatballs. It was fascinating except I felt very much like throwing up.

"You done?" he said, weakly.

When I looked up, I saw that he looked pale and faint. All the blood was in his leg. I realized it was killing him.

"Yes, yes!" I said.

And instantly, he flopped back down on the bed and put the leg straight up in the air. And, just like that, you could see the blood leaving his leg and returning to his face.

"When I shower," he said, "I have to do this three or four times. Stand up for a while, soap up, then lie down, so the blood can leave the leg, then stand up again and soap some more, and on like that. And that's in a 10-minute shower."

I no longer wanted to know how he plays golf on that leg. I wanted to know how he *walks* on that leg.

He takes 12 to 14 Advil a day. He sleeps in two-hour chunks, swallows a couple Advil, and tries again. To Casey Martin, standing around waiting is like anesthetic-free dental surgery to you and me. His critics need to spend a day in Martin's orthopedic shoes.

One time, in Omaha, he was playing in a tournament with a real turtle. Standing around on the tee hurt, but waiting for this guy was killing him. "This guy was adjusting his hat, adjusting his glove, just everything. So finally I said, 'I'm going.' And the guy goes, 'What?' And I said, 'I'm going.' And I stuck the tee in the ground. And he goes, 'No, you're not going.' And I said, 'Yeah, I'm going. I'm fighting for my career here and you're taking forever.' And I pured one down the middle. The guy about flipped. But I remember I shot 29 that nine."

Uphill lies hurt the leg. Downhill lies. Getting in and out of the cart. Off-balance swings. Swinging too hard. Martin is one of the purest strikers of the ball on any tour and it may be for the simple reason that anything but a perfect swing hurts like the bejesus.

"You want to know what hurts absolutely the most?" he said. "I'll be sitting there at a restaurant or in the clubhouse, and somebody will come up and slap me on the knee and go, 'How ya been, Case?' The pain is excruciating. I feel like I'm going to black out."

Even better news? He thinks he may have diabetes. "I get this metallic taste in my mouth. I pee nine times a day. I get the sweats. I get tired so easily. And my grandpa died of diabetes at 58."

The thought of it seemed to take the starch out of him, and as he said goodnight and closed the door, I realized that tomorrow he was going to take that body and try to beat some of the best golfers in the world with it.

ON WEDNESDAY, I tried to sneak into Media Parking because Caddy Parking was, like, in Tibet. I was stopped at a checkpoint.

"Can I help you?" said a rather large rent-a-cop.

I told him I was from *S.I.* "Here to cover the tournament."

He didn't believe that for a second, perhaps on account of he'd never seen *S.I.* take a monstrous interest in the Richmond Buy.com stop before.

"You need a media parking pass," he said.

"Right. I'm supposed to pick that up this morning," I lied.

He noticed the two towels, water bottle, and yardage book in the front seat.

"You're not a caddy are you?" he said.

"Well, yes, but I'm writing a *book* about caddying. See, I'm *both.*"

He glared at me. "Turn it around before I call in backups. Caddy parking is back that way."

Caddies are the lowest form of life.

Since Martin was the biggest name, he drew the big shots of Richmond for amateur partners—the guy who runs the big bank, the big jeweler in town, those kinds of guys. Nice fellas.

On the 6th hole, a photographer came, took the obligatory five-some picture, and then left—in Casey's cart. That left Casey to drive around for a hole and a half in a cart full of photo equipment. And my question was: *Can I ride in THAT cart?*

Martin is warm and available to anybody, anywhere. (As you

know, he calls everybody "Buddy," and starts any important or declarative sentence "Buddy," as in, "Buddy, I'm about to hit us a leaner." It's like spending time with Jimmy Dean.) He is especially helpful to amateur playing partners, who generally ask to play with him in order to see the leg up close. He's used to it. Every day I caddied for him, there was somebody at the range with some kind of disability, hoping for a moment with him. On Wednesday it was a young man with a prosthetic left leg, obviously wanting an autograph or an interview or just some advice. He stood behind us as we hit balls.

"How tough has that gotta be?" one caddy said to me. "Here's Casey trying to get ready to compete, you know? Trying to get ready for his round. And there's a guy standing right behind him with that leg, reminding him of what could happen to him any day."

That day is obviously coming. It almost came the year before at the L.A. Open in Riviera, when he tripped on a hidden sprinkler head on the 10th hole. "Buddy, I thought that was it," he recalls. "It happened and I thought, 'Oh, my God, it could've busted right there.'"

So he's got some tough choices ahead, ruling or no ruling. The doctors tell him if the leg breaks below the knee, they would amputate and he could get a good prosthetic that would allow him to still play golf—but not at this level—and even perhaps run. He's got an economics degree from Stanford. He could get a good job, be a regular Joe. If it breaks *above* the knee, though, they would amputate and his golf days would be over and the leg would be even more painful, subject to infections and far more trouble.

"So, the question is," he said to mostly himself one night, "how do we get ourselves a below-the-knee break?" He could choose to have it amputated now and guarantee himself recreational golf from here on in. But he can't bring himself to do it. "I'm an addict.

I love golf. I *still* think I can play at a very good level. I'm rolling the dice here, I know it. But I want to do it."

Martin gave the prosthesis guy a few minutes between the range and the putting green, though I can't think of any other player who would've done it before a round. Later, I asked him if he sees himself as a symbol of what people with disabilities can accomplish with talent and tenaciousness.

"I don't see myself that way, no," he said. "I don't see myself as disabled." He very much didn't want to talk about it. He resents his leg. In fact, Martin won't even use the disabled parking placard they send him each year.

He's always denied his disability, which he's had since birth. It's called Klippel-Trenaunay-Webber Syndrome. What happens is the veins leak, blood goes everywhere, causing swelling and pain. And because the bone is soaked in blood all the time, it becomes brittle and, eventually, snaps. "It's like if you put a piece of wood in a tub of water for 25 years," Casey explains. "It would be so soggy it could break."

"When I was a kid, I'd run and run until I'd run my leg into the ground. You know, playing basketball and tackle football. I'd come home crying. And I'd have to stay inside for a bunch of days and rest it. But as soon as I felt slightly good I'd be out there again. And then I'd come home crying again."

For every woe, there's a joy and every joy, a woe. If he hadn't had a bum leg, it's quite possible Martin would've never become a terrific golf stick. "No way," he admits. "I loved basketball too much. I'd have been playing that all the time." With a cart, golf was one game he could excel at, and he did. As a Stanford junior, he helped win the NCAA team championship, along with Notah Begay, Brad Laning, William Yonigasawi, and Steve Burdick. But the next season, all anybody wanted to talk about was an incoming freshman, a certain Eldrick (Tiger) Woods.

"I remember the first time I played with him," says Martin. "It was me, Notah, and Tiger. He got out there with us and he called every shot—cut, draw, high, low—didn't matter. He had everything. And distance-wise, buddy, he was in a different league. They'd just aerated the greens and he still shot 68. Hit every green, never made anything, and still shot 68. Wow.

"Notah wasn't afraid to kid him, but the rest of us were. Notah figured, 'Hey, he's a freshman. We gotta get on him.' So he'd make fun of his big teeth and his glasses. He called him 'Urkel.' He'd make fun of how cheap he was.

"I remember, I beat Tiger out of $25 once at a U.S. Open practice round and he said, 'I'll get it to you.' And I said, 'No way, dude. I gotta have it now. I beat you.' It was like you had to pry it out of his wallet. One time I ended up getting $190 off him. He finally wrote me a check. I Xeroxed it and put it in my scrapbook."

Woods went on to greatness, Begay went on to good-ness, and Martin went on to the Nike Tour, which would become the Buy.com. Somehow, despite the pain, despite not being able to grind on the range or on the putting green, Martin actually won the 1998 Lakeland (Fla.) Classic and finished in the top 15 on the then-Nike money list, which got him his PGA Tour card, which is when the world found out about the cart and the wheels came flying off.

Every town he showed up in that year, a columnist or a feature writer wanted an interview, a disabled person or group or charity wanted time, hundreds wanted autographs and hugs. Every name in golf weighed in with an opinion—except his old Stanford teammate, Tiger, who straddled the middle.

If it had been under a tent, you could've easily called it a circus.

There were critics everywhere, in the gallery—"My parents heard it all the time," Martin admits—and even among the guys in his group. But it was funny how people's principles changed. One day, at the Bay Hill Classic, Martin was playing behind Arnold Palmer, who had vehemently argued against the cart. There was a big backup at No. 6, a long par 5, so all eight players were on the tee box at once. The caddies were 250 yards down the fairway, forecaddying, when Arnie snapped one into the water. Feeling his pockets, he realized he didn't have a ball.

"Don't worry about it, Mr. Palmer," Martin said, helpfully. "I can drive up and get you another ball." Casey Cart to the rescue. Arnie nodded sheepishly. Martin drove up, got a ball from Arnie's caddy, drove it back, and tossed it to Palmer.

Martin played like a wreck that year. Put it this way: If you could've turned the newspaper upside down, he'd have been in first place many weeks. He wound up 179th on the money list and found himself back in the bush leagues, playing in pro-ams in Richmond and wondering if he'd ever get back.

"I could still blossom," he said that night at Arby's, his leg propped up on the booth seat across from him. "Like Tom Watson did." Watson was 34 years old before he won his first tournament, then went on to win 33 more.

Buddy, it was all going to start this week.

EVERYTHING WAS DIFFERENT Thursday. For one, I was on time. For two, Casey suddenly started playing like a yak. For three, I started caddying like a drunken yak.

All of a sudden his irons were way off. All of a sudden the belly putter became a pain in the ass.

We played with two Buy.com regulars—Tim (Petro) Petrovic, a 6-4 beast with tons of game, and Charles Raulerson, a dapper, chain-smoking finesse player who'd left an executive job in the railroad industry to try his luck on a lot of courses with railroad ties.

Both of them were shorter than Casey. In fact, on the first hole, Casey hit his drive 346 yards—a little downhill—but 50 yards past his playing partners. And yet he missed the green, short and right, which led to another little problem involving yours truly, Gagger Vance.

I gave him his wedge and walked 20 feet away from him and toward the next tee box, where I was going to deposit the bag and then bring him his putter. But after he took his practice swing, he motioned me over.

"I need the towel," he said, so I offered the towel and he wiped the six or eight blades of grass off his wedge. Again I walked 20 feet away. Another practice swing. Another motion to have me come over. "The towel," he said.

OK, so I'm a slow learner.

He'd never needed to wipe off his wedge after practice swings before. Aaron didn't either. He'd just . . . I don't know what he'd do. Wipe the blades on his pants? Not care? Turns out, when it counts, Casey Martin definitely does care about those blades of grass. And now, forever more, shall I.

Problem was, all day we took way too many chip shots. We kept missing greens. We shot 75. We were miles behind. It didn't look good for the three-legged twosome.

That night at dinner (Arby's, again) I tried to cheer him up a little.

"If, for just one day, you had two perfectly normal legs, what would you do?"

"Oh, man," he said, rubbing his hands together. "Ohhhh, mannn! OK. Wake up and play dunk hoops with my buddies. Then go throw the football around in the park. Then I'd go for a long, long run. Then I'd ride my bike up to the mountains and go skiing. Then I'd go dancing. Buddy, I love to dance. I'm a very good dancer. Ask anybody. I used to be able to get down. Oh, then I'd go work out. Do an aerobics class. Then, let's see . . ."

That answer made me feel so guilty. I've got two healthy legs. I'm lucky to do all that in a *year.*

Casey limped out of the restaurant and went home to bed. Like basketball's A. C. Green, Martin is that rarest of animals—a professional athlete who is still a virgin. He doesn't believe in premarital sex. He believes in long-term relationships, preferably with a Christian woman, followed by marriage, followed, presumably *very* soon after, by sex. And it's hard to have a long-term relationship when one week you're in Aiken, South Carolina, and the next in Richmond, Virginia.

"I want to meet somebody so bad," he says. "But how can I out here?"

He's tried everything: churches and Christian singles groups and setups. Zilch. Seems hard to believe. Handsome, neat, kind, funny, talented, absolutely wonderful piano player, and with a real fear of *noncommitment,* you'd think the guy would have to fend off women like the chief of pardons at a women's prison. But no.

Hey, you Christian women. Get *with* this guy. Be fruitful and multiply.

ON FRIDAY—Zero Hour for us—it was clear that something was bothering Casey. His swing seemed off. His stride seemed funny. His irons were wayward. He kept fussing with the top of his backswing. He even enlisted the help of a buddy the evening before, after I'd left, driven back to the course, and hit some balls, hoping the guy would see something in it.

Apparently he didn't.

I should've had somebody look at my caddying. Maybe somebody could've seen what I was doing wrong. For instance, after we hit balls, I went straight to the first tee and started gathering my bib and ball markers, tees, towels, etc. When I looked up, I had a panicky feeling. Two minutes to our tee time, and no Casey. And no Petro. And no Charlie.

"Whoa!" I said to another caddy standing there. "Where's my guys?"

"Are you sure you're not starting on 10?" the volunteer woman in the obligatory large straw hat said.

Oops.

I sprinted over to 10 tee and there they were, waiting for me. Casey was just smiling. Note to Vatican: Canonize this man.

Then, walking down the cart path to the right of that fairway, after he airmailed his 3-wood right, I was trying to tie my bib and stuff a club in at the same time and somehow managed to get the bag tipped the wrong way and *all his clubs* came splattering out of the bag *onto the cart path.* Not quietly onto the acres and acres of grass or woodland or sand. Right on the freaking cement cart path.

It sounded like Gatling gun fire.

Casey spun around and said, "Are you OK?" with real concern.

I've just dumped all his clubs on a cart path and he wants to know if I'm OK.

Anybody else, I'd soon enough been injured. Then fired.

As the day wore on, I seemed to be farther and farther behind. For one thing, he usually hit last, which meant I couldn't get the good jump off the tee box like the other caddies. For two things, because he hit it so far, he'd hit last, which meant that I was still getting the divot and the club when everybody else was off to the green. One very embarrassing and awful instance, on the third to last hole I had to be a good 100 yards off the green when everybody else was on the green. That's when I saw a terrible thing. Casey was giving *another* caddy his ball to clean. I was so jealous. It was like seeing somebody else kissing your girlfriend. And from 100 yards away, as he was grabbing the OTHER caddy's towel, he gave me the big wave, like you might from a seagoing cruise ship, and yelled, "Hi, Rick!"

Very funny.

We did nothing on the front nine. The only thing of interest was a big, big woman came up to Casey and said, tears in her eyes, "Can I kiss you?"

It was sort of a shock. Petro tried to stifle a laugh and Charles' eyes bugged out of his head. This is the kind of thing that happens to Casey Martin and only Casey Martin on the course. Freddy Couples gets knockout strippers who want to kiss him. Casey gets 300-pound women.

She started coming at him and Casey took a step back and said, "Maybe after the round, OK?"

As we were riding/walking down the fairway, he was overcome with guilt. "Buddy, what would you have done? I don't want to make her feel bad, but I don't want to get kissed in the middle of the round by Jaba the Hut, either!"

Somewhere around there, Casey seemed to get his bulldog up. He started making some beautiful swings. He hit a 5-iron to three feet and we made that for birdie.

As we were riding/walking to the next tee box, I asked him how good he could've been with two strong legs. "I could've been good, but I know I could be good with one leg, too. That's the frustrating thing. I could be good just the way I am."

As long as the leg holds up, Martin could stay on the Buy.com Tour indefinitely, since there's no limit to the number of exemptions a player can take in one year. *If the leg holds up.* It clearly wasn't going to.

"If you told me right now that I wasn't ever going to play the PGA Tour again, then I'd quit," he says.

I'm sure it's wonderfully helpful to have your caddy talking about the end of your career as you're trying to play golf, but Casey kept hitting it long. We knocked it on that par 5 in two, but then, tragically, three-putted. That might have done it for us.

Still, we had a chance as we came to our 17th hole. I'll never forget that hole. He hit a beautiful drive, right down the gut, and we had 165 to the hole, 8-iron. He took it back and then came through as though somebody had stuck a snake in his pants. He lurched at it. Then he limped back to the cart worse than I'd ever seen him limp.

He wouldn't talk about it. We made bogey there. On the last tee box, he made just an awful swing. It looked like a man trying to swing with an alligator biting his knee. The ball went, seriously, maybe 200 yards, duck-hook left, nothing on it. We made bogey there, too.

We missed the cut.

Bye.com.

I walked silently to his trunk and said, "Man, you looked like you were hurting on those last two holes."

He put his hands through his hair. "Something happened to my leg on 17. I don't know what it was. I could barely swing."

I asked if we should see a doctor or a trainer or anybody. He said no, happens a lot, just have to live with it.

For my last question, I asked him to rate me as a caddy. "If you're going to caddy for some other guys, you probably ought to start running and walking a ton. You looked like you were spent out there at the end."

That's a complete lie! I wanted to say. *I did NOT look like I was spent out there! I WAS spent.*

A WEEK LATER, the Supreme Court ruling came down. He won. By a vote of 7–2 (Scalia and Thomas), the high court ruled that walking was *not* integral to the game and that Martin had the right, under the ADA, to take a cart, and that Finchem and his staff had brains made of lint for putting everybody through it to begin with. Or something along those lines.

I called Casey on his cellphone. He was in Portland and he was going nuts. I have no idea what he said.

But I think he called me "Buddy."

POSTSCRIPT: MARTIN DIDN'T *break an egg on the Buy.com circuit in 2002, either, but he went to tour school in December and played great. In fact, he was 21st going into the final day at the brutal PGA West course in La Quinta, California. The top 35 would get their PGA Tour card. But he made two straight double bogeys on the 13th and 14th holes, shot 77, and missed his card by three shots. He said the PGA West course, built by Pete Dye, is murder on his leg because of the deep bunkers you must climb in and out of. "Anything Dye builds kills the leg," he admitted. He faced another year in the bush leagues in 2003.*

If the caddy says . . .

"Man, I shoulda shut my piehole today. We got 250 layup or 300 carry and I go, 'C'mon, let's go WMD.' And he finally buys it but then he gets at the top and just kinda runs outta oxygen. Next thing you know, we're 404 in the nasty muff and wind up shootin' three-quarters."

He means . . .

"Friend, I shouldn't have spoken to my player today. We had the choice of hitting a 250-yard shot off the tee to lay up safely in front of a lake or hitting a driver that would have had to carry 300 yards in the air to be safe. My player agreed with my suggestion to hit the Weapon of Mass Destruction, which is what we caddies sometimes kiddingly call the driver. But he did not perform well under the pressure. Next thing you know we were in the deep rough in a 404 situation, which is the computer message one sometimes gets that reads: '404: File Not Found,' which is to say, we could not easily find the ball. We wound up shooting 75."

10

BOB NEWHART

The Anti-Trump

If I were to pick one club to caddy at the rest of my life, it would not be Pine Valley. Or Cypress. Or Augusta.

It'd be Bel-Air.

There is no cooler membership in golf than Bel-Air, the club of the stars above Sunset Boulevard. You can't throw a bucket of birdseed at Bel-Air without hitting somebody famous. Over the years it's had members like Jimmy Stewart, Katharine Hepburn, Howard Hughes, Gary Cooper, Clark Gable, Carole Lombard, Andy Williams, George C. Scott, Richard Crenna, Glenn Ford, Edgar Bergen, Spencer Tracy, Jerry West, Jim Garner, Adolphe Menjou, Dick Rowan, Dan Martin, and Joe Pesci, to name but 18.

"I remember the first time I played Bel-Air," says Tom Poston, the longtime TV character actor *(The Steve Allen Show, Newhart, Home Improvement)*. "I didn't know anybody yet, so they sent me off No. 10 by myself. When I got to 11, there were four guys standing there, asking me if I wanted to join them. It was Fred MacMurray, Fred Astaire, Randolph Scott, and Ray Milland. I was struck dumb, frozen. I couldn't say a thing. So they played on without me."

There are more stories about Bel-Air than Titleist has dimples.

One time, W. C. Fields had just teed off by himself, the way he liked it, when a rather oily member of the club came running out of the locker room and asked if he could join him.

"Sir," Fields said, "if I wanted to play with a prick, I'd play with my own."

Dean Martin used to bet like a casino at Bel-Air. He'd come out in cool slacks, a buttoned knit shirt, two-tone black-and-white golf shoes, smoking cigarettes and betting guys into the thousands. He was good, too. They say his opponents used to get up early and soak down the hill at No. 4, just so Martin couldn't get up it and beat them.

Jack Wagner, the actor, is the new Martin now. He plays to a scratch and will bet you for your house. One time, John Daly supposedly lost $10,000 to Wagner with a bogey on the 18th and was so pissed he broke every club in his bag in half and threw them down the ravine. After Daly left, his Bel-Air caddy scrambled down the ravine, got all the clubheads and had them reshafted in the shop. Thanks, Long John!

Any Hollywood star worth his shoe lifts has played Bel-Air. Matt Damon happens by. Bob Hope used to. Jack Nicholson still does. They say he was there the day he beat a man's Mercedes with a 2-iron in a traffic argument. Apparently, Jack told the Bel-Air guys, "OK, so I overclubbed."

Hal Roach dealt cards there until he was 100. Joe Namath still limps around there a lot. Elizabeth Taylor married Nicky Hilton at Bel-Air. They say you could come in most any Friday night and Hoagy Carmichael might be playing the piano, or Johnny Mercer, with maybe Bing Crosby leaning on it, singing something by Rogers and Hart.

Les Brown (but not his Band of Renown) was a member. Vic Damone, too. Glen Campbell still is. Johnny Carson used to play a lot of tennis at Bel-Air. So did Mary Tyler Moore, George Kennedy, and Pat Boone.

OK, so maybe it's Old School, but I happen to like Old School. Frank Sinatra was Old School, and Sinatra's used combs are still cooler than most stars today.

Did I mention that Robert (Marcus Welby) Young was a member? Conrad Hilton? Michigan great Tom Harmon? Wimbledon champ Bob Falkenburg? Or the great *L.A. Times* columnist Jim Murray, who campaigned for years to get the club to fill in the giant cavern in front of the par-3 10th because he couldn't quite get over it?

They say the best thing about Bel-Air, though, is that *nobody's* a star. You're not a star, you're the guy they're trying to beat out of a $10 Nassau. Nobody asks for autographs. Nobody is particularly well dressed. They say the place is about as stuffy as an Applebee's.

Not only that, but it's the only place I know where you can see the Masters, U.S. Open, British, and PGA trophies in one place, unless you happen to dust Tiger's coffee table. It's got a U.S. Open from Ken Venturi, a British Open from Greg Norman, a Masters from Arnold Palmer, and a PGA from Byron Nelson. Kinda makes your club's photo of Andy North look a little lame, huh?

So, figuring the closest I'd ever come to getting into Bel-Air is caddying there, I called up a guy who knew a guy who knew a few stars. He said he'd try the one guy who might do it, Bob Newhart, the genius stand-up comic, TV psychiatrist, and Vermont TV inn owner.

The guy called me back and said, "Boy, Bob's mind must really be going."

"Why?" I said.

"He said 'yes'. "

. . .

ME DRAWING BOB NEWHART was like Amarillo Slim drawing aces and jacks, or somebody asking George Foreman if he'd had lunch yet, or a bank robber handing a bag of jewels to Butch Cassidy.

I'd practically memorized his career. I owned every one of his comedy albums. The best, of course, were *The Button-Down Mind of Bob Newhart*, which went to No. 1 in 1961, and *Button-Down Mind Strikes Back*, which went to No. 2 at the same time. Nobody before and only Guns N' Roses 30 years later has been 1 and 2 on the charts with new albums at the same time. How about that? Axl Rose and The Original Mr. Square, together forever.

Bob Newhart has been on TV more than Dial soap. He had two hit TV shows—*The Bob Newhart Show* and *Newhart*—which ran a total of 16 years. Plus he did two others—*Bob*, and the underappreciated and quite hilarious *George and Leo*, which didn't catch because some smart-aleck studio honk decided to get too clever with the title.

What I always loved about Bob Newhart was that he was once an unemployed Chicago accountant who became a star and still looked like an unemployed Chicago accountant—kinda short, not much hair, a little stammer. But out of that plain little mouth kept coming the most hilarious things.

The world found that out when he and a partner taped some imaginary phone calls he'd written for a Chicago radio station. They wanted more, so Bob wrote more. Then a talent scout wanted them to try it at a club and Newhart said, "A club?" He'd never been up in front of his relatives, much less a club. But they did it. Then, one night, the partner got sick and Newhart did it alone—letting the audience guess what the other party was saying. "That worked," Newhart says, "because you give the audience credit for understanding what the guy on the other end is saying. Really, they're applauding *themselves*." Lo and behold, you had Bob Newhart, smash comedy hit.

Naturally, he moved to L.A. and joined the local golf club—Bel-Air. Forty-one years later, he was walking in the door on a January day, 2002, meeting his white-overalled, Frisbee-eyed caddy. This time, he looked like a retired 72-year-old unemployed Chicago accountant: He had on a checked sweater, black-and-white shoes, not much hair, and a few more wrinkles. He still had that sparkle in his eyes, though. You meet him once and you can never call him anything but "Bob." Busboys call him Bob. He is just naturally and happily and forever a Bob.

Bob let me have lunch with him in the grill, which overlooks the first tee, and, beyond that, all of greater Los Angeles.

"The first time I ate lunch in here, in 1961, I'll never forget it," he said. "The guys who kinda ran the place then were Dean Martin, Bing Crosby, Jimmy Stewart, Clark Gable, and Adolphe Menjou, people like that. I mean, these people were 12 feet tall to me! And all of a sudden, they're sitting next to me, eating a tuna-melt sandwich!"

I asked him if he, himself, still gets excited about seeing stars. "Oh, sometimes," he said. "It's funny, though. We're all celebrities here, but the sight of a touring pro just throws us into fits. It's like, 'Oh, Christ! That's Tom Kite!' "

I tried to give the joint a once-over, very coolly. I could see L.A. Dodger broadcasting legend Vin Scully. And former CBS golf producer Frank Chirkanian. And Jerry West out putting on the practice green.

Very cool.

None of them were playing with us. Bob doesn't generally play with too many people. Apparently, he's perfectly happy with his own company and the workings of his endlessly fertile mind. I also heard he doesn't take caddies. I asked him why.

"One time I was playing in the Glen Campbell L.A. Open and I asked the caddy what the line was (for the tee shot). This caddy says, 'Hit it at the eucalyptus tree.' So, as luck would have it, I happened to hit it perfectly, right at the tree. And the caddy goes, 'Oh, man, that's the garden spot! You couldn't have hit it any better than that, Mr. Newhart! That is perfect-o! . . . Hey, wait. Hold up! Stop!!!! Damn, that's o.b.!' I went from the garden spot to o.b. on the same ball. I guess I just haven't found them that useful ever since."

Over the years, there have been wonderful Bel-Air caddies. Corey Pavin was one when he played for UCLA, which is about two good drivers down the hill from Bel-Air. Greg Puga was another. Puga won the U.S. Mid-Amateur a few years ago, thus earning a trip to Augusta. But he shot 80-76 and missed the cut, possibly because, as he admitted, he felt so awkward taking a caddy. He'd never had one before.

But there have also been some you wouldn't exactly try to run for Senate. The most famous of these was a caddy named Snake, who had one tooth on the top and one on the bottom. Snake used to enjoy the recipe, if you know what I mean, and would occasionally suffer lapses in concentration.

Bob: "One time Dean had Snake out for a round—he always took Snake—and they were playing 11 when Dean looked up and noticed Snake walking down the 15th fairway with another group! Dean yelled, 'Snake! What are you doing?' Until Dean yelled at him, Snake hadn't realized he'd completely osmosissed into another foursome!"

There was also the time Snake and Martin were looking for their ball when Martin finally said, "Screw it, Snake. Let's go." But Snake kept looking. Martin said, a little louder, "Forget it, Snake. Lost ball." And Snake said, "Hell with the ball. Where's the goddamn bag?"

Sober, Snake was actually a very good player and gave the members putting lessons. Anytime Bing Crosby broke 70 with Snake he'd buy him a new suit. One time Crosby shot a 69 and asked Snake what color suit he wanted this time. Snake looked like a man who'd gotten up on the wrong side of the Dumpster that day: no socks, an elbowless sweater, shoes that looked like they'd been to Bataan and back. So Snake says, "If it's all the same to you, Mr. Crosby, could you just slip me the cash this time? My tailor's out of town." And Crosby did.

It reminded Bob of something he overheard once walking to his accounting job in Chicago. "I'm walking along," he says, "and there's these two derelicts sitting against the wall. Just real bum, skid row types. And all I heard—I'll never forget this—all I heard was just part of the conversation, just a snippet, in which the one guy says to the other, "When the hell were YOU ever the goalie for the Montreal Canadiens?!"

That's a Bob kind of story. If you buy the premise, then it's funny. If you don't, it falls like a lead flapjack.

People were starting to wonder why a caddy was eating lunch with Bob Newhart in the men's grill, so we set out. There's no real range at Bel-Air. You just lace 'em up and go. Bob said we'd start on the back nine and then play the front nine. But somebody was playing the famous 10th, the long, uphill, and brutal par 3 that begins right next to the pro shop and requires a carry over a hellacious barranca of at least 150 yards. The saving grace of the hole is this gorgeous, white, elegant swinging suspension bridge that spans the gulf and is the signature of the club. It seems to be something out of *Brigadoon.* But since the hole was very full and very hard, we skipped it. Good thing. Jim Murray always contended that until the bridge was built, Bel-Air members had to play it by mule. We also skipped 11 and started on 12, where I asked Bob what his handicap was.

"Nine," he said. "Nine was the lowest handicap I ever got to, so I say I'm a 9 no matter what I am. I like being a 9."

And I was thinking, Hey, if you've got millions, you can afford a cocktail 9. But right off, Bob proved he wasn't a 9. He was more like a 4. He hit a perfect drive and then a perfect 5-wood toward the Mae West green at 12. It's called that because it used to have two huge humps guarding it. The humps are gone now, but then so is Mae West. He was on in two but three-putted.

Does golf drive stars crazy, too? I asked.

"Oh, yeah," he said. "Like, I'll come home after a bad round, swearing. And my wife [Ginnie, with whom he has four kids and three grandkids] will say, 'I thought you played golf to relax?' And I'll snap, 'Dammit, honey! You don't know the first thing about the game!' "

On 13, he three-putted again. I was giving him reads and they weren't working. Why a man who's never played a golf course was giving reads to a man who'd played there 41 years is a mystery, but I suppose Bob is just so damn nice, he didn't want to spoil my fun.

I'm not sure he was all that interested in my trivia knowledge about the 13th hole, which is that the 13th has been aced by more famous people than any hole in history—Clark Gable, Fred Astaire, Ray Bolger, Mike Douglas, Lloyd Nolan, Howard Keel, and Lawrence Welk.

Bob said he knew that and wondered if I knew the famous Fuzzy Zoeller story about 13. Zoeller was playing with *Laugh-In*'s Dick Martin when Martin pointed out his house on the hill above. Zoeller said he figured he could hit one into Martin's living room. Martin said try. So Fuzzy killed a 2-wood that people say had to go 300 yards. And sure enough, plop, it landed on Martin's porch. "World's only house-in-one," Bob said.

Bob lives among the mansions in the Bel-Air hills. "We live next to the house Dean Martin owned," he said. "Then Dean sold it to Tom Jones, who sold it to Nicolas Cage. Right next to that is one Clark Gable and Carole Lombard lived in. It sounds glamorous, I guess. But sometimes, I'll be doing some menial task and I'll say to my wife, 'Hon, do you think Carole Lombard ever asked Clark Gable to take out the recycling?' "

He was still hitting it sweetly at 14, where he made a par 5 and could've had birdie. Bob's was not all that pretty a swing and didn't have much clubhead speed, but everything was coming right out of the slot and right down the sprinkling system.

The mood seemed right so I asked him if he had a favorite golf joke.

"A guy is playing golf by himself," Bob began. "He's trying to decide what to hit on 17 when he hears this soft whisper of a voice in his ear, saying, 'Hit the 7-iron!'

"And he goes, 'What? Who is that?'

"Again, the voice says, 'Hit the 7-iron!'

"The guy is kind of scared not to, so he hits the 7-iron. And the thing goes in the hole!

"Next hole, the guy says to the voice, 'What should I hit here?'

"And the voice goes, 'Cut the driver around the tree!'

"Well, he believes now, so he tries it, gets on the green in one, and makes the putt for eagle!

"The guy can't believe it! Eagle-eagle finish! It's the greatest golf day of his life! He says to the voice, 'How can I ever thank you?'

"And the voice says, 'Go to Vegas!'

"So the guy jumps in his car and heads straight to Las Vegas. He gets a room and says to the voice, 'What do you want me to do now?'

" 'Go to the roulette wheel,' the voice says.

"So he gets there and the voice goes, 'Place it on 14.'

"Sure enough, it hits 14 and the guy makes $1,000.

" 'Let it ride on 14,' the voice says.

"So the guy lets it ride and it hits again! He's up $38,000!

" 'My God,' the guy says. 'This is enough to pay off my house! Thank you so much!'

" 'Play it all on 9,' the voice says.

" 'All of it?' the guy says. 'But it's so much money!'

" 'Nine!'

"So he puts it all on 9. And it comes up 23.

"And the voice whispers, 'Shit.' "

ONE OF THE jaw-dropping things about Bel-Air is that in nearly every group you see, there's a celebrity of some kind or another. Up ahead of us on 15—the hole Alfred Hitchcock used to live on—there was a threesome holding us up, so I asked Bob if we should play through. "No," he said. "In three holes, they'll be done.'

But the three waved us up, and reluctantly, Bob hit. It was a blade, a real Skulldonia, a completely different pass than he'd made all day.

When we got to the green, I noticed the threesome included James Garner and singer-songwriter Mac Davis, who had his own variety show for a while. The third guy was a dentist of some kind or other. What, you never played through two TV stars and a dentist?

They were nice, friendly fellows who knew Bob well, but something about playing with them caused Bob to come apart like a 99-cent headcover. On 16—where Red Skelton used to come out of his house and chat up the members—he got stuck in the kitty litter and never got out, sticking it in his pocket. On 17—where Bobby Jones, W. C. Fields, and Groucho Marx once made a series of golf films—he hit a complete Boston Carver dead right and before it was even 100 yards away from the tee, had another one out to hit again.

"That's ol' Bob," Davis laughed. "Bob is the only guy who can have his second ball out and on the tee before he's finished his swing on the first one." Bob sort of murmured, shyly, "I'd be a 5 handicap on my second ball."

He just didn't seem himself around the other stars. There were more whip-out seconds on 18, which we "bogeyed" (cough, cough). Then Garner and Davis went on to 19 and we went on to 1. Bob got more comfortable when it was just us again. And it struck me that Bob may be just too nice and decent for golf. To play with your pals, to handle the needle, to bet, and to compete, you've got to have a little edge to you or you get swallowed whole. Guys like Donald Trump, Dewey Tomko, John Daly—they have that edge. Bob doesn't have that edge. Bob isn't within a toll call of the edge. In 20 years playing the Pebble Beach Pro-Am, Bob never made the cut.

It's like nothing has changed about Bob since he was that humbled, out-of-work accountant. When Bob was just starting to hit it big in 1963, he got a huge Las Vegas gig opening for Peggy Lee. He made $300 a week. It was so much money he thought you were supposed to go into the casinos and lose it back. So he would. He was uncomfortable gambling, but he did it. But he was such a hit, he was soon making $2,000 a week. Finally he told the club manager, "I'm not sure I can lose that back." The guy was dumbfounded. "Lose it back? You don't have to lose it back. Go put it in the bank!"

In this way, Bob is the perfect Chicago Cubs fan. He knows they're going to lose, they *do* lose, but he keeps showing up, quietly hoping.

"But don't forget, I was a Cubs fan in 1945," he says, "when they won the NL pennant. Remember Andy Pafko?"

Now, of course, he is a halfhearted L.A. Dodgers fan. "There's a difference," he says. "They remember things differently. In Chicago, life is simpler. If you ask somebody in Chicago, 'Hey, when's the last time you went to a Cubs game?' the guy will kind of scratch his head and go, 'Oh, not since Tommy was 10, at least.' But in L.A., if you ask somebody, 'Hey, when's the last time you went to a Dodger game?' the guy will scratch his head and go, 'Oh, not since I was married to Elaine, at least.' "

Speaking of which, I asked him if he ever saw his ex-TV wife, Suzanne Pleshette. "Oh, sure," he said. Turns out, one of his best friends, Poston, ended up marrying Pleshette in 2001. I asked if I could call Poston and he gave me the number. "But, remember, if somebody answers with a voice lower than Tom's, don't hang up. It's Suzanne."

We bogeyed 1 and 2 and then he hit his best shot of the day at Bel-Air's terrific par-3 3rd, a beauty nestled in against a hill. This is the hole Richard Nixon aced in 1961. Bob hit it in there four feet, then blew the putt. Crap.

He was happy and whistling, though, and I figured if that wasn't going to bother him, nothing would, so I hit him with the annoying questions.

You remember those 'Hi, Bob!' parties they used to have at colleges? You know, where everytime a character said 'Hi, Bob!' on your show, everybody at the party had to chug a beer? Did you ever go to one of those?

"Never did," Bob replied. "It's kind of a left-handed compliment, those parties, when you think about it. But they sounded fun. It's just that nobody ever invited me to one."

What's it feel like when people call you the greatest comic mind in American history?

"I don't believe it. Not for a second. To me, brilliance was Richard Pryor. I mean, I'm funny. But that guy was beyond belief."

Did anybody ever tell you to fix that stammer of yours?

"I remember the first week on my first show. The director called me aside and said, 'Could you run your words together a little faster? We're coming up against a time problem.' And I said, 'Look, this stammer has gotten me a house in Beverly Hills. I'm not changing it.'"

We bogeyed the hardest hole on the course, the uphill 4th, the hole Robert Redford used to sneak on and play by hopping the fence when he was a kid. It also used to be the home of the dreaded Newhart Tree on the right, so named for the large number of balls Bob hit into it. Since it was struck down by lightning mysteriously one night, Bob's scores have come down. Bob was questioned, of course, but cleared of all wrongdoing. Oh, and it's also the hole where they used to film Tarzan movies. Johnny Weissmuller used to play it and give his famous Tarzan yell upon making the putt. Other than that, the hole has no history.

We parred the 5th, the par 3 Fred MacMurray once aced by ricocheting it off a portable toilet. *Take that, Uncle Charlie.*

We bogeyed the 6th, where Elvis used to have a house, parred the 7th, where Dick Powell once made an eagle, and then bogeyed the 8th, the hole where Howard Hughes once landed his plane because he was late to pick up Katharine Hepburn for a date. Bel-Air yelled at him for it and Hughes responded with, "I'll never play here again." And he didn't. But he kept paying his dues. Hepburn, by the way, was a very good golfer who shot in the mid-80s. From the men's tees.

With a hole to go, I asked him to name his favorite routine he ever wrote.

"Well," he stammered. "It was this bit about a guy who gets swooped up by a UFO. He's gone for awhile and then they bring him back. He's pitched back on the earth and he's dusting himself off and the newsmen all gather around him and they ask him, 'Is the civilization incredibly advanced up there?'

"And the guy goes, 'Yeah. About six weeks.'

"And the reporters go, 'Six weeks?'

"And the guy goes, 'Yeah. Like, all the stores up there already have the latest disposable razors.' "

I WAS HAVING so damn much fun I hated to see the round end. We bogeyed nine and that was the end of it. In 16 holes, he'd hit seven out of 13 fairways, six out of 16 greens, and shot what probably would've been an 88 if we'd have counted everything and played 18 holes. On his second ball, though, he was probably more like 81. But aren't we all?

Bob invited me to stay for a beer and I nursed it like I was in prenatal care. Finally, as we looked over L.A., the sun itself not really wanting to leave, either, I asked him if he could guess my favorite Bob routine.

"Well," he asked, "Abe Lincoln?"

Nope.

"The driving instructor?"

Nope, I said. *It's the only one you ever did that mentions golf.*

He looked at me blankly.

The witch doctor, I said.

He started howling. "I haven't heard anybody mention that in *years!*"

Bob always set it up by saying that witch doctors are probably quite a bit like regular doctors. They're valuable in their own communities, and yet stuck with the same complaints our doctors have. Like, for instance, the 2 A.M. phone call. Naturally, we only hear the witch doctor's side of the call:

"Yello," says the witch doctor, sleepily. "Oh, hi, Mrs. Kumba. No, no. That's all right. I'd have been getting up in another 5 or 6 hours anyway."

(Pause.)

"Your crops are withering and your son is seeing demons, huh? Yeah, there's a lot of that going around. I wouldn't worry about it. Sounds like a 24-hour curse to me."

(Pause.)

"Well, if you're really concerned . . . Do you have any bark of a tree that was struck by lightning in a full moon in the medicine chest? Yeah? You might sprinkle some of that on him every four hours. Sometimes that helps."

(Pause.)

"Gee, I couldn't possibly come out to the house, Mrs. Kumba. I don't make hut calls anymore. No, no, I haven't danced around a house in years."

(Pause)

"Well, Mrs. Kumba, I can recommend a good demon man. I don't happen to specialize in demon work. He's pretty good."

(Pause.)

"I tell you what you could do. You might wrap him in some mud and put some leaves around him and put him in a field where the hyenas congregate. Yeah. It won't help the curse but sometimes their laughter can become infectious. Might make him feel better."

(Pause.)

"Well, if he's not feeling better in the morning, why don't you bring him in?"

(Pause.)

"Oh, that's right. Tomorrow *is* Wednesday, isn't it? Well, tell you what, we don't tee off 'til 1:30, why don't you bring him down in the morning?

"OK, bye-bye, Mrs. Kumba."

If the caddy says . . .

"We found the Delta ticket counter on 16. I gotta be dead last in Scores for Floors. We spent so much time in the Arab grass, you can call me Achmed. Sumbitch has real warning track power. I swear I'm hearin' Persimmon."

He means . . .

"We found a way to miss the cut on Hole No. 16. I think I rank last in Scores for Floors, which is the traditional caddy game in which the caddy whose player shoots the worst has to sleep on the floor in the caddies' hotel room. I think that's because my player hits his driver so very short. It's as though he is not using a metal driver, but a wooden one instead. Of course, I am only kidding as a way to emphasize my point about his lack of distance."

11

JILL McGILL

Where's Your Caddy?

It's hard to say what makes the LPGA's Jill McGill so sexy. Some people think it's that she's blond, gorgeous, hazel-eyed, and 5-12, as she says, with most of that being legs that are longer than Yao Ming's.

Me, I think it's that her average drive is 268 yards, second on the LPGA Tour behind Grace Park.

For *Playboy*, though, it's definitely the legs and eyes and blond thing. They offered her a reported $500,000 to take off her glued-on shorts and T-back tops after she finished second in Playboy.com's Sexiest LPGA Player poll. The winner was Sweden's Carin (The Face) Koch, who said she would pose showing only one thing (the face).

So McGill said, "Maybe I will." Suddenly McGill was very controversial. Columnists asked: *How could an athlete let herself be objectified by men? How could a woman do this to her gender? How could I, personally, get a copy of the magazine?*

She asked her family. "My mom was way opposed to it. My dad was like, 'You're 30 years old, you make your own decisions.' My sister was all, 'Yeah, do it!' and my brother said it was up to me. I ended up asking *Playboy* if I could pose nude but not show anything and they said no. Now, I'm *soooo* glad I didn't do it. I'd have lived with that the rest of my life."

OK, but would she have shown the "Fore USC!" tattoo on her butt?

"Sure!" she says.

As it stands, only she and her caddy will get to see it, since she sleeps with him. Not that she sleeps with *every caddy,* just *this caddy,* 6-1, dark, 25-year-old part-time golf pro, full-time-caddy Adam (A-Bomb) Hayes.

This came as news to me when I knocked on Room 234 at the Residence Inn in Toledo, Ohio, ready to start working for her at the Jamie Farr Kroger Classic. A-Bomb answered the door.

"Hey, how are you!" he said, extending his hand. "Jill's just getting out of the shower." And soon, there was Jill, wrapped in a towel. The surprising part was that I knew Jill to be married at the time, to a San Diego stockbroker she'd wed in 1998. "Separated," she said. "Waiting for the divorce papers. Should happen in four months."

She said the problem was she wasn't willing to compromise her golf game in order to be home more. And he wasn't willing to travel more to be with her. "Plus, he's just a little introverted. I like to travel and party. Our lifestyles just don't mesh."

But aren't there complications dating your caddy?

Caddy: What do you want to hit here?

Player: What do I want to hit here? (Pause.) I don't even know who you are anymore!

Plus, how weird would it be to pay your boyfriend every week?

OK, here's the money for this week. I had to take out $100 because you weren't hearing my emotional needs. And another $50 for that blond you flirted with going up No. 7.

Luckily, it seems to work for them. Adam is her coach, caddy, roommate, traveling partner, psychologist, lover, and crying shoulder. He is a terrific player himself, just not good enough to make a living at it, so he seems happy to be the wind beneath Jill's wedges.

When I butted between them, they had good *wa* going, as the caddies say. Jill had just come off her finest U.S. Open at Prairie Dunes in Hutchinson, Kansas. She was paired in the final twosome with the LPGA's best player—maybe best ever—Annika Sorenstam, one shot back. It was her first final-group pairing, ever.

"People were giving me all this advice the night before," she remembered. "They're like, 'Just pretend it's any other tournament.' And I'm like, 'It's the last day of the U.S. Open! There's going to be huge crowds! TV cameras everywhere! Photographers! And I'm playing in the last group with Annika Sorenstam! And you want me to pretend it's just another tournament? What are you smokin'? 'Cause whatever it is, I want some.' "

Going into that Open, Jill had missed seven cuts out of 14, was 142nd in putting—which a person could do wielding a large vacuum-cleaner attachment—and 136th in fairways hit. But suddenly she put together three great rounds and voila, you're on NBC!

And that's when the world found out just how slow she plays.

Johnny Miller ripped her for it. And she *was* slower than a French film festival. She and Adam kept looking at the ball like any minute it might sprout legs and evolve. Adam was lining her up for every single shot, putt or otherwise. The USGA put her on the clock, which was nothing new. She'd been docked two strokes twice before and would end up being on the clock three days out of four at the Jamie Farr. The woman plays slower than hairlines recede.

She wound up with a disastrous 79 and finished 12th.

Eventually, we both would decide it was her mother's fault.

EXAMPLE NO. 1 how the LPGA Tour is different from the PGA Tour: Clothes.

It's Wednesday, and Jill is warming up on the range when she has the following discussion with Tour pro Joanne Morley:

Jill: Is that skirt Banana Republic?

Joanne: No, this is The Gap, I think.

Jill: It's darling.

Can you see that on the men's tour?

Tiger: Is that shirt Tommy Hilfiger?

Phil Mickelson: No, this is Boss.

Tiger: It's darling.

The other thing you notice right away is that the caddies give far more help and practice instruction. "Lots more," says Adam. This is why LPGA caddies tend to think they're the best pro caddies in the world. Maybe they are.

"We have to be," says Thayne Aalyson, a law school graduate who loops for Donna Andrews. "The guys on the men's tour don't want any help. These women do. And the men don't have to play on shitty tracks every week, courses with three kinds of sand in the bunkers. And our rough is longer because the courses we're on don't have as much manpower to mow it."

Everything's a little tougher out here. There's almost no courtesy cars. No jets, either. There's nobody in the locker room setting up flights for the players. They often divide up an $800,000 purse for the week. That's not even a top first prize for the men anymore. There's not many Ritz-Carltons or Four Seasons, either. It's a lot of conversion vans and Motel 5s.

"But it's a helluva lot more interesting out here," says Aalyson. "Every day, there's new rumors, new gossip. Lots of drama. Every day is a soap opera out here. It's just an odd mix. It's a lot of silver-spooned rich girls being caddied by degenerates. You got convicts out here, drunks, drug addicts, everything."

And now, God forbid, sportswriters.

JILL'S BAG WASN'T any lighter than any male pro's and, in fact, was damn near as heavy as many women's purses. Some of this was from all the food she packed in it. Just before we teed off she said something else you never hear on the PGA Tour: "OK, I'm going in to make us our sandwiches!" And she came out five minutes later with two peanut butters, one for her and one for me, and they both wound up getting crushed by you-know-who.

Wednesday is pro-am day, which takes on a little edge when the ams are all men who aren't sure how much they like having to depend on a female pro.

"Most of the time, they're great," Jill says. "But they all want to think they hit it farther than you." One time on a par 3 during a pro-am, a rather macho guy asked Jill, "So, what you gonna hit?"

"Seven-iron," Jill replied.

The macho man turned to his caddy and said, "Better bring me an 8."

To which Jill added, "Bring him a sand wedge, too, then, 'cause he'll need it."

Jill: "Sometimes men will find out I play on tour and they'll go, 'Really? Can you make a living at it?' And I just want to say, 'No, pal. I drive a bus when I'm home.' "

Actually, Jill made about $360,000 in 2001, but spent $150,000 to do it. For her career, I noticed she was $19,000 short of a million dollars.

"Damn!" she said. "I've been out here seven years and that's all I have? What the hell is taking me so long?"

Once I saw the way she struck the ball, I was surprised myself.

She has an odd little lurch at the bottom, but the shots come off pure and straight and hard. No wonder she was the 1993 U.S. Women's Amateur champ and the '94 U.S. Publinks champ.

But once I saw her putt, I wondered how she made any cash at all. She studies them too long. Changes her mind on reads. Steps up to them and steps back. She looks like somebody trying to decide where a lamp should go in a living room. In fact, we missed a crummy little four-footer on the last hole to tie for first in the pro-am.

Not that it mattered. On the LPGA Tour, unlike the men's tour, the pros don't make a dime in the pro-ams.

Men are pigs.

EXAMPLE NO. 47 how the LPGA Tour is different from the PGA Tour: The Period Factor.

Actually, not the period itself, the week before the period. "Your timing just isn't there," Jill says. "Your body just feels kind of out of balance."

"To me," says 1994 U.S. Amateur champ and LPGA veteran Wendy Ward, "it's a rhythm thing. It just throws you all off. I mean, I've tried to psych myself out of it. I've tried to pretend I don't have it. I'm like, 'This does not exist. I'm the same person. Same clubs. Same swing. Nothing is new.' But then you get out there and you can't."

They speak of how your hands swell up, so your feel is literally off; how your actual *weight* is different, so your turn is *literally* different; how your mood resembles that of a glue-sniffing drifter.

Upon research, the Period Factor is an absolute consideration for the caddy, too, no less than the wind or the yardage. "When I start a job," says Aalyson, "the first question I ask is, 'When's your period?' "

"Me, too," says colleague Jeff King, Heather Bowie's caddy. "You need to know when they're on it, because if they are, we ain't gonna be hitting any half shots or punches. And we're not going to hit it 20 yards in front and try to get it up and down. Because when they're on it, they got no clue for feel."

The women all have different names for it—"Aunt Flo," "the evil twin sister"—but whatever they call it, they almost all feel differently when it's coming. "That's the week my caddy becomes my punching bag," says Swedish star Helen Alfredsson.

Many LPGA players are on the pill, but not because they're trying to break all of J-Lo's records. It's to more precisely control their period. That way they can time what weeks they'll take off and what weeks they won't. "You can manipulate it that way," Ward said. "If you need it to start a week later, you start the cycle a week later."

This is also the answer to why Nancy Lopez's remarkable string of five straight wins as a rookie in 1978 might be as good as Byron Nelson's 11 in 1945. For one thing, it wasn't done at wartime, and for two, Nelson never had to beat Aunt Flo.

UH-OH. IN our group for the first two days will be Charlotta Sorenstam, lesser known sister of Annika.

"Don't expect a lot of chitchat," Adam warns me.

Seems Adam used to caddy for Charlotta before he jumped to (and on) Jill. He's sensed some hard feelings ever since, as though Jill stole Charlotta's man instead of her caddy. Of course, as we've learned, sometimes the line blurs.

Listen to an unnamed LPGA star tell about her problems trying to fire her caddy and see if it doesn't sound like a woman trying to dump her boyfriend:

"So I tell the guy, 'Look, I think it's time for us to move on, you know? We're done. I think it's time for us to go in completely different directions.' I figure he gets the message, right? So when I get back out there two weeks later, what happens? He's in the parking lot waiting for me! He goes, 'Hey, some guys are saying you fired me. I told 'em they're crazy, right?' And I go, 'Yeah, I did! I fired you!' And he's like, 'You did?' And I go, 'Yeah! What did you think I meant that day?' And he says, 'Well, when you said it's time for us to go in different directions, I thought you meant you were going home and I was going home and then I'd see you here.' And I can't believe this is happening! So I say to him, 'But I told you we were done! What did you think *that* meant?' And he goes, 'I thought you meant we were done, we weren't going to hit balls after the round."

Let's all slap our foreheads in unison.

Right away, from the first tee, you can see there's still some left-over mad with Charlotta. She seems to be wound tighter than Annika, although neither sister is exactly Whoopi Goldberg. She yells at her ball more, looks around less, says not a word to anybody except her caddy. "She's a good player," Adam says of Charlotta, "but it's hard to be Annika's sister. I mean, she's constantly getting, 'Great win last week!' And 'Way to go, Miss 59!' And she has to say, 'I'll tell my sister.' Or she'll go to the range and they'll put out the Sorenstam sign and all of a sudden a big crowd will gather to watch her, thinking it's Annika. I think it's really affected her career."

It didn't affect her on Day One of the Jamie Farr, though. She kept hollering at her putts, "Find it!" and the ball kept obeying. I guess it's OK for women to put their mouth on the ball. She wound up with a two-under 69.

That was a whole helluva lot better than we were playing. The main problem was Jill kept thinking she was going to throw up for the first 12 holes. Not morning sickness. The greasy Italian dinner the night before. We hit it lousy for the first six holes and were lucky to be even par. She turned to me after six and said, "Uh, on this book you're doing, what's been your success rate?"

Sounds ominous for a certain wannabe looper.

Plus, I hadn't caddied in a while and was a little rusty. Apparently, I was shirking some of my group duties.

"Hey, Rick," Jill asked, walking away from one green. "Do you know how much a flagstick weighs?"

"No," I said.

"Well, go try picking one up once and find out."

Bada-bing!

On the 7th, a par 5, it looked like we were going to take two scoops, as the caddies call double bogey. We hit a lousy drive in the left rough, punched out, then hit a smother-hook 4-iron way left, down a steep bank, leaving us an impossible 50-yard chip and no view of the pin. Naturally, she holed it. As she was acknowledging the crowd's applause, she said out of the side of her mouth, "That's a little whipped cream on shit."

EXAMPLE NO. 3,489 how the LPGA Tour is different from the PGA Tour: Bugs.

On one green, Jill gently flicked a bug away from her putting line. On the men's tour, they just crush 'em.

THE BEST THING about caddying on the LPGA Tour is that it hits you that, maybe, just possibly, if you worked at it, you could actually, once in your life, have a round this good.

Watching Jill, you understand it doesn't take a god to break par. I know that I would've been past Jill on some of her drives. Not often, but once in a while. And yet, she's under par three days out of four. And it occurs to you that breaking 70 is, well, do-able! You don't believe that when you're caddying for Lehman or Duval or Nicklaus. With them, it's like hearing Pavarotti. You know you can't hit those notes. But with the women, you realize it's not the length, it's the accuracy. It's knowing exactly how far you hit your irons, where you want to land the ball, how far it tends to release. The men are immortals, you think. But the women, they're *us!*

And then she makes a 3-iron dance the watusi with the flagstick from 210 yards and you think: Nah.

THE THIRD MEMBER of our group was Kelly Robbins, 32, one of the top 10 or 15 players out here. She started the day driving it wildly, but after about six holes, she started striping it. "Man, you're really driving it good now," I told her on one tee box. "When you started out, it seemed like your driver was all over the place." And she said, "It's that time of the month. You start your backswing and you never know what you're going to get."

Here, finally, was a topic I knew something about and was ready to launch into it when I noticed everybody, including Jill, looking at me oddly. Turns out a caddy *never* talks to the other player during a round and if he should break that rule, he would *never* talk to them about their golf game. That can get you a spiked foot.

Robbins is a fascinating player. A biography of LPGA superstar Karrie Webb, written by Charles Happell a few years ago, alleged that Webb and Robbins are in a long-term relationship. Happell says Webb broke off an engagement to her caddy before she began dating Robbins.

It's amazing when you think about it—the tour's No. 2 and 13 all-time money winners, sleeping together. On the men's tour, that would be Phil Mickelson sleeping with Mark O'Meara. On the Senior Tour: Gil Morgan and Isao Aoki.

Feel free to shudder.

All this is Jill's least favorite subject. "I just think it's unfair," she says. "The LPGA takes all the heat for all of women's sports on the lesbian issue. You never hear it come up in tennis, but there's plenty of lesbians on the tennis tour, much more than out here! And what about basketball? You telling me there's not a lot of lesbians in the WNBA?"

She's right. But the LPGA is stuck with lesbianism because every year they go to Palm Springs and play a major, the Nabisco Classic (used to be the Dinah Shore), that turns out to be a kind of national convention for 20,000 lesbians. Strip bars suddenly cater to women. Hotel pools become no-man's-land. Corporations like American Airlines actually cater to the demographic. And no matter what week the LPGA picks, the lesbians turn it into their quasi-convention.

It's a helluva scene—a lot of hiking boots and tank tops and Marine flattops and it makes some of the LPGA straights want to gag. "It's like they're sailors who haven't had shore leave in a year," says one straight player. "They sit on the hill behind the 17th with their legs spread wide open so you can see. It's gross!"

Now Jill is squirming. "This is the all-time no-no subject," she moans.

Well, maybe it shouldn't be. Maybe if more players would live openly, it would keep the press from constantly trying to find out the secret. Tennis superstar Martina Navratilova came out of the closet early in her career. At first, the media wanted to talk to her about it, but after that, the story was done, old news, and they got back to her tennis. It's the LPGA's whole "Lesbianism? What lesbianism?" that gets the media's noses twitching.

Somewhere, right now, Jill McGill is pounding her head on a desk.

. . .

WE WOUND UP with 1-over 72 Thursday, which put us more than halfway back in the pack. So Friday meant we had to play some serious Hide Whitey or we'd be trunk-slammin', see ya later, MC: miss cut.

In the newspaper account of the scores, you couldn't help notice how many Korean players were ahead of us. They're big on the LPGA Tour. Se Ri Pak is a star and Mi Hyun Kim may turn out to be even better. In all, there were 11 Korean nationals with their card in 2002, and most all of them good sticks. And yet there was only one, K. J. Choi, on the men's tour.

This might be because of Korean fathers, who wield a huge and dominating influence on their daughters. You see them everywhere, driving their white conversion vans, hanging around the range, watching everything. The last player on the range and the last player on the practice green are generally Koreans and always, the fathers are standing there, watching.

"It's a cultural thing," Ward explains. "The Korean ethic is that the parents come over with them. If they haven't succeeded enough at a certain age, they take them home and marry them off."

Those fathers can be a huge pain in the gluteus for the caddies. They are just slightly more demanding than Stalin. Worth Blackwelder, a longtime LPGA caddy, got fired by Kim's dad after two straight second place finishes, worth $289,000 in winnings. Then again, Kim's dad fired a caddy named Larry Smich after they *won* the Rail Classic.

"It's the Korean way," Blackwelder says. "It was her father's idea all the way. If anything at all goes wrong, it's the father's way of taking heat off their daughter. It's not your fault, sweetheart, it's the caddy's fault. That's how she's had 10 caddies in three years."

Of course, it's not just overprotective dads out here. It's moms, too. Well, at least one mom. Karen Pearce's mom, Patricia, has been caddying for her daughter for 17 years now. They fly together, eat together, and room together.

"It's just Karen and I out here," she says. "We leave the dog, the cat, and the husband at home."

Women are pigs.

Karen is 33 and still unmarried, and no wonder. "She can date if she wants to!" says Mrs. Pearce. "Mom can always get out of the house. She just doesn't want to much."

I wonder if Karen Pearce would like to meet Casey Martin?

EXAMPLE NO. 7,409 how the LPGA Tour is different from the PGA Tour: They talk dirtier.

On 9, Jill hit a good drive and as we were walking to it, she said, "That's dead titties from there."

What does that mean? I asked.

"Titties! You know? The hole opens up from there!"

I FELT LIKE weeping at our round Friday. It was the most precise day of ball-striking I'd carried, man, woman, or beast.

We just kept stacking the ball up on top of the pin. We hit it so damn close, you'd think we were in a Titleist commercial. We missed a 7 footer for birdie on 1. Missed a 15 footer for birdie on 2. Missed an 8 footer for birdie on 3. We missed a 14 footer for birdie on 4. We missed an 8 footer for birdie on 7, even though she finally let me read the putt for her. Perhaps she was sick of my begging. I gave her right lip. She agreed. She stepped up to it, backed off, changed her mind to right center of the hole, hit it there, and missed on the left lip. I nearly bit my tongue off.

On 9, we found out we were on the clock. But as we came to 10 tee, the group ahead of us was still teeing off, so I ducked over to the caddyshack to take a leak. Only I couldn't find the bathroom. Turns out it was in the way, way back. Only just as I reached for the doorknob, the caddymaster said. "My daughter's in there." She must've been taking a bubble bath because she took forever. I finally got out, grabbed the bag, and sprinted for the 10th tee, only to see Jill standing there with her hands on her hips. Kelly and Charlotta had already hit.

Oops.

Frazzled, Jill played 10 practically on the run. And guess what? We birdied it! Imagine that. Sometimes, less thinking is better. Then we missed a 4-foot birdie on 13. At this point, a dyspeptic yak could've putted better than us. And still slower than an IRS check. On 14, she was over an iron shot for 70 seconds. You only get 40.

For once, I really felt like it wasn't my fault. In fact, I was having my greatest day caddying. To wit: On the par-5 17th, she drove it in the right rough into a line of trees. She had 235 to the green. The play was obvious: punch back into the fairway, knock it on with a 9-iron, and hope you make the birdie putt. But she started looking at branches and 6-irons and tops of the trees ahead of us in line with the green.

"What are you doing?" I asked.

"I'm thinking I can get a 6-iron out from under here and then over that next tree," she said.

"Are you nuts?" I said.

"No, I think I can!"

"Wait a minute. Even if you could hit a 6-iron out and then high enough to get over the tree, where does it get us? You still aren't on the green."

"But we'll be right in front."

"But you'll still need three to get on, right? And if you just punch out, you'll be on in three. Same thing, only we don't make 7."

"Caddies aren't supposed to bring up negative things," she snapped.

"Sorry, but this is insanity."

"But I can do it!"

"Yeah, but what if you don't?"

I had broken the caddy rule: never be negative. But this was an exception. David Copperfield wouldn't have tried that shot. Begrudgingly, she yanked out the 4-iron and punched out. She hit her third to 12 feet, nearly made it, and settled for par. Then she roped her drive on 18 right down the middle and said, "Good job on 17. That would've been stupid."

Hey, it's what I do.

We birdied the 18th from 12 feet to shoot 1-under 70. We'd hit 16 greens and missed only one fairway. We made the cut, but I swear, it could've been 63.

Charlotta and Kelly made the cut, too. I congratulated Kelly and asked her to give an honest critique of my caddying.

"I think you're a good writer," she said with a grin, "and I would strongly suggest you stick with that profession."

Later, she told a *Toledo Blade* reporter that she was bothered by my incessant pencil-writing in my pad while she was trying to hit. Also the sound of butterflies burping on the petunias two fairways over were a distraction. And an ice floe shifting in the Bering Strait. Give me a freaking break.

As long as we were critiquing, Jill mentioned that perhaps it was not generally the wisest idea to disappear at the 10th tee when your player is trying to hit and happens to be on the clock. "But," she said, more happily, "it made me think of a better title for your book."

"Yeah?" I said. "What?"

"Where's *Your Caddy*?"

. . .

EXAMPLE NO. 11,321 how the LPGA Tour is different from the PGA Tour: Pregnant players.

Packing her car in the parking lot Friday was Connie Masterson, five months pregnant. She'd shot 76-82 and was going home for the season, tired of playing for two.

"For awhile, you play better pregnant," she said. "You get better extension going back, because your arms are naturally farther away from your body. But then you get too big and you're swinging kind of around yourself. You get too flat and you have no idea where your hands are. Plus, my ankles are swelling. I get cramps walking. And the heat is too much. And the baby is kicking me in the bladder all the time as I pull it back. And I've got to go to the bathroom all the time."

Yeah, but have you ever tried to play with 5 o'clock stubble?

THE OTHER BIG news Friday was that the living legend, 45-year-old Nancy Lopez, playing in her final season, finally made a cut after missing nine out of nine. Not only that, but she'd made an ace on Friday.

And if you think all the players would be happy for her, you don't know LPGA players. One rather famous player could be heard grousing on Thursday, "I'm so sick of this. Every week, it's the same thing. Nancy shows up. Nancy gets a plaque. Nancy cries. Nancy misses the cut. God, call it a career already."

Man, it's a catty place.

EACH MORNING AT the range was Check Out Everybody's Outfit and Make Snide Remarks time. Jill's outfits were often a topic. "I hear it all the time," Jill says. "From players and also from the old ladies in the gallery. 'Oh, there's Jill McGill. She's the one who wears the miniskirts.' "

For the record, they're *not* miniskirts. They're *skorts.*

It doesn't bother her. For one thing, LPGA commissioner Ty Votaw, a married man with two kids, seems to want her to dress like this as part of his famous "summit meeting" to find ways to make the Tour more *fan-friendly.* He didn't say anything about sex appeal, but everybody knew what he meant. A lot of players were offended and a lot of players said, hell yes, it helps. "People who don't think sexiness matters in sports ought to pull their heads out of their butts," Jill was quoted as saying.

And so they're trying. When Tour star Laura Diaz gets sent her shorts from her clothing sponsor, she hems them higher. Swede Catrin Nilsmark wears shorts some days that contain less material than a pair of men's Speedos. One player once asked of them, "I wonder where she puts her tees," and another replied, "You don't want to know."

And why *not* talk of sex appeal on a tour that is so full of, well, sex? Adam was gesturing down the line with his eyes.

"You see that woman?" he said, pointing to a shortish blockish woman. "She's gay and so is her caddy [a younger, thinner woman]."

They sleep with each other? I asked, thinking they were the gay pride version of Jill and Adam.

"Nah, the caddy sleeps with another gay caddy out here and the player sleeps with another gay player."

After quite a lot of discussion, Adam and I got it down to a single LPGA Tour Sex Scoresheet:

There are . . .

. . . straight players sleeping with male caddies.

. . . female gay caddies sleeping with female gay caddies.

. . . gay players sleeping with gay players.

. . . gay players sleeping with gay caddies.

but no . . .

. . . gay male caddies sleeping with gay male caddies . . .

. . . as far as we know.

That's about when the flamboyant redhead Alfredsson happened by and wanted to know what we were talking about. When we told her, she announced, rather loudly, "Well, I'd never sleep with a caddy, but for a lot of us out here, where else are we going to meet men?"

Warming to the subject, she then proceeded to ask Jill and Adam, "Are you going to have sex after the round? You should! It should be on the schedule, you know? 8:10: golf. 1:30: lunch. 2:15: sex. 2:19: it's over! We can still make the movie!"

JILL AND I went off Saturday morning to try and put her over the $1 million mark. And again, she hit it straighter than a clothesline. And again, she putted it more crooked than a corkscrew. We still wound up shooting 68, but it should've been 64.

This is where the whole Mom Factor plays in.

"You'd have to know her," Jill said that night over a beer. "My dad is a great guy, but my mom [Mary Beth] is just different. The only time I got approval from her was for achieving things. It was never good enough that I was just me, her daughter.

"I guess maybe she thinks of it as tough love. Maybe she thinks it's the way to motivate me. But she doesn't call me and I don't call her much. One time she said, 'You know, those young guys that came out of school, they've all really turned into something. You know—Tiger, Mickelson, Leonard. But the girls who came out, you know, like you, never really made much of yourself.'

"And I'm like, 'Gee, thanks, Mom.' "

Golf played Jill, not the other way around. She went to the range to be with the boys, then found out she could beat them. She played No. 4 on the boys' team at Cherry Creek High School in a Denver suburb. "The guys on my team liked me, but the guys on the opposing team hated it. It was always, 'Who has to play the *girl?'* And I'd usually beat them and the guy would have to hear it from his buddies the rest of the week."

Unlike most of the women on Tour, Jill never had any dream to be a pro. "Everybody kept telling me, 'Do you know how many people would die to be in your shoes? You HAVE to get out there.' So I did. I guess I felt like I owed it to my mom."

That's funny, because that's exactly how her mom felt. Just after Jill turned pro, her mom presented her with a bill for $15,000. "This is for our expenses to send you to all the tournaments after your senior year in college," she said.

"I was shocked! Dumbfounded! I mean, I didn't know what to say, so—I wrote her a check."

In her mother's defense, a couple years before, Jill's dad, Gary, went suddenly broke and her mom had to work as an assistant manager at Perkins restaurant. "She'd always say to me, 'I'm only working so you can play golf.' Do you know how much guilt comes with that?"

Lately, Jill has been going to therapy, reading books on self-esteem, and falling asleep to positive-thinking tapes given to her by sports psychologist Jay Brunza, who also happened to work with Tiger as a teenager. "I realized I stand over shots for so long because I'm afraid to make a mistake," she says. "I feel like I have to be perfect. That's why I play so slow. But I'm working on it."

She's also trying to work on her relationship with her mom. "I called her up one day and said, 'Mom, if the way we communicate doesn't change, I think we'd both be better off if we didn't talk anymore.' And she said, 'Well, I can tell *somebody* saw their psychiatrist today.' "

I called her mom to get her side of it.

"She shouldn't care if she doesn't have my approval, she should have her own approval," Mary charges. "But I've never really felt she had the passion to play. Like, you look at her stats. If she could putt, she'd be in the top 10. Wouldn't someone who is really passionate about what they do find a way to fix that? And the way she plays so slow. That would drive me up a wall! HIT THE BALL! JUST HIT IT!

"So you have to ask yourself," Mary said, "does she really *not* want to do well? I think a lot of people *don't* want to do well because then they're stuck in it. I mean, golf was never a goal of Jill's. I always thought she'd do it in college and then go get a real job."

Gee, I don't see a problem here, do you?

IT WAS SUNDAY morning and I was waiting on the putting green when suddenly Jill was asking me, "Rick, look at this and see if you can figure out what's causing it."

And she was pulling down the top of her short shorts to show me an itchy spot that was developing, er, well, kind of along the bikini line.

"What is that?" she asked.

Man. There are people that live a lifetime and never get a setup line like this.

Still, I bit my bottom lip and replied, "Well, uh, I think it's a rash."

Turns out it was from her metallic player i.d. badge, which she'd stuck in her beltline. The sun was kind of cooking it to her skin.

"Thanks," she said, yanking the badge off and rolling her shorts back up.

Sigh. A caddy's work is never done.

AS WE WERE about to set off Sunday, only seven shots behind the leader, Jill had a good, long talk with her golf ball.

"C'mon, Mr. Ball," she cooed. "It's so hot out. Wouldn't it be nice and shady in the hole? Wouldn't it be nice for Mr. Ball to meet Mr. Hole?"

But Mr. Ball did not want to meet Mr. Hole. In fact, Mr. Ball and Mr. Hole were hardly speaking. We missed four very makable birdie chances in the first seven holes again—two inside six feet, two more inside 10. We were even par through 9.

She was getting more and more hot, and not just from her rash. At one point she yelled, "Pull your head out of your ass and start playing!"

Memo to Mary McGill: She cares.

On 12 we missed the green and hit a bad chip that left us 12 feet from the hole. I was holding the bag as she slammed her wedge into it, nearly crushing my pinky. But then she made a rare putt, walked over to me with the putter, and said, "Maybe I should have mentioned for you to watch your fingers."

Seeing as how I was having one of the worst caddy days in golf history, I would've deserved it.

First, with about 10 minutes to go before our tee time, I couldn't find my stupid bib. Wasn't in the bag anywhere. Adam ran madly out to the car but came back empty-handed. So I gave him $20 to go get a new one from the caddymaster and he got back with it within 30 seconds of tee time.

Then, as we were walking off the first tee with maybe 500 people watching, a bunch of stuff fell out of the pockets because I'd stupidly left them open searching for the stupid bib.

Plus, I kept dropping the towel, the headcover, and the water bottle. I kept adding and subtracting wrong, putting the bag in the wrong spot, forgetting to get the flag, you name it.

Finally, she said, "What's wrong with you today?"

"Just got my period," I confided.

. . .

EXAMPLE NO. 14,810 how the LPGA Tour is different from the PGA Tour: Elves.

There are far fewer players sponsored by beers, cars, and banks on the LPGA and far more sponsored by foods, kitchen appliances, and cleaning solvents, stuff that, rightly or wrongly, sponsors think might appeal to women golfers. Laura Diaz has little Keebler elves for headcovers. But not one player had what I would think are the obvious perfect LPGA headcovers: little toasters, refrigerators, washers and dryers.

Wouldn't that be great? You could then have conversations like this:

Player: What do you think we should hit here, the Amana?

Caddy: No way. It's the Kenmore at least. If not the Jenn-Air.

THERE WERE MORE male fans than women in Toledo, and the men were fascinated. For instance, Jill just flat nuked a 316-yard drive on the par-5 17th and made a two-putt birdie to get us to five under for the week. Some guy stopped me on the way to the 18th and said, "Hey, caddy, how far did she hit that drive?"

"Three sixteen."

And his face kind of fell and his shoulders drooped. He looked like the bottom had just fallen out of his vial of testosterone. He was obviously a man who no longer could tell his friends, "You know, we hit it longer than those bitches. They just get it up and down more."

We wound up finishing two-under 69 for a week's total of 279, placing us 21st for the tournament, nine shots back of the winner, an Australian named Rachel Teske. Out of the 78 who made the cut, Jill finished 9th in greens hit, but 53rd in putting. The world is a cruel place.

She won exactly $10,000, which means she still wasn't over the

$1 million mark. If I were a real caddy, I would've made the $800 weekly fee plus 5 percent of the $10,000, which was $500, or $1,300 total. Of course, if I were a real caddy, we might've won the thing.

"Actually, this worked out great having you this week," she said, cheerily, packing the car. "This proves to me that I can play with a mute on the bag, if I have to."

Gee, well, thanks.

"You know what I mean. It means I don't have to be so dependent on Adam. I can trust my own decisions more. And that will speed me up. And it was good you came the week after the Open. I was so mentally exhausted, I didn't see how I was even going to be able to play this week. But having you around gave me a new set of problems, you know. Got my mind off it."

And that, I think, might be the lasting contribution my caddying made to the game of golf and its players: a whole new set of problems to take their mind off the old ones.

Always glad to help.

If the caddy says . . .

"Did you hear Reilly got whacked? Dude is such a tool. His man is comin' down when Reilly yells, 'Eat hot titanium!' and his man carves a Rick Flair into prison. And Reilly goes, 'I don't care if that thing's wrapped in bacon, Lassie ain't findin' it.' His man volcanoes right there and sacks him. Should be some pamphlet the fishhack pens, huh?"

He means . . .

"Did you hear Reilly got fired? The man is quite a fool. His player was in the middle of his downswing when Reilly yells a phrase to encourage him to hit his driver a long way. Rattled by this, his player hits it deep into the rough. And Reilly says, 'That is very far into the rough and we're probably not going to find it.' This makes his player so mad he fires him then and there. It will be a very short book the sportswriter produces, don't you think?"

12

BOB ANDREWS

The Blind Approach

One day at the Broadmoor resort in Colorado Springs, I caddied for a 30 handicap who scraped it around for a 118. He hit it halfway decent, but he three-putted an acre of greens.

Then again, he *was* blind.

Bob Andrews' sight was blown out of his head on a June morning in 1967, on Marine Corps patrol in Vietnam. He was walking along a river about 25 yards behind a rookie sergeant and his last thought was, "That sumbitch is walking down the path!" Walking down a trodden path in Vietnam was like walking down the middle of the Holland Tunnel at rush hour. He tripped a wire that sent two hand grenades swinging out to Bob Andrews' feet. By all rights, he should've been dead, but another sergeant got him, carried him over his shoulder—Forrest Gump–style—to a clearing.

Medevac choppers came and radioed down that there was no way they could land with so much fire in the area. The sergeant pointed his huge M-79 grenade launcher at them and radioed back, "You're coming down here one way or another."

Bob was unconscious for two and a half months. He had 29 operations on his eyes, face, and knees. He was given last rites three times. Bob's father, disguised as a doctor, snuck into Vietnam, made off with his drugged-up son, and spirited him back to the States.

But Bob was so far gone when he came home that his mother called Bob's 21-year-old girlfriend, Tina, and said, "Don't bother coming to see him, honey. He's not going to wake up."

Tina sat in a rocking chair and didn't move for three days. Her mother finally screamed, "If you don't get up out of that chair and cry or move or do something, I'm going to come over there and slap your face!"

Tina went to him that day. "I had to," she says. "My whole life was lying in that bed." Together with his parents, she nursed him back to life. Of course, there were times when Bob wished they hadn't. "I can't see!" he cried. "What can I do?"

And Tina said, "Look, we're two people. We're a team. We can do anything we want!"

Since then, they practically have. They married within two months. Bob became a building contractor. "Can you imagine?" says Bob's friend, Tom Sullivan, the blind actor, author, and recording star. "You're about to build your dream house and the guy they bring in to draw up the plans is blind!"

You rarely see Tina without Bob and Bob without Tina. Together, they live with the Fun Meter pegged. They sail, fish, bodysurf, and golf, all around the world. They have three healthy sons. It's very hard to keep people like Bob and Tina Andrews down long.

I've always been fascinated by blind golfers. The Tiger Woods of blind golf, Pat Browne, once shot four rounds in the 70s at Mission Hills Country Club in Palm Springs, California. He once won a blind tournament with an 86-83–169, and that included an even-par 36 on one of the nines. In my entire sighted life, I've shot even par for nine holes once. Browne once challenged the late, great

Payne Stewart to a nine-hole blind match. Pat shot 47. Stewart, the pro, shot 61.

So I e-mailed the U.S. Blind Golfers Association and asked the president if they could find somebody that would let me caddy for them. And the reply came back: "Yeah, me."

Turned out the president was Bob.

I caddied one round for him, but it was enough to realize that nowhere else in the whole realm of golf—not in junior golf, not in senior golf, not even on Tour—is the caddy more important than in blind golf.

Bob Andrews turned out to be a handsome, thickly built, outrageously fit 57-year-old—maybe 5-10 and 175, in big, black Ray-Bans and brown bangs that swept across his forehead. He was open and funny and completely unafraid of life, much less golf. "Blind golf is great," he said. "I don't have to watch my bad shots. You do."

He handed me his business card, with the blind golf motto: "You don't have to see it to tee it!"

"Nobody likes to lose money to a blind guy," he said, stretching. He has proof. Sometimes, when he's into the pockets of buddies back home in his regular game in Tallahassee, Florida, they'll start driving the cart in circles half a dozen times to get him disoriented.

Golfers are cruel.

To get even, he stages midnight golf tournaments. The "sighteds" use glow balls and the holes are marked with glow sticks. Naturally, Bob slays them.

"They get all discombobulated in the night," he says with delight.

His goal in life now is to buy state-of-the-art night-vision goggles for Tina, his caddy (in blind golf, they're called "coaches"). "Wouldn't it be great?" Bob said. "It would open up all the greatest courses in the world! Do you have any tee times for midnight?"

Now, wait a second. One of the things that makes a course fantastic is the scenery—the oceans, the cliffs, the mountains, the bunkering, the lakes, whatever. But the blind can't see that. Pebble Beach becomes just another par-72 course, right? Might as well play the Dubuque municipal links and have someone fake wave-crashing noises, right? Save the $350.

"Not at all!" says Bob. "You feel the breeze, you hear the water, you can feel this is different. I played Pinehurst once, and I could feel the fog, smell the pine. It was dead quiet, wonderfully silent, except for the hollow crack your ball makes when you hit it. And, of course, the people you're with come to every tee box and go, 'Oh, wow! Wouldya look at this?!' You don't have to see to know you're somewhere special."

Ask a stupid question, get a wonderful answer.

OK, we were on the range and he looked like he was ready to start hitting balls. I watched him. Nothing happened. There was an awkward silence. What was he waiting for? Then I could feel his eyes on me and Tina's eyes on me and I thought, "What?"

"Uh, blind golf is a team sport," she said.

Can I just tell you how hard it is to line up a guy's clubface *every shot?* And line up his shoulders, hips, and feet *every shot?* And pick the right club and get the right distance and get his hands the right length away from his body and gauge the wind and gauge the lie *every shot?* And that's just on the range.

Tina seemed delighted to have a sub "coach" for the day. "Bye, honey," she sang. "I'm going shopping!"

Wait! Can't I come with?

We made our way to the first tee of the East course at the Broadmoor with his sighted buddy, Scott, who would play along with us. Scott caddied for him once at the TPC course in Ponte Vedra, Florida, where Bob knocked it onto the island green 17th hole on his third try. First time I played it, it took five tries.

As I prepared to get him off that first tee, Bob could tell I was nervous. "OK," he said. "Let's talk about the bet: Today, we'll play a blind Callaway."

Funny.

We did not do well at first. In fact, we did not even do crappy at first. We wouldn't have made the cut at the Suck Invitational. We started triple-quintuple-triple-triple. I kept forgetting that he was relying on me for nearly everything. He could feel the wind, of course. And he would bend down and feel the grass around his ball to get an idea of the lie. But elevated green? Uh, forgot to tell him. Trap in front? Yeah, I shoulda mentioned that. Pond behind? My bad.

See, it's easy to forget Bob is blind because of all the little tricks he plays. We'd get out of the cart and I'd walk to the ball and he'd walk with me and put his club down right behind it! And at first you think that's normal, and then it hits you that he can't see, and you're flummoxed.

"How do you keep *doing* that?" I asked.

"It's easy," he said. "Every time you get out of the cart, you go to the ball and I follow your voice. Then your head dips down to look at the ball and I can guess about where you're looking."

Freaky.

We were playing so badly that the group behind us played through—on the second hole. I felt bad, but Bob said not to worry. Happens all the time. He said sometimes people will yell at him from behind. "Hey!" they'll call up. "This is no place for lessons!" He said they'll play through all huffy, point at the caddy, and say, "You don't bring your pro out here!"

And Bob will say, "He's not a pro. He's a coach."

"Well, I don't care if he's a damn butler! Save it for the practice range!"

And then, suddenly, they realize that Bob is blind.

"Then they either apologize profusely or run and hide," Bob said.

Sometimes, just for kicks, Bob will go by their group later *driving* the cart, with his buddies whispering directions. That blows their minds. Or he'll start lining up putts, plumb-bobbing 'em, giving his hat the Tiger shade, stuff like that. And they'll get all indignant again and roar, "Hey, I thought you said that guy was blind!"

Sometimes, at restaurants, he'll point to an item on the menu and say, "I'll have that." Bugs the waiters out a little. Or he'll come up in his glasses and his white cane, point across the room to the brunette Tina, and say, "That's my wife, the blond one." He loves it when they stammer, not sure how to break the bad news to him.

Guy is more fun than redheaded twins.

Anyway, once it hit me that I was absolutely half responsible, 50-50, for how he played, we improved. Once I realized that his mistakes were my mistakes, his great shots my great shots, our numbers came down. For instance, one time I set him up for a little lob-wedge shot, maybe 50 yards, over a nasty bunker with a Mick Jagger of a lip on it. He took his practice swing and I just knew it wasn't enough.

"Bigger," I said.

He swung bigger.

"Little bigger," I said.

He swung a little bigger.

"Perfect," I said.

Then he stepped up and hit a perfect shot over the bunker to about 10 feet. When I told him, he said, "That helped me. You gave me a picture of the shot I need to make. That gave me a lot of confidence."

I put my foot in my mouth once. He hit a drive that stopped

short of a hill and I was trying to describe to him what he had left. "You've got kind of a blind approach shot here and . . ."

Pause for awkward silence.

"Hey, Rick," he said, grinning. "They're *all* blind approach shots to me."

Putting was the most excruciating part of it all—and yet the most exhilarating. On each putt, Bob and I would stand next to his ball and face the hole, with my right arm lightly guiding his left elbow. In his right hand, he held his putter out parallel to the green. We would pace the putt off carefully until his putter clanged the flagstick. Then we'd walk back. And he'd say things like, "This is definitely right to left here." Or, "OK, this is going to be downhill and quick!" Or, "Double-breaker."

"How the *hell* do you know the breaks?" I asked.

"With my feet," he explained. "I read greens with my feet. I can feel the change in terrain as I walk."

And I remember Nick Price saying that once. He said, "Trust your feet. They don't lie." And ever since Bob, I've putted better "trusting" my feet. If my eyes tell me it's a straight putt and my feet tell me it's left to right, I play it left to right and usually it'll be correct. Sometimes I'll even close my eyes and walk the distance of a putt. It really helps—until your buddies goose you in the crotch with the flagstick.

On the short putts, Bob had me hold one of his hands over the hole and the other hand over the ball. That way he could know the exact length of it. He always looked like a tailor measuring somebody's wingspan. Then he'd have me line it up and he'd try to put a square putt on it.

We were on the 4th hole and we hadn't holed a single putt (hey, blind people get to play "leather," too). So we had this four-footer and I read it left-lip and he hit a perfect putt. And the sound of that little beauty plunking into the cup was like hearing a slot machine jackpot. Because that's all Bob gets for a payoff—the delicious sound of it. His face lit up like Wyoming fireworks when he heard it, and come to think of it, so did mine.

We made the turn in 63, not a good nine. This is a guy who once shot 43 on a single nine holes, and who has won the Florida State Blind Championship three times. I felt sort of bad once we added it up and Bob tried his best to make me feel better.

"One rule," Bob said. "Any bad shots are blamed on the caddy."

On the back nine we made a huge comeback. On the par-3 12th we made a quite gorgeous bogey and beat Scott's 5! I could've kissed him.

When you're caddying for a blind guy, very strange thoughts come over you. For instance, I kept having to fight the urge to line him straight up into a lake, just to see what his face would do when he hit it perfectly and then heard the distinctive *glop!* of a burial at sea. At heart, I guess I'm just evil.

On the par-3 16th, Bob hit the shot of the day, the most gorgeous little 7-wood you ever saw, even if he didn't. This was the Halle Berry of 7-woods. It damn near went in the jar. I thought my heart was going to stop. I kept screaming, "Oh! Oh! Oh!" and he's going, "What? What? What?" It's kind of like a radio play-by-play guy going, "Wow! Look at that!" and his listeners are going, "What, you moron?" It ran right past the hole and finished four feet by.

Sadly, I misread the putt and we missed it right. Bob looked bummed. I could've hung myself. Not far in the distance at the Broadmoor stood the famous statue of Will Rogers. And I had the feeling Bob, like Rogers, had never met a caddy he hadn't liked—until this day.

Still, we shot 55 on the back for a total of 118. Scott played well and shot 89. The whole thing was fulfilling, frustrating, and, most of all, fascinating. I think I learned more about golf in those 18 holes than I have in a month of lessons. In fact, I made a list . . .

WHAT BLIND GOLF TEACHES YOU ABOUT GOLF ITSELF . . .

1. *All puts are straight.* "Every putt is straight to a blind man," says Bob. All day, I tried to line up his putter on the line I picked for him. Then his job was simply to putt it dead straight. The break would take care of itself. I forget that sometimes. I know it's going left so I subconsciously try to yank it left. Or it slides right so I try to cut it in there right. Bob simply tries to bang it dead straight every time and hopes I've picked the right line. Half the time, his hopes were crushed.
2. *See every shot before it's hit.* Bob was always asking me, "Give me a picture of the shot before I hit it." At first, I said, intelligently, "Huh?" And he said, "You need to tell me the character of the green, how high I should hit it, can it hit and then run or should it stop? And if there's big trouble in front, then you definitely need to tell me. You HAVE to hit the green here." And that's a useful tip. Picture what the shot will look like before you hit it. When I remember to do that, I pull the shot off more often than I don't. Figures you'd learn how to visualize from a blind guy.
3. *Be happy. Golf is humbling.* Blind golf is twice as humbling. When Bob whiffs one, which he did twice (and counted them), he laughed and called it a "fresh-air shot."

We had lunch afterward with Tina and you'd have thought Bob had just been released from a POW camp. They sat next to each other like high school sweethearts. I half expected them to put two straws in his beer.

Tom Sullivan said something to me once that suddenly made sense just then. "Every blind person is told at first that he's going to be dependent on others his whole life," he said. "And so they react wildly. They do anything they can to be *independent.* You know, walk into traffic, take up dangerous sports, stuff like that, stuff that will prove to the world that they don't need them. But it only makes them unhappier. Eventually, through love, they recognize that the only way to be happy and at peace is to live *interdependently*, to live knowing that they need others and others need them. And that's what blind golf is, a symbol of that lesson. The notion that we all need each other, blind or sighted."

I saw then what a team they had become—the broken soldier and the lost girlfriend. They were so much greater than the sum of their parts. I couldn't count two couples I knew that would survive one caddying every round for the other, but these two could. I guess they came too close to losing each other to ever let a bad 7-iron break them apart.

And as they walked off together, I thought, "Has there ever been anybody happier with a 118?"

That's when I realized there was one last thing to do.

IT TOOK SOME arranging, but I worked it out. I got some good, tight, airline sleeping eyeshades, a bandana to tie over them, a willing golf course—Columbine Country Club in Littleton, Colorado. I was going to play nine holes blindfolded. Payne Stewart, wherever you are, watch out.

Unfortunately, the only caddy I could get was my longtime confidant and general white-collar hooligan, Leonard (Two Down) O'Connor, the world's most avid golf gambler.

Two Down is a wiry little mook with perpetually twitching eyebrows—one of them cleaved in two by a hockey puck when he was nine. He could be described as "energetic" the way a twister could be described as "breezy." He is half man, half cappuccino. Not a moment goes by when he doesn't have some kind of plan, scheme, proposition, bet, or angle. He is the only guy who will sit in church and give you 6 to 5 that the priest will pick his nose sometime during the homily. Everything about him is set on frappé—his swing, his speech, his life. If he were God, the seasons would cycle through about every 20 minutes.

He is much too large a character to have only one name, so he has 23. The list of "approved" nicknames is on the back of his business card. Among them . . . World, Lenny the Brain, Ming the Merciless, and Lenny Gold. The card also lists his dice handicap—plus 2.

He'd caddied for me before—at the Pebble Beach National Pro-Am—and it was a disaster on the order of *Ishtar*. He was more interested in how his bets were coming against other caddies, the sports ticker on his belt, and how he could get Clint Eastwood to read his screenplay on check-dodging than actually caddying. It started to rain once while I was putting on the practice green and yet Two Down wasn't budging an inch toward the bag.

"Hey, Two, it's starting to rain," I said, annoyed. "You wanna get the umbrella?"

"Good idea," he said. He walked the 15 yards over to my bag, opened the umbrella, and held it over *himself*. He seemed pleased.

Still, nobody else would caddy 9 holes for a blindfolded guy. And, of course, I knew why *he* was doing it. He could see some kind of proposition bet coming up in his future. Something involving a blindfold, a hockey stick, and a hard-boiled egg.

Not that people hadn't tried blind proposition bets before. Amarillo Slim, the Texas poker champ and hustler, once bet a champion bowler $10,000 that he couldn't break 90 blindfolded. The champ couldn't get the blindfold on fast enough. He had eight pins on his first ball. But he only downed one on his second. On his next frame, he threw two gutter balls. And he hardly hit another pin. In fact, he barely kept it in his own lane. He threw a 22. "Toward the end, he accidentally put that dang ball through a windowpane!" says Slim. "What he didn't understand is that the first few minutes in a blindfold, you're OK, but as time goes on, you get so discombobulated, you hardly know your butt from a teakettle!" Lesson learned, the bowling champion started betting other people that they couldn't break *60* blindfolded. And he won plenty of money until Slim showed up one night, saying he had a man who could do it. The bet was $20,000. And Slim produced a man in a blindfold, whom he introduced as his driver. The man bowled 92, earning Slim the cash. What they didn't know was Slim's man was blind.

For blind golf, the 18-hole record is 74. As my Sancho Panza and I set out, I made 74 my goal, too—for nine holes.

I learned one thing very quickly. In blind golf, you do *not* waggle. Once your caddy has set the club behind the ball, you must resist the waggle at all costs, because he then has to *reset* the club. This tends to make your caddy very angry, especially if he is also trying to check his sports ticker.

Sure enough, my first shot was beautiful, a 3-wood that went about 240, right down the watering system. Because I'd just seen the world, not three minutes before, it all felt comfortable. I felt the swing, could visualize just where the ball was. It seemed like cake.

But the second shot was pure "fresh air." The third was a top. The fourth a shank right. The fifth another whiff. The sixth could've flown under a '63 Buick.

"For God's sake, keep your head down!" Two Down scolded, tiring of escorting me back to the cart, finding the ball, and setting me up all over again. You'd think I would've kept my head down. After all, what are you gonna see when you look up? But I couldn't. I made a 10.

As my sense of where I was and where the club was became more and more addled, my other senses improved. I could hear lawn mowers, birds, Two Down jiggling his keys. When we were in shade, I felt the cool air. When we were near water, I could smell the streams. I could hear other people's shots on other holes. Felt the sun on my skin. Newly invigorated by the simple joy of all that exists, I went to the 2nd hole and made a 12.

By the 3rd hole, two groups had played through us. On that hole, I whiffed it seven times, including four in a row. I produced more fresh air than photosynthesis. Of course, it didn't help all that much when I whiffed five in a row, to have Two Down lying on the ground, his legs and arms up in the air flailing, trying to get his breath from laughing so hard. I missed a three-footer at the last and made 20.

Q: How'd you make 20, Rick?

A: Missed a little 3-footer for 19.

Another thing that didn't help was that Two kept leading the top of my forehead into tree branches and the cart roof. "Sorry," he said by way of explanation. "My world ends at 5-7."

On No. 4, I made a 15, and again, the only reason I stopped at 15 is that Two Down let me play "leather." Actually, I was learning to hate the leather now. I wanted to hear the sound of the ball rolling into the cup. Through four holes, I lay 57. I would need to make four birdies and an eagle the rest of the way to shoot 74.

It wasn't entirely my fault, you know. My caddy kept making me proposition bets as I played. For instance, on the 4th hole, I was apparently 10 yards off the green when he said, "Hey, I'll bet you $5 you can't get it down in four from here."

My shoulders sagged. "Now why would I make that bet? *You're* the one telling me where to hit it!"

He seemed insulted that I would impugn his integrity. From then on, I felt he was *purposely* guiding my forehead into tree limbs.

On the sixth, Two Down could stand no more and insisted I let him try it. It was a joy to take the blindfold off and strap it over his twitching eyebrows.

Naturally, he creamed his first shot, then proceeded to go completely Gerald Ford after that, employing an impressive assortment of shanks, chunks, and whiffs. Then he got himself in a bunker and couldn't, for the life of him, get out. He kept hitting it straight into the lip of the bunker. Every single time. I lost count of how many times he tried. Ten? Fifteen? "Hey," he said, "it doesn't help when you're laughing hysterically, you know."

Charitably, I deemed it a 20.

I regained the eyeshades. The world refreshed in my brain, I played the last three holes slightly better, including a preposterously lucky 6 on the 9th hole when apparently I flushed my fourth shot, a 6-iron, over a maintenance shack onto the green when I just as easily could've missed it entirely and hit Two Down in the shin.

I putted up to about six feet. Two Down lined me up perfectly from there and I finally hit a solid putt, square in the middle of the clubface. Then I heard Two say, "Listen for it!" Then silence. Then the joyous plastic rattle of balata in the cup.

Hurrah!

At least I *thought* hurrah. As it turned out, Two Down, feeling sorry for me, let me hit my putt and then dropped *another* ball in the cup so I could at least enjoy the happy sound once.

Love that lug.

For the nine holes, Two Down and I combined to fire an impressive and entirely dishonest 121, or three shots worse than Bob's honest 118 for 18. And it only took us three hours and 25 minutes!

I wanted to take the eyeshades off, but Two Down insisted that if

I were going to approximate life as a blind man, I had to carry it clean through to the 19th hole.

That's when things got really hard. Even holding Two's elbow, I was bumping into tables, catching corners of walls, tripping on rugs. It was humiliating. Now I understood what Bob meant when he described why golf is so precious to him. "It's one of the few places I don't need to be hanging onto somebody all the time," he said. "It's wide open spaces. And I get to leave my cane in the car."

As the second beer was coming, I thanked Two for "coaching" me and apologized for laughing at his misfortunes.

"OK," he said, "but now let's do something *I* wanna do."

"You name it," I said, still wearing the eyeshades.

"Dice. $10 rolls. I'll read the numbers for both of us. Deal?"

Afterward, I finally got to take those eyeshades off, gratefully. I said good-bye to Two and took a little walk out to the 18th green.

As much as I admired Bob Andrews for playing blind, I didn't envy him. It took playing nine holes in blackness to make me realize what golf really means to me.

When I started this, I'd always thought it was the challenge of the game or the bets or the handicap or the 300-yard drives or 100-foot putts or the beers afterward or my ridiculous golf towel collection that the wife will only allow me to hang on the wall of our garage that made me love golf. But it turns out it wasn't any of those.

When I took off the eyeshades, I was floored by the color everywhere, the blue of the skies, the hundred shades of green, the aqua of the lakes, the Crayola set of flowers, the crisp, whipping flags on the sticks, even the caramel brown of the bunkers.

You know you've missed golf when the bunkers start looking lovely.

You forget what a rush it is to send a tiny little white ball hurtling great distances and to be able to watch it fall against sky, cloud, and mountain.

Being suddenly sighted again after three and a half hours was like being suddenly returned to Bedford Falls. I vowed never to take the game for granted again, not as a player, not as a caddy, and not as a writer.

See, George, golf really *is* a wonderful game.